ALL ABOUT AIDS

JAY S. ROTH

Professor of Molecular and Cell Biology
University of Connecticut
Storrs

Lifetime Fellow
National Cancer Institute

harwood academic publishers

chur london paris new york melbourne

© 1989 by Harwood Academic Publishers GmbH, Poststrasse 22, 7000 Chur, Switzerland. All rights reserved.

Harwood Academic Publishers

Post Office Box 197
London WC2E 9PX
England

58, rue Lhomond
75005 Paris
France

Post Office Box 786
Cooper Station
New York, New York 10276
United States of America

Private Bag 8
Camberwell, Victoria 3124
Australia

Library of Congress Cataloging in Publication Data
Roth, Jay S.
   All about AIDS.

   Includes index.
   1. AIDS (Disease)—Popular works. I. Title.
RC607.A26R67   1988   616.97'92   88-21456
ISBN 3-7186-0488-4

CONTENTS

3. Nature of the Beast / 45

4. Transmission and Spread of the AIDS Virus in the United States / 71

patient and doctor confidentiality–*225;* American Civil Liberties Union stand on AIDS–*226;* Children with AIDS going to school–*226;* Should sex partners of AIDS victims be informed?–*228;* Supplying condoms to federal prisoners–*230;* Legal aspects of AIDS: Divorce–*231;* Rights bill on AIDS–*232;* Should free needles be given to drug addicts to help curb AIDS?–*233;* AIDS and the right to die–*234;* Other types of legal issues involving AIDS–*235;* Anonymity of blood donors–*235;* The Catholic Church's stand on AIDS–*236;* Corporate policies toward AIDS–*238;* Should physicians (or dentists) with AIDS be allowed to practice?–*239;* Responsible behavior for AIDS victims–*240.*

PREFACE

AIDS has become one of the primary health concerns in the United States. Although at present, heart disease and cancer kill far more people, projections of future deaths from AIDS indicate that by the year 2000 it could rank third in cause of deaths in this country, behind heart disease and cancer which rank one and two, respectively. Unless the spread is checked and a cure or effective treatment is found by the year 2000, deaths from AIDS could surpass the deaths caused by any other past epidemics in this country including tuberculosis, polio and influenza or, in fact, the total of all three.

Understandably, therefore, the public is highly alarmed at the apparent inexorable spread of the disease. As is usually the case in a highly complex medical problem, misinformation, exaggeration and unsupported statements abound. There are many unanswered questions as well. Because of these alarming projections and the myths and misconceptions regarding the disease there is a pervasive air of fear among the general population. This fear finds expression in prejudice against and shunning of those with the disease, and its victims are not only affected with an incurable and progressively worsening malady, but become outcasts of society, the modern day lepers, at a time when they most need support.

The purposes of this book are to help those free of AIDS to remain uninfected and to help those who have AIDS to obtain the best treatment and care.

An effective way to give this help is to present the large body of relatively stable information concerning AIDS in a carefully ordered way and at a level that everyone can understand. Careful attention has been given to many pressing questions which are answered as fully as possible. If there are presently no answers to some of these questions, this is clearly indicated. It should be stressed that considerable controversy surrounds many aspects of AIDS. An effort is made to present different points of view regarding controversial matters and although the author occasionally presents his own point of view, this opinion is clearly indicated as such and it should be recognized that a whole range of opinions exists on most controversial questions.

It is hoped that this book will remove the fear from victim and potential victim alike and will point the way for everyone in order to prevent the spread of this desease. If this way is followed then the dire projections of increasing cases will never come to pass and it will only be a matter of time before effective treatment and care is achieved. This may be sooner than we now think but in the meantime our entire population will have to obey the strictest behavioral precepts to which they have yet been subjected to minimize further spread of AIDS.

JAY S. ROTH

Note: This book has been prepared with the help of electronic printing facilities. Although carefully edited and proofread, it has been made from final laser-printed typewritten pages prepared by the author. The time from submission of final copy to offering the book for sale has been greatly reduced, insuring that the latest data available is presented. Any errors which might still remain are those of the author and not of the publisher or editor.

Acknowledgment

My sincere appreciation to Mrs. Ruth Shephard of The Job Shop, who never complained about my handwriting or the numerous changes necessary and without whose help this book could not have been done.

GLOSSARY

Acute disease: A rapidly occurring disease.

AIDS virus (HIV) **:** A retrovirus, human immunodeficiency virus, formerly called HTLV-III, LAV, or ARV.

Allele: A particular type of gene.

Amino acid: A simpler chemical building block for proteins. There are 21 different amino acids in proteins.

Anemia: A deficiency in red blood cells.

Antibody, immunoglobulin: A protein made by B lymphocytes specifically engineered to attack and inactivate a single foreign protein or other invading substance.

Antigen: Any foreign substance that causes an immune reaction.

Avirulent: Not causing a disease.

B lymphocyte: A white cell with the primary function of making an antibody.

Cachexia: A wasting of the body.

Chancre: A sore, usually of the genital organs.

Chromosome: A structure in the cell nucleus containing a large number of genes arranged in tandem. It is highly extended in a resting cell and highly folded in a dividing cell.

Chronic disease: A long-term, slowly developing disease.

Clone: Cells or virus particles that are all of one type (genetic strain).

Codon: A sequence of three nucleotides carrying a message for a particular amino acid.

Complement: A group of at least 9 proteins in the blood that interact with each other in complicated ways to produce C-9, a protein that punches holes in cells targeted by white cells as dangerous.

Cytoplasm: The material of a cell between the nucleus and the membrane bounding the cell.

Dementia: A decrease in the ability to carry out higher mental functions.

Endogenous: Related to or occurring within the body.

Endothelial cell: A cell that lines an organ.

Enzyme: A protein catalyst capable of facilitating a metabolic reaction in a cell.

Epidemiology: A study of the causes of disease, its locations and, in general, all disease statistics. One who studies these matters is called an epidemiologist.

Etiology: The cause of a disease.

Exogenous: Related to or occurring outside the body.

Exon: A portion of a gene that codes for part of a protein, a domain or part of a protein with a specific function.

Genome: All the genes of a microorganism, plant, or animal.

Golgi apparatus: A collection of membranes found in most cells where proteins are processed by adding various groups and sorted out.

HIV-2: Human immunodeficiency disease-2. A retrovirus similar to AIDS but more closely resembling SIV (STLV-III). It may cause a disease similar to AIDS infrequently.

Hormone: A chemical messenger produced by a gland. It circulates in the blood and may affect most cells or special target cells.

HTLV-I: A human retrovirus causing a usually fatal T-cell leukemia in a small percentage of those infected. It is related to HIV.

HTLV-II: A human retrovirus causing a less aggressive T-cell leukemia. It is related to HIV.

HTLV-III: The AIDS virus, HIV.

HTLV-IV: Name formerly given to what is now believed to be HIV-2 or a variant of it. Related to SIV: it does not appear to cause disease in humans.

HTLV-V: A human retrovirus causing T-cell lymphoma or leukemia (mycoses fungoides). It is related to HIV.

Immunogenic: Causing an immune response.

Immunoglobulin: Same as antibody.

Intron: Intervening sequence separating two exons in a gene.

In vitro: In a test tube or petri dish outside the body, as in a tissue culture.

In vivo: Inside the body.

Leukemia: A cancer of the white cells characterized by an increased production of white cells usually of a specific kind.

Leukopenia: A deficiency in white blood cells.

Lymphoma: A cancer affecting the lymph glands. It may be coincident with leukemia.

LTRs: Long-terminal repeats. Similar nucleic acid ends on retroviruses and elsewhere. They function in coding, control of transcription, and inserting gene(s) into DNA.

Lysosome: A small particle (organelle) found in the cytoplasm of many cells. Lysosomes contain a variety of digestive enzymes bound up in a single membrane.

Metabolism: Any chemical reaction carried out by cells in the body.

Monoclonal antibody: A clone of antibodies, each with the same exact specificity. It is made by a clone of B lymphocytes.

Monocyte: An immature macrophage. It develops into a macrophage with the proper stimulus.

Mutation: A change in a gene usually, but not always, inactivating it or making it recessive.

Nucleocapsid: Portion of a virus consisting of the coat proteins and the nucleic acid genome of the virus.

Nucleosome: A roughly spherical structure consisting of eight histone protein molecules around which DNA is wrapped.

Oncogene: 1. A normal cellular gene capable of causing cancer under certain conditions. 2. A mutated cellular gene capable of causing cancer. 3. A gene carried by certain retroviruses capable of causing cancer in animals and possibly humans.

Organelle: A small particulate within a cell with defined function.

Pathogenesis: How pathology develops or is brought about by a virus, bacteria, and so on.

Pathogenic: Disease-causing.

Pathologist: One who studies the effects of disease on body organs and cells and who identifies disease (cancer, etc.) by the microscopic examination of cells.

Pathology: The effects of disease on the body and cells.

Peptide: Two or more amino acids joined together in a chain. Dipeptide: 2 amino acids. Polypeptide: 3 to 60 amino acids in a chain. Protein: more than 60 amino acids in a chain.

Phagocytize: To take inside a cell and digest.

Phagocytosis: The process of taking into a cell and digesting.

Placebo: A pill containing no medicine or drug.

Polymerase: An enzyme or structure that makes a polymer or a long chain from chemical units. DNA polymerase makes DNA from deoxynucleotides; RNA polymerase makes RNA from ribonucleotides; a ribosome makes proteins from amino acids.

Receptor: A protein usually located on the outer membrane of a cell capable of binding a particular molecule with great specificity.

Recessive gene: A gene that is not expressed.

Reverse transcriptase: Enzymes found in retroviruses that copy RNA into DNA.

Sarcoma: A malignant cancer arising in connective tissue or bone.

Seropositive: Giving a positive test for AIDS virus antibodies.

Seroconversion: Going from a negative to a positive test for AIDS virus antibodies.

Syncytia: Giant cells made by fusing many single cells.

Syndrome: A collection of symptoms.

Synovial: Of or related to membranes and other sheaths surrounding tendons that secrete a viscous fluid used for lubrication.

Tissue culture: Growth of separated cells in a petri dish, test tube, or special culture flasks called chemostats.

T4 or CD4 lymphocyte: A helper lymphocyte.

T8 or CD8 lymphocyte: A suppressor lymphocyte.

Transcription: The use of DNA codons to make RNA.

Transformation: A change of a normal cell to a cancer cell.

Translation: The use of messenger RNA to make protein. It occurs in the cell cytoplasm.

Vaccine: A preparation made from a disease organism which when injected confers immunity to a disease on a human or animal without producing the disease.

Virion: A single virus particle.

Virulent: Highly capable of causing a disease.

CHAPTER 1
SOME GENERAL ASPECTS OF AIDS

Introduction; A brief description of AIDS; Naming the AIDS virus and related viruses; AIDS-like viruses in other animals; Possibility of human infection by animal immunodeficiency viruses; The origin of AIDS virus; What is AIDS?; AIDS related complex, ARC; Who has AIDS?; Infection of hemophiliacs by AIDS virus; Sex ratio of AIDS patients; Age distribution of AIDS patients; How AIDS is spreading in the United States; Distribution of AIDS cases in the United States; Ethnic breakdown for AIDS cases in New York City; Costs of AIDS; Additional hospital beds for New York City AIDS patients; Spread of AIDS in Africa; AIDS in children; Will all individuals infected with HIV get AIDS?; Will all those with active AIDS die?

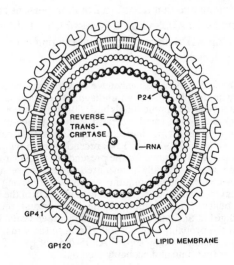

1

SOME GENERAL ASPECTS OF AIDS

Introduction

Acquired immune deficiency syndrome (AIDS) appeared in the United States, almost entirely unnoticed, in a few male homosexuals in 1981.*

There were approximately 200 cases diagnosed that year. The number of cases rapidly increased, roughly doubling each year from 1981 to 1987. In 1987 alone, at least 28,000 new cases were observed, as many as the total of all cases through 1986. The total number of cases by the end of 1987 was more than 50,000 with about 30,000 deaths registered.

It has been estimated that from 1 to 2 million persons in this country are now infected with AIDS virus. It is possible that all or nearly all of them will develop AIDS after a lag period ranging from a few months to more than a decade.

---

*In retrospect a much earlier case may have occurred involving a 15-year-old male patient who died in 1969 of an undiagnosed disease. Doctors were so perplexed that they saved samples of his body fluids and tissues. A pathologist, Dr. William Drake, found small, purplish lesions at the autopsy which he correctly identified as being indicative of Kaposi's sarcoma, a cancer commonly found in AIDS victims. Tests recently run on the patient's blood and tissue samples were positive for the presence of AIDS virus. The patient also had *chlamydia*, a sexually transmitted virus disease and there was virtually no evidence that his immune system was blocking its spread. If confirmed, this would certainly be the first case of AIDS in the United States. The patient believed his disability came from sexual relations with a neighborhood girl in St. Louis, but this and any other sexual encounters he may have had are probably untraceable. Because the virus present in this youth probably was not widely spread AIDS did not get a foothold in the United States at that time and probably died out.

The disease has been referred to as a pandemic (worldwide epidemic) and compared to the Black Plague of the Middle Ages, which devastated Europe and parts of the Near East. Even President Reagan has referred to it as the Black Death.

Such comparisons are entirely incorrect and even harmful. AIDS was shown in 1985 to be caused by a new retrovirus while the Black Plague was caused by a bacterium, *Yersinia pestis*. The plague spread rapidly, mostly by bites from fleas infected by rats or other rodent carriers. AIDS is spreading slowly, and is not easily transmitted. Most cases have resulted, from the passage of body fluids, principally semen or blood from an infected person to an uninfected one as a result of various sexual practices or from the use of contaminated needles during intravenous injection of drugs. Once infected with the Black Plague a person got sick within a week or two and developed a high fever and other well defined symptoms, and a large percentage, perhaps 25 to 50%, of those infected died. Some, however, recovered and were then immune to the disease. Others may have escaped the disease by not being bitten by an infected flea.

It is probable that the small number of persons who were infected by the Black Plague and were able to resist the disease entirely did so by virtue of having a well-functioning immune system. We do not know if *anyone* can resist AIDS virus once infected, because the virus *attacks the immune system* and even a well-functioning one can be destroyed. In comparison to that of the Black Plague, the onset of AIDS is generally very slow, and the rate of spread is also slow. Many persons have harbored the virus for years and still have not shown any symptoms of the disease.

The actual percentage of those with the virus who will contract the disease is not known, but as time progresses it appears that this percentage is increasing and may eventually attain a high value — 50, 75, or even close to 100%. It will take at least another 5 years to obtain a good estimate of how many of those infected will get AIDS.

We do not yet know if there will be any lifelong survivors of AIDS who will be cured and free of the fear of recurrence or of the ability to transmit the disease sexually. Thus far, more than half of those with the full-scale disease have died.

Today a person who becomes infected with *Yersinia pestis* can be readily cured with antibiotics and other supportive hospital care. Antibiotics so far have been useless against AIDS virus, although they may help to cure so-called opportunistic infections that accompany AIDS. Thus far, no ideal antiviral chemical has been found, and although azidothymidine (AZT) has been shown to be helpful to many AIDS victims, it has several drawbacks and cannot be used by all patients.

There are many other points of difference between AIDS and the Black Plague, and comparisons should really not be made at all. They only result in further scaring the public which visualizes the disease as a rapidly spreading Black Death when in reality it is rather difficult to transmit AIDS virus and its spread is very slow in comparison with the spread of most contagious diseases in a susceptible population.

At this moment AIDS has affected mainly small, specialized segments of the U.S. population. Over 90% of the cases have involved male homosexuals, male intravenous drug users, and a smaller number of female intravenous drug users. The disease has the potential, however, for spreading to the general population, particularly the sexually active population. It is very important that this be prevented not only in this country but throughout the world and the best means of prevention is education.

A Brief Description of AIDS

Acquired immune deficiency syndrome (syndrome = a collection of symptoms) is a disease new to the United States and was first observed here in 1981. It is caused by a virus called a *retrovirus* that uses ribonucleic acid (RNA) for its genetic material instead of the usual deoxyribonucleic acid (DNA) – which is the genetic material of all animals, plants, and bacteria.

AIDS virus is almost unique in directly attacking the immune system which is all important in defending the body from viral, bacterial, and parasitic invaders. Specifically, it attacks a special kind of white cell called a helper T4 lymphocyte which is one of the most important white cells needed to initiate an effective immune response against a large variety of disease organisms. Without these T4 cells the immune system of the body essentially falls apart, and the AIDS victim becomes prey to a large number of disease organisms which normally never create the slightest trouble. Most AIDS patients die not from the AIDS virus but from these opportunistic infections, the most common of which is a form of pneumonia caused by the protozoan *Pneumocystis carinii*.

Quite a few AIDS victims develop a rapidly spreading, highly lethal cancer called Kaposi's sarcoma and they may die from this affliction. This cancer, which was very rare before AIDS appeared, and almost unknown in this country, was previously observed in a relatively mild form in a few men along the Mediterranean shores of Africa. Why this one particular cancer is associated with AIDS is unknown, and how it is caused is also unknown.

AIDS virus also appears to attack at least one other important white cell, the *macrophage*. Macrophages have a large variety of important functions in providing protection from disease. They can also migrate to all parts of the body and may be responsible for spreading the virus to cells of the central nervous system, brain and spinal cord. Brain cells of several kinds may also be directly attacked by AIDS virus, giving rise to nerve disorders and mental symptoms ranging from mild to severe. In addition, the virus can infect and hide in cells of the skin, lung, intestine, colon, rectum, cervix, and heart, sometimes producing a fatal infection of the latter organ.

The AIDS virus appears to cause a general deterioration of all the blood-forming elements, including the red cells, and anemia or a low number of red blood cells is a common finding in AIDS patients.

AIDS virus is the most complex retrovirus known, and its actions in the body and manifestations of its disease are highly complicated.

Naming the AIDS Virus and Related Viruses

In May 1986, AIDS virus was given a new name, human immuno-deficiency virus, (HIV) which supplanted the three names formerly used.

Lymphadenopathy virus disease (LAV): The designation given the virus by Dr. Luc Montagnier, co-discoverer of HIV, and his colleagues at the Pasteur Institute in Paris. (Loosely defined "lymphadenopathy" means a disease involving lymph glands and white cells.)

Human T lymphotrophic virus III (HTLV-III): Used by Dr. Robert C. Gallo, co-discoverer of HIV, and his associates at the National Cancer Institute (lymphotrophic = attracted to white cells).

AIDS-associated retrovirus (ARV): The name chosen by Dr. Jay Levy and his co-workers at the University of California School of Medicine in San Francisco.

Dr. Luc Montagnier isolated a different strain of virus in West Africans that may cause an AIDS-like disease although only about 20 active cases have been found. This is now called HIV-2 and it appears to be spreading slowly through Africa and Europe.

Examination of large numbers of samples of blood from different African countries (Chapter 3) indicated that many were infected with an AIDS-like virus initially called HTLV-IV, a name since discarded. None of the persons infected showed any signs of disease. This virus may be HIV-2 or a variant of it. HIV-2 resembles SIV — simian immunodeficiency virus (Chapter 3).

AIDS-like Viruses in Other Animals

AIDS-like virus in simian species
Many different species of monkeys have been found carrying an AIDS-like virus. The nature of all these viruses and their relationships to one another and to HIV is not yet clear. Some of them cause disease in their simian hosts; others do not. The chimpanzee has been suggested as a test animal for human AIDS virus. When HIV is injected into chimpanzees they develop antibodies to the virus but do not show any symptoms of AIDS except in rare instances. They cannot, therefore, serve as effective test animals. There is considerable enthusiasm for the use of either pigtailed or Rhesus macaque monkeys, which are relatively abundant, as test animals. They can be infected by SIV and some of them develop a disease similar to AIDS which includes infection of the brain. One problem has, however, arisen: When a pure SIV (consisting of only one type of particle) was injected, it did not produce disease. This is one example of why vaccine research and testing are proceeding slowly.

AIDS-like virus in cats
A retrovirus causing an AIDS-like disease in cats has been discovered by Dr. Niels C. Pedersen, professor of veterinary medicine at the University of California at Davis. The cat virus is genetically distinct from the human virus but causes a similar disease in the animals. There is no indication that the cat virus can infect human beings.

The new cat virus is classified as a *lentivirus,* and it appears to be distinct from another well-known retrovirus that can attack cats, feline leukemia virus. Feline leukemia virus, in common with most leukemia viruses, causes cancer of the lymph glands, leukemia, and immune deficiencies, but none of the cats infected with lentivirus showed any signs of leukemia virus.

The new virus is called feline T-lymphotrophic lentivirus, (FTLV), and it attacks the same T-lymphocyte white blood cells as AIDS virus. The extent of the disease in cats and the threat it poses to the cat population is not known. The new virus was discovered in Petaluma, California, in a colony of 42 homeless cats retrieved from veterinary hospitals, pounds and homes. The cats had only normal mild illnesses during a 14 year period until a female kitten from San Francisco was placed in one of the enclosures in 1982. The cat had intervals of diarrhea and infections for 2 years, and in the third year became thin and anemic before developing abnormal neurological signs and dying. Other cats in the same pen developed similar symptoms in 1985, and 10 died. Of the 15 remaining cats, 13 are sick and 8 have tested positive for FTLV.

Since this virus appears to cause a disease similar to AIDS, cats may be a useful test model for the human disease. Although they do not resemble humans as closely as monkeys do, they are much easier to obtain and care for. In general I do not favor using animals for research, but AIDS is a pressing human emergency, and one can rationalize, in addition, that FTLV may become a real menace to cats as well. Further research on the cat virus as a model for AIDS virus has shown, paradoxically, that the virus that grows in the animals doesn't cause disease! According to Dr. James I. Mullins, an associate professor of virology at Harvard University, the disease is caused by defective virus particles. Dr. Mullins has isolated a highly immunosuppressive feline lymphadenopathic virus from cats that induces a fatal AIDS-like disease in these animals. The virus isolated by Dr. Mullins is apparently different from the one obtained by Dr. Pedersen, however, and the complexities of these discoveries will have to be resolved in the future.

AIDS virus in African insects

A group of French scientists from the Pasteur Institute have reported finding the AIDS virus in mosquitoes, cockroaches, tsetse flies and antlions from Zaire and in mosquitoes, ticks, and bedbugs from the Central African Republic. The virus was found integrated into the insect DNA, but there was no indication that it could multiply in insect cells or that insects could infect humans. In fact, epidemiological data suggest it cannot. Otherwise far more children would be getting the disease. All the data from Africa, as from other parts of the world, suggest that AIDS is confined to the sexually active population and that only children born to AIDS-infected mothers or who have received contaminated blood or blood products have the disease.

Many scientists are puzzled by and skeptical of these results with African insects and think it is possible that there may have been errors in the testing. Although transmission by insect bite remains a possibility, all the present data indicate that insect transmission of the disease is not a factor in its spread. Further work and confirmation of these reports is necessary.

AIDS virus in American mosquitoes

Dr. Robert C. Gallo of the National Cancer Institute, working with the Federal Centers for Disease Control, has studied the fate of AIDS virus in blood ingested by mosquitoes. The virus is retained, apparently, in a viable state for 2 or 3 days, but there is no evidence that it can be passed on to another person or that it can remain viable or grow in mosquito cells. Even in areas where mosquitoes are prevalent children are not affected, and the results of these studies confirm those of the French scientists mentioned above who studied AIDS virus in African insects.

Is cattle virus linked to AIDS?

There is a retrovirus that infects cattle, called bovine lymphadeno-pathy virus (BLV) which is distantly related to HIV. Jeremy Rifkin, an outspoken critic of genetic engineering experiments and biotechnology advances that could conceivably affect humans adversely, has suggested that the cattle virus is a progenitor of HIV. He has speculated that BLV might have infected cell cultures used to make some human vaccines, perhaps contributing in this way to the global spread of AIDS.

In a petition submitted to the U.S. Department of Agriculture, the Federal Centers for Disease Control, and the National Institutes of Health, Mr. Rifkin called the cattle virus "an extraordinary potential threat to public health."

There are several scientific papers in the literature that point out the resemblance between BLV and HIV, and these articles were cited by Mr. Rifkin in his petition. He also cited a paper reporting that the bovine virus can infect human cells grown in the laboratory.

Two of the scientists whose papers were cited were interviewed. Dr. Matthew A. Gouda and his co-workers at Program Resources Inc., which conducts research for the National Cancer Institute in

Frederick, Maryland, propose in their paper that the cattle virus be used as a model for studying AIDS virus. He does not believe BLV can cause AIDS in humans. "It is not something that somebody should be afraid will jump into humans or that should make people fear cows," he says. The second expert, Dr. Martin J. Van der Maaten who was the first to isolate BLV from cattle, believes there is very little chance of it infecting humans and that it is far-fetched to speculate that contaminated vaccines have spread the virus to humans.

A bovine retrovirus more closely related to HIV and called BIV was recently discovered by Dr. Gouda and his colleagues. This cattle lentivirus looks very much like HIV under the electron microscope, causes the same changes in cattle cells and gives the same response in cattle that is seen in AIDS virus infected humans. Studies of the genetic composition of the bovine virus showed that it was similar to HIV. The relationships of BLV and BIV to HIV are shown in Chapter 3, Figure 4.

Possibility of Human Infection by Animal Immunodeficiency Viruses

There is a popular theory that humans developed AIDS somehow after being bitten by a monkey carrying simian immunodeficiency virus. If this is true, then it would be a prime example of a retrovirus crossing a species barrier. In theory, at least, retroviruses should be capable of crossing species barriers. We presently have no strong evidence that they do, but I believe that they can, and probably have, gone across species barriers in the past and may do so in the future.

A detailed explanation of how this could happen is given in Chapter 2. For now it is only important to know that for a virus to infect a cell it must enter the cell. HIV gets into human cells by attaching itself to a particular human cell surface protein, called a receptor, found on T4 lymphocytes and a few other types of human cells. AIDS virus attaches itself by means of a protein in its outside membrane coat called glycoprotein 120 (gp120). Attachment of gp120 triggers a reaction within the cell that pulls the virus inside. For this reaction to occur the human cell receptor and the virus gp120 must form the right combination. In other words, they have to fit together. Most human cells are not infected by AIDS virus because they do not have the T4 receptor. Another retrovirus, FTLV, does not infect human cells because it does not have a glycoprotein that fits T4 receptors. Apparently BLV glycoprotein can interact with human T4 receptors, however, at least in tissue culture.

We know that the glycoproteins of retroviruses are capable of continuous mutation (change that may lead to varied properties). Sometime in the past a single simian virus particle (virion) may have mutated in such a way that its glycoprotein changed and became capable of combining with human T4 receptors. If a monkey bite conveyed this single virus particle to a human the mutated monkey virus could have begun spreading in humans. Further mutation could result in a better fit, a more virulent virus and finally one we now recognize as human AIDS virus, HIV.

The French investigators who examined mosquitoes in Africa reported HIV was integrated into the DNA of mosquito cells. If this is true it must have entered these cells and this may have occurred by the mechanism already described. Although being inside the cell is not necessarily equated with multiplication of the virus, the virus has the potential to do so.

Finally, it has to be said that there are undoubtedly many unwritten chapters on the immunodeficiency viruses yet to come in the future. While it is unlikely that we will have to worry about getting AIDS from monkeys, cats, cattle or mosquitoes, we must be ever alert to these and other possibilities and be ready to combat anything that Nature may throw at us. More research and experimentation will provide answers and give us the means to prevail.

The Origin of AIDS Virus

The thinking of a majority of scientists today is that AIDS virus probably originated in central Africa.

It has already been mentioned that monkeys carry viruses similar to AIDS virus. One of these monkeys, the African green monkey found throughout much of equatorial Africa carries simian immunodeficiency virus, (SIV), a relative, but not a close relative of HIV.

The hypothesis has already been stated that SIV somehow entered humans, possibly as a result of a bite or during butchery of a green monkey. In the monkeys, or subsequently in humans, a series of mutations may have previously taken place yielding intermediate viruses of lesser virulence but finally terminating, after many passages, in the deadly pathology of HIV.

Tests on blood stored in Africa during the 1970s have detected no antibodies to HIV except in samples from a small region in central Africa where the earliest signs of infection have been found in blood taken in the 1950s. After remaining localized for some time the virus probably began spreading to the rest of central Africa in the late 1970s. Later in that decade it probably spread to Haiti and from there to the United States, and then to Europe and South America. The mutation(s) that resulted in the present day virulent virus may have occurred sometime in the late 1970s, for there is no evidence that Africans were being killed by the virus in large numbers before that time. Admittedly, statistics on causes of death are not generally available in much of Africa, but some indications should have appeared in hospital records.

There are two additional retroviruses related to HIV that have been known for a somewhat longer time: HTLV-I and HTLV-II. HTLV-I causes a usually fatal leukemia called adult T-cell leukemia, (ATL), involving the same T cells that are attacked by HIV. HTLV-I causes these cells to proliferate wildly and results in other harmful effects on the immune system. HTLV-II differs from HTLV-I in causing a less aggressive leukemia, and the virus particles of each are slightly different. At present HTLV-I and II are found principally on the two southern islands of Japan, Kyushu and Shikoku, in Jamaica and Haiti, and, possibly in a small section of New Guinea and on two southern Philippine islands. Tying together all these unlikely locations are sixteenth-century Portuguese traders who traveled to Japan and stayed on the islands where HTLV-I is prevalent. They brought African slaves and green monkeys with them, and one or both may have carried the virus. One fact that does not support this theory is that the Ainu people living on Japan's northernmost major island, Hokkaido, are also commonly affected by HTLV-I, and this was an area the Portuguese did not visit. It has been suggested, therefore, by Dr. H. Taguchi, from the Department of Internal Medicine, Kochi Medical School, Japan, and others that HTLV-I was originally carried by prehistoric Japanese including the Ainu and that it was spread by fishermen to various areas in Japan where the infection is endemic and to North American Eskimos who also have a high prevalence of HTLV-I. There is a close correspondence between ATL and the occurrence of the virus in patients. The reverse is also true. HTLV-I appears to be transmitted in the same way as AIDS virus (Chapter 4), mostly through sexual contact and blood transfers, but in addition there is evidence that infants can ingest HTLV-I in their mother's milk (this is true of AIDS virus also), and even more recent findings suggest that HTLV-I may be carried by mosquitoes. This observation has to be confirmed because AIDS virus, as already noted, has been found in mosquitoes in Africa and in the United States. Once infected, a child may harbor the virus in a latent state for 40 or more years. In an adult the latency may be as short as a few years. Although HIV, as already stated, is related to HTLV-I and -II, this relationship is not close, and the mechanisms of action of the two kinds of viruses in their common host, humans, are quite different (Chapter 3).

What is AIDS?

The Federal Centers for Disease Control in Atlanta are attempting to keep a close watch on the spread of AIDS and on all other factors concerning the disease. Since other diseases can mimic AIDS, the centers have carefully defined the conditions required to give a positive diagnosis. This is helpful to the individual physician confronted with a possible case, and also to local, state, and federal governments that administer the many assistance programs for AIDS victims (Chapter 8).

The initial case definition was approved in 1981 but was revised thereafter. Under current criteria, for a diagnosis of AIDS, a patient must show evidence of a damaged immune system and either the presence of at least one of the officially recognized cancers, for example, Kaposi's sarcoma (a cancer of the skin and internal organs), or opportunistic infections, for example, *Pneumocystis carinii*. A revision in 1985 added patients who had a positive test for antibodies to AIDS virus and non-Hodgkin's lymphoma (cancer of the lymph nodes), but there were not many in this classification. By the end of 1987 about 50,000 patients had diagnoses meeting these criteria, and more than 30,000 of them had already died.

AIDS Related Complex, ARC

There is another group of patients with AIDS who may not show either the cancers or infectious diseases AIDS patients usually have. Those in this group, referred to as having AIDS-related complex (ARC), develop dementia (loss of brain function), severe emaciation, and possibly anemia. These latter three symptoms may also be exhibited by patients with a diagnosis of AIDS in addition to the cancers and infectious diseases. Since ARC patients were not previously included in the official AIDS classification, demented and emaciated patients, who could not work and often could not take care of themselves, were denied the full social and disability benefits given AIDS patients. In New York City an ARC patient could qualify for a rent subsidy of only $196 a month from the Human Resources Administration, while patients with AIDS could receive $500 to $600 per month in rent subsidies along with monthly Social Security disability benefits and several home care services.

In May 1987 the Federal Centers for Disease Control officially recognized ARC patients as AIDS victims, and with the approval of Congress and state governments these patients receive the same benefits and care as the initially defined AIDS patients. It is estimated that this change has added about 7000 persons nationwide to the number of those officially having AIDS. The increase is about 25%, a considerable number, and the projected number of future cases will have to be revised upward to include those with AIDS related complex since most of these projections do not include such patients.

Who Has AIDS?

The percentages of AIDS cases reported for the United States are given in Figure 1-1.

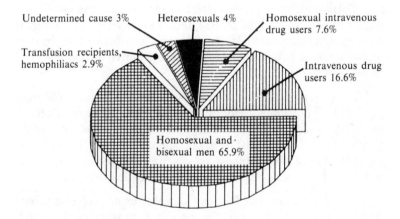

Figure 1-1 Distribution of AIDS in the United States. Persons with disease as defined by the Federal Centers for Disease Control, 1986.

Usually intravenous drug users of all kinds are lumped together in a single group, accounting for 24.2% of the total. These figures change fairly rapidly, with homosexual and bisexual men showing a decreasing percentage and intravenous drug users an increasing percentage of the total cases. At present the values are probably close to 60% for homosexual and bisexual men and about 30% for intravenous drug users nationwide.

The reason for these changes is believed to be that homosexuals, in many cases, have adopted a restrained sex life with single partners the rule and the widespread use of condoms. On the other hand, intravenous drug users, according to social workers and others who care for them, are continuing their use of contaminated needles and few of them will consider using condoms.

The prevalence of AIDS in the heterosexual population is increasing, and was up by about 135% in 1987, but AIDS cases in this group still make up only a small percentage of the total number. A rapid and widespread increase in the number of heterosexuals with AIDS is not expected, however.

Infection of Hemophiliacs by AIDS Virus

Hemophilia is a disease in which the blood does not clot properly. Like many human diseases, it is due to a genetic deficiency, most often failure to produce von Willebrand's factor (factor VIII), a protein essential to the clotting process. The lack of this factor can range from slight to complete, and the disease, therefore, from mild to severe. It is primarily a disease of males. Females may have hemophilia, but it is probably due to a different condition than failure to produce normal amounts of factor VIII.

Hemophiliacs had been supplied with factor VIII prepared from pooled blood donations. Before 1985, blood donors were not screened for AIDS virus antibodies, and consequently many, if not most, of the preparations of factor VIII were contaminated with AIDS virus. As many as 1000 blood samples were sometimes pooled to prepare the factor, so the chances of AIDS virus contamination were high.

The Federal Centers for Disease Control estimate that among about 10,000 Americans with severe hemophilia, approximately 70 to 90% are now infected with the virus. In the remaining 10,000 with mild to moderate forms of hemophilia, the rate of infection is from 30 to 50%. Interestingly, although these groups are highly infected, the number of cases of active AIDS is low, — only 370 in adults and 30 in children, or about 2% overall among the 20,000 hemophiliacs. In other AIDS groups, such as homosexuals and intravenous drug users, it is estimated that 20 to 30% of those infected will come down with AIDS in about 5 years. Many hemophiliacs have been followed since 1980, but they still show no signs of AIDS. Passage of the virus from hemophiliacs to others via sexual contact also seems to be much less frequent than in other risk groups. The reason for this is not clear, but a reasonable suggestion is that during the processing of blood to produce factor VIII, the AIDS virus is subtly altered so that it is no longer so infective; also, it can perhaps act as a vaccine, causing immunity to the overt expression of AIDS with its debilitating symptoms. It is obviously of interest to determine the cause of the low incidence of AIDS in infected hemophiliacs, as it may be possible to use this information to protect other risk groups in the same way.

Federal experts have pointed out that the risks to others from hemophiliacs are very low. The popular conception is that hemophiliacs bleed easily and excessively from minor cuts and scrapes, but this is not true. Their chief problem is internal bleeding, which can be treated by quick injection with factor VIII.

It is indeed sad that so many people are uninformed or misinformed about these facts. In Florida, three young brothers with hemophilia who tested positive for AIDS virus were to enter school, but there was a tremendous outcry from parents in the community who were opposed to their attendance. Death threats were telephoned to the boys, and finally their house was burned to the ground by a fire of suspicious origin. It's bad enough to have a severe disease like hemophilia *and* a potentially fatal infection by AIDS virus, but to be subjected to total ostracism and violence by the community one lives in is certainly more than anyone should have to bear. The family left town, and the new town in which they settled has treated them well and with compassion.

It is fortunate that hemophiliacs no longer have to worry about AIDS virus infection from contamination of their life-saving factor VIII. The protein is now made by recombinant DNA technology using bacteria or yeast, and there is no possibility at all of AIDS virus contamination.

Sex Ratio of AIDS Patients

Figure 1-1 does not show the ratio of males to females with the disease. In the United States it is approximately 13 males to 1 female. This lopsided ratio can be explained by several observations. First, although it is possible, it is unlikely that sex between two lesbians transmit the disease if one member of the pair is infected. To the contrary, a large percentage of the male homosexuals in San Francisco already carry the virus and any anal or oral sex with an uninfected partner carries a high risk of infection if condoms are not used. If they are used, the risk will be considerably less but not zero. Since male homosexuals make up the largest group of those infected, this accounts for a large part of the discrepant sex ratio. Second, published data for New York City (Table 1-1) indicate that male intravenous drug users outnumber females considerably. Consequently those with AIDS outnumber females by about 4 to 1, which further adds to the discrepancy.

In Zaire, the Central African Republic, and Haiti, countries with large populations infected by AIDS virus, the sex ratio, in marked contrast to that in the United States, is about one to one. This has puzzled researchers and epidemiologists, and the only explanations are highly conjectural. Several that have been offered are the following. In Africa medical equipment and facilities are primitive, and injections and blood sampling are often performed with nonsterile needles and syringes. As a result, it would be expected that equal numbers of males and females would be infected. Also, it has been found that in Rwanda there is a high correlation between a history of infection by sexually transmitted agents and infection by AIDS virus. Consequently, many more women in Africa may have less effective immune systems as well as vaginal tract sores, and on both counts they are probably more susceptible to AIDS virus. We know that in different parts of the world the sex ratio for various diseases, including cancer, may differ appreciably. It is possible that certain still unknown factors, such as genetic ability to resist AIDS or environmental or dietary conditions, may also affect the sex ratio for AIDS. Much additional work in this area is obviously required.

Age Distribution of AIDS Patients

In 1986, the age distribution of AIDS cases was as shown in Figure 1-2 for 26,000 patients.

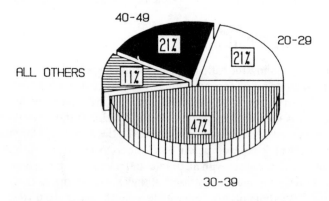

Figure 1-2 Age distribution of AIDS

It is clear that AIDS is striking the most productive young workers in our nation. Sixty-eight percent of the victims are in the age range of 20 to 39 years. This represents a great loss of talented people, many of whom are highly skilled or artistic. The next group that may be hard hit, depending on how effective education is, are the teen-agers, those roughly 15 to 19 years of age, a group noted for sexual activity. Many members of this group may not be well informed on how best to minimize infection, and much will depend on how well the schools get the message about AIDS across.

How AIDS is Spreading in the United States

The number of cases of AIDS occurring during the first 7 years of the epidemic is shown in Figure 1-3.

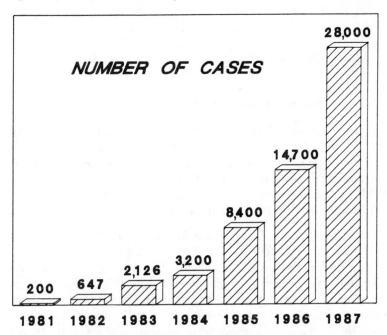

Figure 1-3 Number of cases of AIDS in the United States (not counting ARC). Data courtesy of Federal Centers for Disease Control, Atlanta. Figure for 1987 estimated by the author.

Except for 1984, the number of cases has roughly doubled each year since 1981. The figure for 1984 may be underreported or lower than expected because of some other artifact. This doubling is not expected to continue much longer, as shown in Figure 1-4, which gives projections up to 1991. Although not doubling, the figure for each year after 1987 indicates an increasingly larger total of new cases, thus in

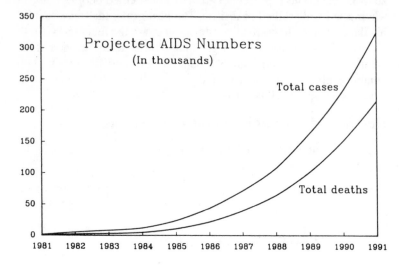

Figure 1-4 Projected numbers of AIDS cases

1990, approximately 90,000 new cases are expected. The total number of cases by 1991 is expected to be about 324,000, with approximately 215,000 deaths. At its worst, in 1952, paralytic polio struck 21,000 Americans and in peak years killed between 10,000 and 18.000 victims. This comparison indicates, at least, that a few superlatives describing the deadliness of AIDS are appropriate.

As already noted, it is estimated that there might be between 1 and 2 million persons infected with AIDS in the United States at present. This could increase to 3 to 4 million within 5 to 10 years. A lot will depend on the behavior of promiscuous people with the disease. Even assuming a best case scenario, the epidemic is bound to cause far more damage in the next 10 years than it has so far. Eventually, it is hoped, with the application of common sense, altruism, safer sex practices, and effective vaccines and medicines, the curves in Figure 1-4 will level off and start to go down, possibly by the year 2000. Before that time, however, more than 1 million Americans are doomed to die, and the costs to and burden on our medical facilities will be overwhelming. The above figures, while correcting for previous underreporting of AIDS, do not include ARC cases which would, if added, bring the projections for 1991 to over 400,000 cases and about 250,000 deaths.

Distribution of AIDS Cases in the United States

Three major centers of AIDS cases exist in the United States. Numerically, New York City and its environs is the most important with about 13,000 cases (including ARC) — nearly one-third of the total for the United States. San Francisco has about 6400 cases of AIDS and the highest per capita number. The third center is in southern Florida, especially Miami, which has 3000 cases. The fourth largest is Houston, Texas with 1200 cases, and Newark, New Jersey, is close behind. The remainder are distributed throughout the country, with all states reporting at least some cases. A heavier caseload is found across the tier of southern states; Alabama, Mississippi, Louisiana, Texas, and southern California, with fewer cases in the sparsely populated northern states. However places such as Milwaukee, Minneapolis, Chicago, Portland, Oregon, and many other major cities are showing rapidly increasing numbers of victims.

Ethnic Breakdown for AIDS Cases in New York City

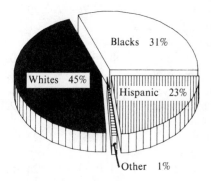

Figure 1-5 Percentage of AIDS cases in major ethnic groups of New York City.

Figure 1-5 shows that blacks and Hispanics carry the major burden of AIDS in New York City, namely, 54% of the cases. It is a heavy burden to carry. Poor socioeconomic conditions, with an attendant lack of access to education and health care are undoubtedly the major causes of the disparate distribution of AIDS. The poor, with less stable family conditions, inadequate diets, and unhealthy environments, are always subject to higher disease rates. All these factors also contribute to higher drug use. Improvement in the socioeconomic conditions of minorities would undoubtably slow the spread of AIDS in these groups.

Although this improvement will be expensive to society, it will be even more expensive not to improve them when just the costs resulting from this one disease are considered.

The patient profiles for New York City illustrate some interesting facts, some of which have already been mentioned.

Table 1-1 New York City AIDS Cases: Patient Profiles[a,b]

Patient category	Males (%)	Females (%)	Total (%)
Homosexual/bisexual not intravenous drug user	5101 (55.5)	0 (0.0)	5101 (55.5)
Homosexual/bisexual, intravenous drug use unknown	138 (1.5)	0 (0.0)	138 (1.5)
Homosexual/bisexual, intravenous drug user	451 (4.9)	18 (0.2)	469 (5.1)
Intravenous drug user, heterosexual	2086 (22.7)	544 (5.9)	2630 (28.6)
Intravenous drug user, sexual orientation unknown	93 (1.0)	11 (0.1)	104 (1.1)
Born in a country where heterosexual transmission is believed common	159 (1.7)	39 (0.4)	198 (2.20
Recipient of transfusion	38 (0.4)	35 (0.4)	73 (0.8)
Hemophiliac, or other blood factor deficiency	17 (0.2)	2 (0.0)	19 (0.2)
Sex partner of person from known risk group	4 (0.0)	209 (2.3)	213 (2.3)
Interviewed, no risk factor determined	44 (0.5)	23 (0.3)	67 (0.7)
Unable to interview adequately	51 (0.6)	24 (0.3)	75 (0.8)
Under investigation	74 (0.8)	27 (0.3)	101 (1.1)
TOTAL	**8256 (89.8)**	**932 (10.2)**	**9188 (100.0)**

[a]Number of cases of acquired immune deficiency syndrome as of February 25, 1987, by patient group and percentage of total cases.
[b]Source: New York City Department of Health.

One anomaly which is difficult to explain is that individuals born in countries such as Zaire and Haiti where the sex ratio of AIDS is one to one nevertheless do not adhere to this ratio in New York City. In Table 1-1 the ratio is close to 4 males to 1 female (159 males, 39 females). This value, intermediate between the African ratio (1:1) and the United States ratio (13:1), suggests that at least some of the factors affecting it may be environmental, for example, medical care, diet, and the presence of disease.

Table 1-2 Costs of AIDS (Estimated Figures)[a]				
	1985	1986	1987[b]	1991
Victims (not counting ARC)				
Cumulative number of cases	19,000	35,000	60,000	324,000
Cumulative number of deaths	9,000	18,000	35,000	215,000
Medical care (in millions)				
Care of AIDS patients	$630	$1,119	$2,532	$8,544
Other medical costs	$319	$542	$795	$10,869
research, health education, blood				
testing, and support services				
TOTAL	$949	$1,661	$3,327	$19,413

[a]Data from the U.S. Public Health Service and a study done for the agency by Anne A. Scitovsky, Palo Alto Medical Foundation. Costs estimated by Dorothy P. Rice, University of California, San Francisco.
[b]Figures for 1987 estimated by the author.

Costs of AIDS

By any reckoning, the costs of AIDS are staggering, even now. They will become very much worse before they get better. AIDS has struck mostly the younger, sexually active generation, those between 20 and about 45. More than half of these people with AIDS have died, and among them have been some of the most promising artists and professionals of our time. Writers, painters, sculptors, choreographers, actors, lawyers, doctors and many others have not lived to fulfill their destiny. Many would have become great, and some had already been recognized as highly talented, highly creative people.

The economic totals for several years past and future are given in Table 1-2.

The Figures for 1991 are highly speculative and at worst could total as much as $16 billion according to data from the U.S. Health Service. Not included in these figures are the earnings and output lost as a result of the long sickness and premature death of AIDS patients. This will total $55 billion in 1991, far more than the direct medical costs.

Paradoxically, the use of new therapies which prolong the lives of patients but do not cure them, will increase the total cost of caring for AIDS victims. AZT is such a drug. Its use, moreover, will cost each patient, or the agency providing the drug, about $10,000 a year.

New York City, which at present has about one-third of the total number of AIDS victims in the United States, is particularly hard hit. Although it seems unlikely that it will continue to retain this proportion of the total in future years. Hospital costs alone could be more than $2 billion by 1991. Although most of this money will come from the federal government, New York State and New York City will have rapidly increasing bills for their share of the costs.

The state of New York would like to turn St. Clare's hospital into the first one in New York City devoted entirely to the treatment of AIDS cases. This proposal is meeting with strong resistance from the entire staff of the hospital, and just the suggestion of this idea is already scaring people away. A partial conversion to AIDS care is probably not realistic, because it is unlikely that many voluntary patients will want to go there. St. Clare's may have no alternative but to convert to an AIDS hospital, and, unfortunately, many others will probably follow.

The unpleasant prospect of treating more AIDS patients is also a difficult problem for other hospitals in the city. Many have seen large sections of their medical floors taken up by increasing numbers of AIDS patients. At present, St. Clare's, a private Roman Catholic hospital, and Bellevue Hospital Center, a New York City hospital, each admit more AIDS patients than any other hospital in the country.

Cases involving drug users are more costly for several reasons. Homosexual victims have access to outpatient care and social services usually not available to drug users. In addition, drug users tend to have more associated health problems, so their medical condition is generally worse than that of homosexuals at the outset of the disease. Drug users are also less likely to be employed and less likely to have health insurance. Since New York City has more drug users with AIDS than other cities, costs are higher. For example, in New York City the average hospital stay for an AIDS patient is 11 days compared to 2 days in San Francisco.

Individual hospitals, particularly city hospitals that will have the largest share of AIDS patients, face steeply escalating costs. For example, Parkland Memorial Hospital, a 760 bed public facility in Dallas, estimates its costs for treating AIDS as $1.2 million in 1986, $2.9 million in 1987, and $10.8 million in 1989. Gregory G. Graze, a vice-president of the hospital, points out that local taxpayers will have to shoulder much of the cost because most of the patients have lost their insurance by the time they enter the hospital.

The saddest tale with regard to AIDS hospitals is that concerning the nation's first hospital devoted solely to AIDS patients—the Institute for Immunological Disorders, a private research and treatment hospital in Houston, Texas. It lost more than $8 million its first year and shut down by the end of 1987.

Its rapid demise was due to the fact that it could not attract enough paying patients to keep its doors open. Most AIDS patients are indigent at the start, and many others lose their jobs or exhaust their insurance or both. The costs of treating AIDS are understandably very high—up to $1200 a day for inpatients and $400 a day for outpatients. Although the hospital's research was supported by a $5.8 million contract, the facility failed to attract enough paying patients to remain open. As a private hospital owned by American Medical International, it did not have access to federal or other subsidies. The thought of AIDS being a money making proposition seems perverse, although the pharmaceutical companies that market useful drugs like AZT will certainly do well financially. The obvious answer for the treatment of AIDS patients is to have the federal government take over, either directly to run hospitals dedicated to AIDS or through subsidies to allow nonprofit operation. Where possible, state and city governments should also contribute funds.

As AIDS patients live longer as a result of using various drugs such as AZT (Chapter 7) and by virtue of improved supportive care, they unfortunately tend to develop neurological problems, many of which require nursing home care and occasional hospital treatment. Both of these factors obviously can greatly increase overall treatment costs.

Additional Hospital Beds for New York City AIDS Patients

Reversing a long-standing policy of closing hospitals and reducing the numbers of beds in others, New York City Health officials plan to add 500 new beds for AIDS patients. There were 1335 AIDS patients hospitalized in October 1987, with 2500 expected by 1989, which would amount to 9% of all patients. Hospitals are already overcrowded, particularly municipal ones that treat 50% of the AIDS patients and there is no place to put the additional expected influx. In New York State about 26 hospitals have applied for designation as AIDS centers.

So far only 3, St. Clare's and St. Lukes-Roosevelt in New York City, and University Hospital in Stony Brook, New York have been approved, but the 11 additional acute-care municipal hospitals in New York City will probably soon be added to the list.

Spread of AIDS in Africa

The World Health Organization has estimated that at least 50,000 Africans may have AIDS and that between 1 and 2 million Africans may be symptomless carriers of the virus. These figures contrast sharply with official figures provided by nine African nations which have reported only 378 cases among them. Initially many governments of African countries denied the presence of the disease despite ample evidence of it, but more recently they have acknowledged the threat. Most African countries are now cooperating with international efforts to track and combat the disease. The heaviest infection is probably in central Africa, which includes the countries of Zaire, the Central African Republic, and others.

The most serious aspect of the AIDS problem in Africa is that the most simple means of limiting the spread of infection are not routinely used in African countries. There is no screening of blood donors, and sterile needles are rare. It is probable that condoms are seldom used in sexual encounters. Education programs are getting under way, but many Africans are illiterate. Although the data coming from Africa are very limited and possibly not representative or accurate, the available information suggests a very high rate of infection in particular areas. For example, serum samples collected from prostitutes in Kenya in 1984 showed 51% infected with AIDS virus. In Rwanda 10.5% of a sample of 258 blood donations contained antibodies to AIDS virus. In Rwanda, Africa's most densely populated country, the capital, Kigali, is a tidy, well run city, but it has one of the highest rates of AIDS virus infection in the world. Approximately 12.5% of the blood samples collected are contaminated with AIDS virus. Blood for transfusions is now mostly collected in the countryside where people are not yet affected. In February 1987 Rwandan authorities banned the use of blood that had not been tested for AIDS virus. One problem with this testing, however, is that its accuracy is uncertain.

Kenya and Rwanda have been trying to avoid damage to their tourist industries. They require that all information concerning AIDS in their country be channeled through national AIDS committees, and this information is almost completely censored. In contrast to its suppression of scientific information, Rwanda has begun an excellent AIDS education program. In 1986 the national radio broadcast a series of 10 public health programs on AIDS. Early in 1987 the Rwandan Red Cross started distributing 25,000 brochures written in the national language explaining the dangers of AIDS. They plan to distribute hundreds of thousands of one page pamphlets. Other measures are being taken and their efforts appear to be having an effect, as indicated by a large increase in the sale of condoms.

#	Country	HIV-1	HIV-2
1	Egypt		
2	Libya		
3	Tunisia		
4	Algeria		
5	Morocco		
6	Mauritania		
7	Mali		
8	Senegal	0	L
9	Gambia	0	L
10	Guinea Bissau	0	L
11	Rwanda	M	L
12	Guinea	0	L
13	Djibouti		
14	Burkina Faso	L	0
15	Sierra Leone		
16	Liberia		
17	Ivory Coast	L	0
18	Ghana		
19	Togo		
20	Benin		
21	Niger		
22	Nigeria		
23	Chad		
24	Sudan		
25	Ethiopia		
26	Somalia		
27	Central African Republic	H	M
28	Cameroon	L	L
29	Equatorial Guinea		
30	Gabon	L	L
31	Ngo		
32	Zaire	H	L
33	Uganda	M	L
34	Kenya	M	L
35	Tanzania	M	L
36	Mozambique		
37	Malawi		
38	Zambia	H	L
39	Angola		
40	Namibia		
41	Botswana	M	M
42	Zimbabwe	M	M
43	South Africa	M	M

L = Light
M = Moderate
H = Heavy
0 = None
No entry = Unknown

Figure 1-6 Distribution of AIDS viruses in Africa

AIDS virus is now spreading to the countries of West Africa. Nigeria, Togo, Ghana, Ivory Coast, Gambia, and Senegal. These countries, as well as others, have started to report the disease and have blamed prostitutes for its spread. "AIDS; Fear of the Unknown," was the headline of a recent article in an Ivory Coast newspaper after a study found that 60% of lower class prostitutes were infected with one or the other of two strains of AIDS virus. Despite these fears, health experts predict that West Africans will not change their sexual habits in time to avoid a widespread epidemic.

"People are afraid, but they are not well informed," says Odehouri Koudou, an infectious disease specialist who heads Ivory Coast's newly formed work group on AIDS. An article published in the *Lancet*, a British medical journal, predicts that the number of AIDS cases in the Ivory Coast "will within a few years be as high as it already is in Central Africa." The same is probably true of the other countries of West Africa. The French government has announced a $2.8 million emergency program to distribute public information and to screen blood for the probable presence of AIDS virus, and the World Health Organization is also contributing money and experts to West African nations to combat the disease.

AIDS in Children

Approximately 1000 children in the United States are now estimated to have AIDS, and the number is bound to increase rapidly. The U.S. Public Health Service expects the number of AIDS cases in children under 13 to grow to 3000 by 1991, and some experts predict as many as 10,000 to 20,000 cases in children by that year. In New York City of 50,000 women of reproductive age, approximately 3% are infected by HIV. From 30 to 50% of the children born to these mothers may be infected. Hospital care can cost more than $200,000 per year for each infected child. Children can become infected at birth from mothers with AIDS, from a past blood transfusion, or from the use of a contaminated blood product such as factor VIII (von Willebrand's factor) in the case of hemophiliacs. Since blood for transfusion is now carefully tested for AIDS virus and this factor is no longer obtained from blood, these two avenues of infection are essentially closed. Being born to an infected mother is a potent threat, however, and experts have suggested that women infected with AIDS virus defer pregnancy. They also recommend that an early test for AIDS virus infection be encouraged for pregnant women so that, if it is positive, they can consider abortion.

Will All Individuals Infected with HIV Get AIDS?

Actually, no one knows the answer to this question. However, the answer will do much to determine the ultimate toll of the epidemic. Also, the fate of millions who are infected with HIV but are not sick will be determined by this answer. The opinion of knowledgeable scientists ranges from fairly optimistic—no more than 20 to 30% of those infected will come down with active disease—to highly pessimistic—perhaps in two decades nearly everyone infected will suffer from the serious disease effects. Also unknown at this time is how many of those infected now or in the future will be spared the active disease by drugs or vaccines now or soon to become available. Even if repressed, the infection is believed to persist for life, and even if active virus is not present in blood or semen, infected cells may be passed via these fluids. In other words, an infected person may always be contagious, and sex without the most stringent safeguards may always be risky with such an individual.

The best estimates of the climbing toll of the disease have been made using a group of homosexuals in San Francisco who volunteered for a hepatitis study in the late 1970s. The blood specimens from this group were saved, and using the blood test for antibodies to AIDS virus that became available in 1985, it was possible to determine which of these patients were infected with HIV and when they showed active disease. Among them, the rate of progression of AIDS has not fallen off with time. After 5 years, 15% had AIDS; 6 years, 24%; 7 years, 33%; and 88 months, 36%.

In another study using 63 patients who had been infected for 76 months, 30% had developed AIDS, 21% had fever, weight loss, thrush (a whitish growth in the mouth and throat), diarrhea, and other symptoms associated with ARC, and 27% had swollen lymph nodes throughout their body, a probable sign of beginning AIDS. Only 22% of this group were symptom free. Homosexuals may not be the best groups to use for this type of study because many of them have had multiple partners with probable multiple exposure to the virus. Many also have a history of other venereal diseases, parasitic infections of the bowel, hepatitis, and other infections common among gay men. These individuals may have already weakened their immune systems making them more prone to contract the disease. In addition, it has been shown by a number of scientists that semen itself represses the immune system.

Using data from a group of patients infected by blood transfusions, Dr. G. F. Medley and coworkers at the Imperial College, University of London, have determined the incubation time of AIDS, that is, the time from infection to diagnosis (appearance of disease symptoms) to be approximately 2 years for children up to 4 years old, 8.2 years for persons 5 to 59 years old, and 5.5 years for elderly patients 60 years or older. Dr. Medley notes that the distribution of incubation times in patients infected by blood transfusions is not necessarily the same as in patients infected via other routes. Another factor that might affect infection times is the state of health of the infected person, including the health of his or her immune system.

It is important to point out to AIDS victims that although these statistics look grim, there is considerable hope. Antiviral agents and vaccines may be found that will relegate AIDS to a status no worse than that of herpes, which also persists for life but is mostly only an annoyance.

Will All Those with Active AIDS Die?

Almost all the victims of AIDS who exhibited the disease in the period 1981 through 1985 have died. At present, widespread use of AZT which was initiated in 1986 has prolonged the life of many AIDS patients. Better supportive care and treatments for opportunistic infections have also helped greatly in this respect and it is now known that many patients may survive for quite a few years, even with the active disease. We do not yet know for how many years and we do not yet know if any will be able to survive though their natural lifespan. Even with AZT and better supportive treatment the death rate is still high. It is obvious that it will take many years to get a definitive answer to this question. It is possible to say, however, that the time span for survival is increasing steadily from year to year.

CHAPTER 2
AIDS IS A RETROVIRUS

Introduction; Structure of a retrovirus; How the virus enters the cell; Conversion of virus RNA into DNA and integration into cellular DNA; Latency period of HIV; Activation of HIV–Development of AIDS after other infections; Long-term culture of HIV-infected cells; Types of cells infected by AIDS virus; Giant-cell formation by AIDS virus; Effect of AIDS virus on helper T4 lymphocytes; Effect of AIDS virus on other cell types; Brain cell injury caused by AIDS virus protein.

Dr. C. Everett Koop, Surgeon General of the United States. A leader in the fight against AIDS.

2

AIDS IS A RETROVIRUS

Introduction

The term "retro" means reverse, or backward, and refers to the fact that retroviruses have RNA for their genetic material and from it make DNA. This DNA becomes incorporated into the DNA of the cell and parasitizes the cell's synthesizing machinery to make viral RNA and viral proteins which can assemble to make new virus particles (virions). The cell is sometimes killed when these virions leave the cell.

All other viruses and living things use DNA as their genetic material and from it make various kinds of RNA to carry out their life processes (See What Is a Gene? below.)

Retroviruses (family *Retroviridae*) include three subfamilies, *Oncovirinae, Spumivirinae* and *Lentivirinae*. *Oncovirinae* produce, as the prefix "onco" (meaning tumor) implies, tumors in animals and possibly in humans. Oncoviruses are transmitted as regular infectious viruses but also can be carried in the germ line (the sperm and eggs of animals and possibly humans). In contrast, lentiviruses, which were known to infect only hooved animals (mostly sheep, goats, cattle, and horses), are transmitted only by outside (exogenous) infection from one animal to the next. HIV and HIV-2, are now classified as lentiviruses. (See Chapter 3). *Spumivirinae* are not presently of any importance to humans or animals.

Since retroviruses use RNA as genetic material, their structure and life cycle are somewhat more complex than those of many DNA viruses. Among the retroviruses, HIV and HIV-2 appear to be the most complex, having at least eight different genes.

All retroviruses contain a characteristic gene called *pol* (for polymerase) which codes for an enzyme called reverse transcriptase. This enzyme is able to catalyze the formation of DNA from viral RNA. and the DNA is a complementary copy of the virus RNA. This complementary DNA is able to insert itself into the cell DNA and become part of the chromosome of a human or animal cell. Further details of the life cycle of a retrovirus are given below.

What Is a Gene?

The box What Is a Gene? that follows and the one in chapter 3, Short Review of the Human Immune System may be helpful to some readers lacking background in these areas.

Definition

A gene is the *hereditary unit* – actually a section of a DNA chain that carries coding instructions that enable a cell to manufacture one specific protein or ribonucleic acid (RNA) molecule.

Location and nature

The DNA of genes consists of two chains twisted around one another in a double-helical form. The units of the chains are nucleotides called bases. There are four different bases – cytosine, thymine, adenine, and guanine, abbreviated C, T, A, and G, respectively. In the double helix, C of one chain is always paired with G of the other chain, and A is always paired with T. These nucleotides are called complementary pairs. Three (hydrogen) bonds between C and G and two between A and T hold the DNA double helix together and stabilize it. One chain of DNA is the coding chain, and the other is the complementary chain. Genes are arranged tandemly, with as many as several thousand on a chain forming a *chromosome*. In humans there are 23 pairs of identical chromosomes, including 2 X sex chromosomes in a female. Males have the same 22 pairs of identical chromosomes as females and one X and one Y sex chromosome forming the twenty-third pair. Thus there are 46 chromosomes in all and possibly as many as 100,000 genes in a human. The chromosomes are located in the nucleus of the cell and are mostly in stretched out form, except during cell division when they undergo extensive folding. All the genes of an organism are called, collectively, the *genome*.

Scheme for making protein

In the normal sequence DNA is used to make ribonucleic acid RNA, and RNA is used to make protein.*

---

*RNA is usually a single chain containing the three bases C, A and G as in DNA with uridine, U replacing T. The bases in RNA contain the sugar ribose instead of deoxyribose which is the sugar in DNA.

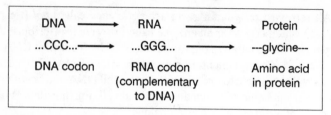

Coding and transcription

Three bases form a codon that specifies one of the 21 different amino acids used to make protein. There are 64 codons altogether, 61 are coding, 3 are stop signals, and the start signal is the code for the amino acid methionine. The code is redundant, with some amino acids having 6, 4, or 2 codons each and methionine only 1. *Transcription* is the use of DNA codes to make ribonucleic acid. Several types are made, among them:

1. Messenger RNA (mRNA): A code for a protein

2. Ribosomal RNA (rRNA): A structural RNA needed for the formation of a ribosome, the protein-synthesizing machinery of the cell

3. Transfer RNA (tRNA): An adapter used to bring the correct amino acids to the ribosome.

All humans have essentially the same genes. There are many complex forms of gene regulation for turning genes on or off or for adjusting their transcriptional activity. Each cell type in a human, liver, lung, muscle, and so on, has a different qualitative and quantitative expression of genes that distinguishes that cell type. Humans differ from one another because of differences in the quantitative expression of many genes. For example, if more growth hormone is produced, a person will be larger and taller, if skin cells produce more of the pigment melanin, a person will have darker skin, and so on.

Control of gene activity

The following methods are known:

1. The DNA chain contains sections acting as promoters or enhancers which speed up transcription.

2. Four nucleotides (and sometimes more) form a TATA box which helps to position the transcription agent (the enzyme RNA polymerase) on the DNA chain.

3. Trans acting factors are proteins that facilitate transcription and possibly translation, which is the use of RNA codons to make protein.

4. Hormones may act in two ways depending on their type.

    a. Steroid hormones enter the cell, after attaching to a cell receptor, and combine with protein in the cell interior. The protein-hormone complex formed migrates to the cell nucleus where it interacts directly with the chromosomes. This interaction may be the turning on of some genes and/or turning off of others.

b. In the case of protein and peptide hormones, the hormone attaches to a cell receptor on the cell surface. This triggers a series of reactions within the cell, usually forming a substance that can interact with genes and produce a change in cell metabolism.

5. Changes in the configuration of the chromosome (folding or unfolding) are important in the regulation of gene activity.

6. Protein repressors are known that regulate gene activity.

7. Small molecules can interact with various proteins which can then affect gene expression.

8. Methylation [placing a methyl group (CH_3, one carbon and three hydrogens)] on the base cytosine inactivates some genes.

9. Antisense RNA (complementary to messenger RNA) is made by some bacterial genes to control other gene activities. It has not yet been proved to be made by higher animals.

There are undoubtedly many other methods of gene regulation.

Packaging of genes
Histones are very old and invariant proteins (they have not changed much for billions of years) that act like a file cabinet, stabilizing and making genes accessible when necessary. There are five major types of histones: H1, H2A, H2B, H3, and H4. Two molecules of each of the last four combine to form an octamer *nucleosome* on which two turns of DNA can be wrapped. H1 may be located on the DNA between nucleosomes (Figure 2-1).

Most genes of animals and plants are split into *exons* or coding sections and *introns* or noncoding sections (intervening sequences). Bacteria do not have split genes.

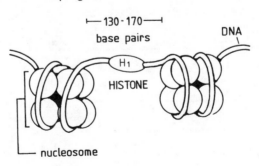

Figure 2-1 Portion of stretched out chromosome

Introns are generally longer than exons. Exons represent a *domain* or functional unit of protein structure, for example, a signal sequence (exon 1) signifying that a protein is to pass through a membrane; a

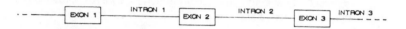

Figure 2-2 Representation of section of a gene

membrane-traversing sequence (containing hydrophobic amino acids) not readily soluble in water but soluble in the membrane to anchor a protein there; a sequence for combining with a metal and so on.

The function of introns is not clear. In some cases, for example fungi, introns may code for a reverse transcriptase enzyme, and in protozoa RNA an intron is known that is itself a catalyst that can remove or splice out itself as well as synthesize RNA from simpler precursors.

Formation of messenger RNA
All exons and introns are transcribed, but introns are removed by looping out intron sections as shown in Figure 2-3.

There appear to be several different mechanisms for doing this, all of them autocatalytic, that is, occurring within the RNA chain itself.

Function of Introns and Exons
The availability of many different exons allows resorting of these protein domains, which may give rise to new proteins possibly with advantageous functions for the organism. The function of introns is not known with certainty, but they are a possible control point for protein synthesis. Also, as mentioned, they have catalytic activities

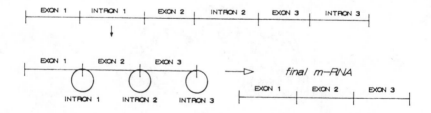

Figure 2-3 Removal of introns to form messenger RNA

Structure of a Retrovirus – HIV

The structure of HIV is shown in Figure 2-4. The shape is spherical, with an outer membrane obtained from the cell in which the virus grows. Like all viruses, HIV is a true parasite and cannot reproduce without using the machinery of the cell for many of its needs.

Into this borrowed membrane the virus inserts a glycoprotein (gp) made up of two parts: One is a stem that traverses the membrane (gp41), and attached to the stem is another larger oval glycoprotein gp120. The number refers to the molecular weight of the protein in thousands. The membrane is constructed from various lipids, and for this reason it can often be disrupted by detergents or other lipid solvents which in some instances can be used as a defense against the virus (Chapter 7).

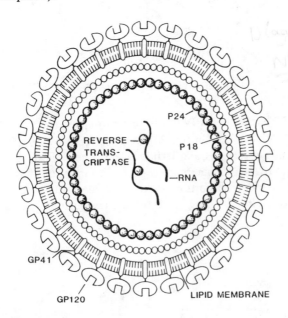

Figure 2-4 The structure of HIV

Between the membrane and the center of the virus, are two protein coats made up of relatively small proteins – p18, the outermost, and p24, the innermost. These coats may be arranged in a regular form, like a crystal with a fixed number of faces. Coat proteins themselves, as well as glycoproteins, may have profound biological actions on the cell. Inside the innermost protein coat are two identical strands of single-stranded RNA which carry the genetic code of the virus. Attached to each strand is at least one molecule of reverse transcriptase enzyme.

How the Virus Enters the Cell

The first step is attachment of the virus to the cell membrane by a combining of the glycoprotein (gp120) with a receptor, T4 also called CD4, on the membrane of a helper lymphocyte, one type of white cell, as is shown in Figure 2-5.

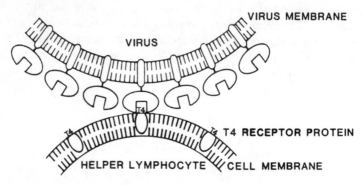

Figure 2-5 Attachment of HIV to a T4 helper Lymphocyte

The HIV glycoprotein (gp120) is not perfectly oval but has clefts, valleys, and depressions, and T4 fits well into one of these. Attachment of the virus to the cell membrane triggers the formation of a coated pit, which is an indented portion of the cell coated with a large protein called a clathrin. The progress of the virus is illustrated in Figure 2-6.

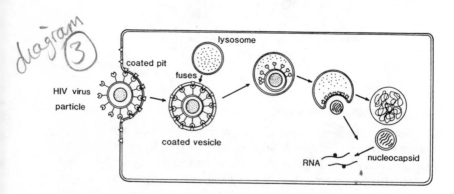

Figure 2-6 How the nucleocapsid enters the cell protoplasm

The pit is carried further into the cell, forming a coated vesicle. The coating is soon lost, and the vesicle fuses with a cell particle called a lysosome. The lysosome is filled with digestive enzymes which, in some way which is not entirely clear, release the inside protein coats containing the RNA into the cell contents. This inner portion of the virus is the nucleocapsid. The protein coats are somehow dispersed, and the RNA is released free into the cytoplasm or liquid portion of the cell with its reverse transcriptase enzyme still attached to it. (Figure 2-6).

Conversion of Virus RNA Into DNA and Integration Into Cellular DNA

The freed RNA, with its attached reverse transcriptase, then begins to utilize some of the cell's components to synthesize a strand of DNA complementary to itself (Figure 2-7).

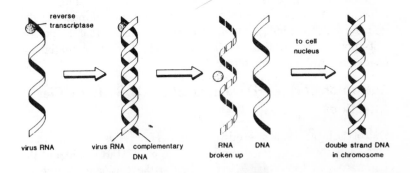

Figure 2-7 Continuing steps in the HIV life cycle

A double helix with one strand of RNA and one complementary strand of DNA is formed. The reverse transcriptase has a second activity (called ribonuclease H) which is able to break up the RNA strand, leaving only the DNA strand. This strand migrates into the nucleus of the cell and, by means of special functioning strand ends called long terminal repeats (LTR) (see Chapter 3), is able to insert itself into one of the cell's chromosomes where it eventually receives a complementary DNA strand to make it conform to the rest of the chromosomal DNA. The chromosome it goes to and the site on this chromosome it selects are both apparently chosen at random. Where it ends up, however, may influence its future activity.

Latency Period of HIV

The viral code, now as DNA in a cell chromosome, appears in most cases to undergo a long latency period which may last years. The length of this period is not known, but some people have harbored the AIDS virus for as long as 7 years without showing symptoms of the disease.

It seems reasonable that when a person is infected by sexual contact, intravenous transmission of the virus by use of contaminated needles, or the use of transfusions of contaminated blood or blood products, not many infectious virus particles are picked up. Perhaps a few thousand at most. This is enough, however, to provoke an immune reaction, so the person will thereafter test positive for HIV antibodies in the blood. Some of the initial virus particles will be destroyed by the immune system, but many will probably have time to insert themselves into the DNA of the helper lymphocytes which are their targets. And there they may reside for many years. There is no way the immune system can recognize these cells with integrated DNA. Probably all the residual HIV proteins initially present are soon digested by the infected cell. By the same token, no antiviral drug can pick out the infected cell (Chapter 7). All one can say at present is that if a person tests positive for HIV antibodies, he or she has the potential for developing AIDS at some future date.

Activation of HIV — Development of AIDS After Other Infections

One of the biggest unanswered questions is, How is this virus activated? One suggestion has come from Dr. Malcolm A. Martin, Chief of the Laboratory of Molecular Microbiology at the National Institute of Allergy and Infectious Diseases. Dr. Martin and his co-workers found that AIDS virus lying dormant in cells could be stimulated to reproduce by at least several other kinds of viruses. The ones they tested were herpes, the cause of cold sores and genital herpes; adenovirus, the cause of respiratory infections; *Varicella zoster*, the cause of chicken pox and shingles; and Jacob-Creuztfeld virus, which causes a progressive degenerative neurological disease. These are all DNA-containing viruses, but many other DNA disease-causing viruses, as well as other RNA viruses, might also be able to activate AIDS virus.

Activation of HIV forces the cell to make many thousands of copies of each of the proteins in HIV using the protein-synthesizing machinery of the cell. Copies of the RNA of the virus, all of its genes, are also made directly from the integrated DNA of the retrovirus. All these components can self-assemble into provirus (early virus) particles inside the cell, and the particles then move to the outside cell membrane from which they bud off, taking along a piece of the cell membrane already containing virus glycoprotein molecules. The cell membrane thus becomes the outer coat of the virus (Figure 2-4).

Other stimuli may activate the virus, such as some of the normal growth factors from white cells, for example, interleukin-2 and colony stimulating factors. Whatever the reason for activation, the virus grows explosively and may spread rapidly to other cells through the blood, via the lymph fluid, and by direct cell-to-cell contact.

Another form of latency was observed by several scientists working with Dr. Anthony S. Fauci, Director of the National Institute of Allergy and Infectious Diseases in Bethesda, Maryland. These scientists found that when a human T-cell line grown in tissue culture was infected by HIV, most of the cells were killed. However, a small number of cells lacking a marker on the cell surface, Leu-3, survived. These surviving cells did not produce virus, nor could they be infected by virus. However, when treated with a particular chemical, (1-iodo 2'-deoxyuridine), virus was made soon afterward, suggesting that the cells contained HIV in a latent form, probably as DNA integrated into the cell genes. This chemical, as well as others, is known to be able to activate various DNA systems to produce messenger RNA and protein. Although not a natural chemical, possibly others like it found in the body, or growth stimulants, might trigger activation of integrated HIV genes. That growth stimulants may indeed activate the virus has been reported recently by Dr. Fauci who found HIV to be activated in tissue culture by exposing infected cells to cytokine, a protein growth stimulant secreted into the blood-stream by monocytes. Monocytes develop into much larger cells called macrophages. Dr. Fauci believes the process is a slow, insidious one that eventually becomes overwhelming.

Long-Term Culture of HIV-Infected Cells

Dr. D. Zagury and co-workers, in collaboration with Dr. Robert C. Gallo, studied HIV-infected white cells from AIDS patients in tissue culture. They utilized white cells from normal donors infected by HIV *in vitro*, as well as white cells from AIDS patients. They found methods for growing the cells for 50 to 60 days. In all cases, stimulation of the infected cells either by an immunological challenge or by the use of chemical growth stimulants led to the secretion of interleukin-2, a growth factor for helper T4 lymphocytes. The production of inter-leukin-2 was followed shortly afterward by the formation of virus progeny, and this led to cell death.

These results suggest how helper T4 cells are depleted in AIDS patients and also how repeated immunological stimulation by an infection such as cytomegalovirus and by venereal diseases can trigger activation of HIV. Foreign blood and semen, which cause immune reactions, may also be important in activating the virus and bringing on full-blown AIDS.

Types of Cells Infected by AIDS Virus

The probability is that AIDS virus is capable of infecting many different kinds of cells. Already mentioned has been any cell type that carries a T4 receptor. Thus far the following cells are known to be infected:

1. Helper T4 lymphocytes

2. Macrophages

3. Follicular dendritic cells in lymph nodes

4. B lymphocytes (some types)

5. Brain astrocytes

6. Endothelial cells of the brain

7. Microglia (brain cells)

8. T8 cells transformed by HTLV-I

9. Cardiac cells

10. Langerhans cells (immune cells in the skin)

11. Rectal cells

12. Colon cells,

13. Cells in the cervix.

The list is increasing in size. It is not always clear whether the infection is direct, by attachment of virus to the cell, or indirect as by fusion of an infected macrophage with one of the above cell types.

Giant-Cell Formation by AIDS Virus

Dr. Jeffrey D. Lipson and his colleagues at Stanford University Medical School in California found that AIDS virus-infected helper T4 lymphocytes in tissue culture could fuse with other T4 cells, either infected or noninfected, to form giant cells with many nuclei. These multinucleated cells are called syncytia, and they produce large amounts of virus and then die after a period of a few days.

Since giant cells can incorporate normal uninfected T4 lymphocytes, this provides one mechanism by which these normal cells may be killed besides direct invasion by the virus. The same types of multinucleated giant cells have been observed in sections of tissues taken from patients with AIDS, so the formation of syncytia can evidently occur in the human body as well as in tissue culture.

The T4 or CD4 receptor on the surface of the lymphocyte appears to be essential for giant-cell formation, because if the T4 receptor is neutralized by a monoclonal antibody to T4 (a very specific protein that can combine with T4), giant cells are not formed. These same monoclonal antibodies to T4 block the infectivity of the virus *in vitro* by blocking the T4 receptor so the virus cannot combine with it.

Effect of AIDS Virus on Helper T4 Lymphocytes

Rapid growth of the virus in helper T4 lymphocytes kills them. It is believed that this killing occurs only in activated T4 lymphocytes, those that have already begun to function in fighting a foreign invader of the body. Activated T4 lymphocytes comprise about 10% of the total number of T4 lymphocytes, and if all these cells were killed, the total would fall 10%. In active disease, however, the total often falls 75 to 90% below normal, leaving so few T4 lymphocytes that the immune system is crippled. It is possible that large numbers of T4 lymphocytes that are infected but not killed bear on their surface various AIDS virus proteins, especially the glycoprotein. These would be recognized by the surviving immune system as foreign, and the cells probably killed by a type of autoimmune reaction. This autoimmune reaction can occur, rarely, in other types of diseases, probably for the same reason — contamination of normal body cells by foreign virus or bacterial proteins. The damage to the immune system caused by HIV is much more pervasive than just the destruction of T4 lymphocytes. Many other cell types in the immune system and throughout the body are also affected and are injured or killed.

Effect of AIDS Virus on Other Cell Types

B lymphocytes that have been transformed (made into precancerous cells) by Epstein-Barr (EB) virus can be infected by HIV. Nearly everyone is exposed to EB virus in the United States by about age 14. This exposure may pass completely unnoticed or at most cause a transient fever or sore throat. In young adults who have not been exposed to EB virus, mononucleosis may occur on infection with it, and in some places, particularly in parts of Africa, EB virus can cause a lymphoma or cancer of the lymph glands (Burkitt's lymphoma) that particularly affects the face and jaw.

There is no easy way to determine how many EB transformed cells are present in a person and how many undergo dual infection with HIV. It is known that B cells are very important, as they produce antibodies in response to an infection that circulate in the blood and are a valuable line of defense against an invader.

Another white cell that is attacked is the monocyte. This cell develops into a larger macrophage cell that plays an important role in telling T4 lymphocytes and probably B cells what kind of proteins to look for and attack. The macrophage travels freely throughout the body and to the brain and carries the virus with it. This may be the source of the frequent infections of the brain observed in AIDS patients that lead to dementia and other mental abnormalities. Macrophages can fuse with brain cells, forming multinucleated giant cells most often in the brain cortex (white matter) or hippocampus (gray matter) deep in the brain. Both these areas are important to higher mental functions, which could explain the dementia and other symptoms observed in AIDS patients. HIV can also produce meningitis, an acute infection of the membranes that line the brain and spinal cord. This affliction is much rarer than dementia which can affect up to 60% of AIDS victims.

In addition to the infected macrophages that reach the brain, it has also been reported that endothelial cells lining capillaries (minute blood vessels) in the brain are directly infected. Dr. Clayton Wiley and his colleagues found that this was a very selective infection, as endothelial cells elsewhere in the body did not appear to be infected.

Interestingly, the degree of mental disease does not appear to be related to readily visible changes within the brain under microscopic or other examination. Persons with severe mental symptoms may show minor changes in brain tissue appearance.

Brain Cell Injury Caused by AIDS Virus Protein

A discovery that explains in part the mental impairment of AIDS victims is that the glycoprotein on the virus exterior (gp120) blocks the action of an important nerve chemical, neuroleukin. The way in which gp120 appears to work is by binding to brain cell receptors for neuro-leukin. This is possible because gp120 protein has some sections in it that closely resemble neuroleukin. The brain cell needs the neuroleukin for its normal functions but cannot obtain it because of its blocked neuroleukin receptors.

Neuroleukin is also secreted by white cells and plays a part in the functioning of the immune system, for example, it is believed by scientists that neuroleukin is needed for antibody production. It thus has a dual role. As already mentioned, AIDS virus may bind directly to brain cells, and some research indicates that infected macrophages located in the brain may secrete toxic substances that harm nerve cells. Blocking of neuroleukin, however, cannot explain all the diverse symptoms found in AIDS patients with mental impairment.

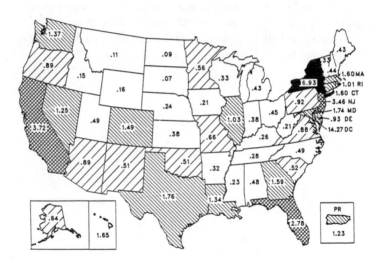

Cumulative reported incidence of AIDS by state as of November 2, 1987. Rates per 10,000 population from *Epidemiology of HIV Infection and AIDS in the United States* by James W. Curran et al., *Science,* **239,** *610-616* (1988) by kind permission of the authors and the editor of *Science.*

CHAPTER 3
NATURE OF THE BEAST

How AIDS virus is put together; AIDS virus genes and what they do; Formation of antibodies to AIDS; Failure of AIDS virus antibodies to control disease; HIV proteins causing formation of antibodies; Classification of HIV as a lentivirus; Nucleotide sequence of HIV; Genetic variation in AIDS virus in a single individual over time; Genetic variation in AIDS virus from the United States and from Zaire; Newly discovered relatives of AIDS virus; Comparison of gene structure of SIV and HIV-2; Isolation of a new virus in patients with lymph gland cancers; Stability of AIDS virus; Suppressive action of semen on the immune system.

3

NATURE OF THE BEAST

How AIDS Virus Is Put Together

The AIDS virus is pictured in Figure 3-1. Genes are generally signified by three italicized letters. A single gene usually codes for a single protein, but many viruses pack a lot more information into their limited repertory of genes than that, and AIDS virus is no exception. One gene, *pol*, has probably three distinct activities and possibly two proteins; the *gag* gene codes for three proteins as well, and there are several overlapping genes.

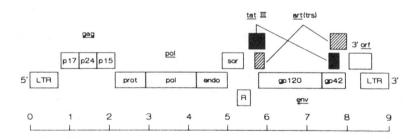

Figure 3-1 Arrangement of genes in HIV

Although the exact sequence of all the nucleotides in HIV (three variants) is known, it is sometimes difficult to sort out all the coding possibilities, especially when there are overlapping codes and bits and pieces that are separated are spliced together. The scheme in Figure 3-1, which depicts eight genes and codes for 10 or 11 proteins, may be revised as time passes and additional proteins may be discovered. Our knowledge of the properties of some of the proteins and exactly what they do in the cell is quite fragmentary at present but is improving with considerable rapidity.

AIDS Virus Genes and What They Do

Long terminal repeats are found at the beginning and end of HIV. They have been given this name because the sequences of nucleotides within each section are similar. LTRs are present in all retroviruses, and they appear to have several functions. At the 5' end, the LTR contains sequences of nucleotides that act as promoters facilitating transcription of the virus genes. They may also contain a sequence which helps to position the cellular enzyme involved in transcription of the virus DNA. This sequence may also help position the virus reverse transcriptase when it copies virus RNA into DNA. In addition, by a mechanism that is not entirely clear, LTRs appear to be able to facilitate the entry of the strand (or circle) of DNA copied from the virus RNA into the chromosomal DNA of the cell. Cellular DNA from higher animals contains LTRs here and there, possibly arising from other retroviruses or perhaps having a natural function of allowing genes or parts of genes to move around to make new combinations. The 3' LTR in HIV contains a major part of the 3' *orf* gene in addition to the above mentioned functions.

gag gene

The *gag* gene codes for three proteins – p17, p24, and p15, in that order. These three make up the two protein coats, inner and outer, found in HIV. Since these coats contain p18 in the outer coat and p24 in the inner coat, it is possible that two molecules, one p15 and one p17, assemble and form one molecule of p18 by splitting off a piece. (In assembly, parts may be combined in different ways.) The *gag* gene appears to have a small piece left over, however its purpose, if any, is not yet known. *Gag* genes are subject to considerable mutation or change during the process of virus replication in an individual.

pol gene

The *pol* gene codes for the reverse transcriptase enzyme (polymerase) of HIV that copies the RNA of the virus into complementary DNA. Since this is a very important step in the life cycle of the virus, this gene cannot tolerate much change or mutation. It is therefore a good candidate for a vaccine source. The first step toward making a vaccine against *pol* has already been taken – a process has been devised for obtaining the enzyme in large quantities from bacteria given one *pol* gene or several. After purification of the enzyme to homogeneity, it could be injected into humans who would develop antibodies to it and thereby might be able to prevent HIV infection by destroying the ability of HIV to use its *pol*.

Reverse transcriptase enzymes are not naturally occurring in humans or higher animals, and they differ considerably in their structure and properties from mammalian polymerases, both DNA and RNA. The HIV reverse transcriptase is therefore also a good target for an antiviral drug, and at least one successful drug, AZT, is now finding extensive use against AIDS virus. The difference in properties between viral and human polymerases allows AZT to strongly inhibit the virus polymerase while only weakly inhibiting the human polymerases.

The reverse transcriptase coded for by the *pol* gene also contains an activity allowing the reverse transcriptase protein to break down the RNA of the virus. This activity is called an endonuclease, or ribonuclease H, and it does not appear to be a separate protein but rather an integral part of the reverse transcriptase molecule. Still another activity, a protease or protein able to cut up larger proteins to make smaller active pieces, appears to be coded for by the *pol* gene. This is apparently a separate protein which may also be useful in cutting the *gag* protein into the three required pieces and the *env* protein into its two different-sized pieces. Although all cells have proteins that are able to cut other proteins to the correct size, it is probably more efficient for the virus to have its own protein cutting enzymes.

env **gene**
The *env*-gene codes for the HIV glycoproteins. These proteins are synthesized as one long piece and then cut at the proper place to make the gp42 stem and the gp120 oval surface piece. When this protein is being made in quantity during an acute HIV infection, it migrates to the cell's outer membrane and inserts itself there so it can be ready to bud off from the cell with an otherwise assembled virus particle. The *env* proteins are synthesized without the carbohydrates (glyco = carbohydrates) attached. The virus uses the cell's equipment, probably the Golgi apparatus (a cluster of membranes in most cells that processes and sorts proteins) to add the correct carbohydrates to form the glycoprotein. How the virus manages to do this is a complete mystery. Often, the carbohydrate portion of the protein is important in forming contacts, in this case a contact between the virus gp120 and the T lymphocyte T4 or CD4 receptor protein. How important the carbohydrate is in AIDS virus contact has not yet been determined.

The ability of gp120 to bind to nerve cell receptors for neuroleukin has already been mentioned. The *env* gene is not as important for replication of the virus as *pol* or *tat III*. Consequently *env* undergoes sizable drift or variation due to mutation. The changing nature of this gene may allow the retrovirus to leap to new species, as from monkeys to humans or from humans to cats. It is also possible that similar changes in the *env* gene of other lentiviruses, allows them to migrate to new species and originate new immunodeficiency diseases.

Although the *env* gene can undergo considerable change, there are some regions that cannot do so without adversely altering the ability of the virus to function. For example, the site where the protein is cut into two pieces cannot be changed, nor can the region that binds to the CD4 T lymphocyte receptor.

tat III gene

The *tat* III gene is coded by two separate parts of the HIV genome. One part is just before gp120 (and overlaps the *art* or *trs* gene), and the other part is within (and overlaps) the gp42 part of the *env* gene. When the messenger RNA is made from these two quite distant parts, it has to be spliced together correctly another complex problem for the virus (and for us to understand).

The *tat* III gene is very important in the production of HIV proteins, and the way in which it works has been clarified in part by Dr. Craig A. Rosen and his co-workers in the Departments of Pathology and Cancer Biology, Harvard Medical School and School of Public Health. These investigators found that the level of virus proteins produced under the control of an LTR was greatly increased in cells making the *tat* III protein. The greatly increased amounts of protein produced were not accompanied by a similar increase in messenger RNA, so enhanced transcription was not the cause of the increase but rather some event or events that occurred after transcription. The increase in protein synthesis was as much as 500- to 1000-fold.

Using a *tat* III gene protein and LTR, other, not normally present genes could be stimulated by this system to give large increases in protein synthesis. The trans acting response sequence of nucleotides was determined to be from -17 to $+80$ (initiation of viral RNA synthesis begins at $+1$). The mechanism by which this posttranscriptional control was exerted was not determined. One suggestion is that the *tat* III gene protein interacts with sequences at or near the 5′ terminus of messenger RNA species and thereby increases the translational efficiency of these species. Other possibilities have not been eliminated, however. The *tat* III protein contains a cluster of positively charged amino acids which would facilitate its direct interaction with viral messenger RNA. It has 86 amino acids, a molecular weight of about 14,000, and a responder element in the LTR (trans-activating responsive sequence). Interestingly, *tat* I and *tat* II proteins, from HTLV-I and HTLV-II with more than 300 amino acids, are much larger than *tat* III and apparently work by a much different mechanism, namely, actual stimulation of transcription.

These studies suggest that useful agents that prevent the action of *tat* III might be found. These agents could be chemical or immunological. In addition, the *tat* III gene might be important in stimulating the production of useful human protein products by bacterial systems. The *tat* III gene is one of the most important regulatory genes of HIV, and for this reason little variation or mutation in its gene would be expected.

art or trs gene

This gene is constructed from a coding section preceding the *env* gene and overlapping the first part of the *tat* III gene. A second, somewhat larger, section overlaps the second part of the *tat* III gene and the *env* gene (Figure 3-1). Both *art* or *trs* and *tat* are absolutely required for the synthesis of gp120 from its messenger RNA. Also, both genes influence the level of messenger RNA made from the *env* gene. *Tat* III is required for functioning of *art* or *trs*.

The *art* or *trs* gene produces a small protein of 116 amino acids which, like *tat* III, has a significant positive charge. It also is believed to function as a trans acting stimulator in viral synthesis. If this factor is absent, *gag*- and *env*-encoded protein synthesis is severely diminished. If a drug could be found that would bind or inactivate this protein, viral replication would probably be inhibited. The exact mechanism by which the *art* protein acts is not known. Since this protein is also important for virus replication, little variation or mutation in its gene is to be expected either.

sor/or A gene

The A gene has been given several names: A, Q, P, ORF-II, and *sor*, and it partly overlaps the *pol* gene. (See Figure 3-1.)

Dr. Klaus Strebel at the Laboratory of Molecular Microbiology, National Institute of Allergy and Infectious Diseases, together with colleagues from several different institutions, attempted to determine the function of the protein product of this gene.

It is known that this protein is present in cells in which HIV is replicating. Mutant HIV which does not have the A gene grows in and kills helper T4 lymphocytes. A particular mutant virus isolated by Dr. Strebel and his colleagues which lacked the A gene was found to produce virion particles normally, but the particles were found to be approximately 1000 times less infective than virions from normal HIV. However, the mutant virus spread efficiently when cells containing it were co-cultivated with normal uninfected T4 lymphocytes, indicating that HIV can spread from cell to cell by a mechanism that does not require the A-gene product and probably does not require the production of infective virus particles. The two mechanisms of spread are by means of complete virus through passage of body fluids (blood, semen) and from cell to cell which can proceed without the A gene.

3'orf, (F/3')

The 3'orf gene turns out to be one of the most fascinating of the HIV genes, and it marvelously complicates the possible actions and abilities of the virus. The gene codes for a protein of 206 amino acids which has myristic acid at the amino terminal end. Myristic acid is a 14 carbon fatty acid, and its function in other proteins is to anchor these proteins into the membrane (which also contains fatty acids).

The 3'orf protein is phosphorylated (has a phosphate group placed on it) by protein kinase C, an important intermediate in signal transduction (transmittal) in cells, including signals to grow and divide.

In addition, the protein can bind the high-energy substance guanosine triphosphate (GTP) and hydrolyze it or break it down, and it can also autophosphorylate itself on the amino acid threonine. These last three abilities are the same as those found in the oncogene v-Ha-*ras*, an oncogene found in a retrovirus capable of causing cancer in animals. Also, the same protein contains a sequence similar to one found in another oncogene, *src*. A viral form of *src*, v-*src*, is present in the retrovirus *Rous sarcoma* virus, and the v-*src* sequence is phosphorylated in the same way as the 3'orf protein.

It appears therefore that the 3'orf gene might have been formed by fusion of the most important parts of *ras* and *src* oncogenes, thus producing a protein which could be doubly active as an oncogene. Exactly what the 3'orf protein does is not known except for one thing: When it is produced in a helper T4 lymphocyte, it causes a down-regulation (decrease) in this cell's surface marker, however, the significance of this action remains unclear at the moment. It is likely, however, that 3'*orf* protein can intervene in cellular regulatory pathways and that it may play a role in the establishment or maintenance of latent HIV infection. In addition, it is possible that it has something to do with Kaposi's sarcoma, a cancer of unknown origin occurring as multiple foci in certain specific cells of some HIV-infected patients.

R gene

A short open reading frame that may encode another protein from HIV. The function of the gene R is unknown.

Brief review of the human immune system

Functions of the system

The immune system has several functions: (1) To recognize and destroy or inactivate any foreign bacterium, virus, protozoan or other microorganism that might enter the body and probably cause harm; (2) To recognize and destroy any cell, tissue, or other substance not native to the body; (3) To carry out surveillance for, recognize, and destroy any cancer cell that may arise; (4) To maintain a reserve force capable of quick attack and elimination of any foreign material that may participate in a second invasion of the body.

That we can stay healthy for 60, 70 or 80 years or more in view of the numerous microorganisms lurking on every dust mote is a tribute to our wonderfully complex but efficient immune system.

A few necessary definitions

Antigen: Any substance that provokes an immune response. Most *foreign* proteins are antigens. The word "foreign" is italicized because it is important to understand that in most instances human protein is not antigenic to the same or another human. There are exceptions to this, for example, *autoimmunity* is a pathological response of the immune system to one or more of its own proteins. This may result in an *autoimmune disease*.

Antibody (synonym *immunoglobulin*): A protein made by the B lymphocytes in the immune system in response to an antigen. An antibody is Y-shaped, and each molecule can combine with two antigen molecules at the ends of the Y, usually inactivating the biological activity of the antigen. The antibody can combine with the antigen because the antibody and the antigen have been constructed to fit together like two pieces of a jigsaw puzzle (Figure 3-2).

Immunogenic: Capable of eliciting an immune reaction.

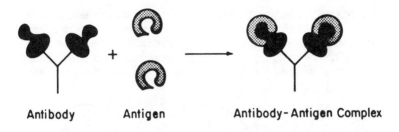

Antibody   Antigen   Antibody-Antigen Complex

Figure 3-2 Combination between antibody and antigen

Divisions of the immune system
The immune system works through two major divisions.

1. *Humoral mediated immunity*: Referring to fluids, particularly (a) lymph, which is the pale, straw-colored liquid that circulates through lymph nodes and between cells, and (b) the blood. The immune components in these fluids are the antibodies and the *complement system* which work together to destroy cells.

2. *Cell mediated immunity*: The various white cells comprise the second division of the immune system. The white cells destroy foreign cells and microorganisms by a variety of methods.

Cells of the immune system
All the cells of the immune system arise from *stem* cells found in the bone marrow, mostly in the long bones of the arms and legs and in the ribs. There are three main series.

1. *Lymphocyte series*

a. T Lymphocytes: T lymphocytes leave the bone marrow and go to the thymus gland where they mature and are processed into several types: (i) T4 (or CD4) cells, helper cells which, as the name suggests, function to assist other cells in recognizing antigens and fighting them; These cells are specifically attacked by HIV. (ii) T8 (or CD8) cells, suppressor cells which damp down the immune reaction to keep it from going out of control. (iii) Natural killer (NK) T cells which attack a variety of foreign cells and microorganisms. (iv) Cytotoxic effector (killer) T cells – go after a variety of cells, infected cells, cancer cells, tissues from another person, and so on.

b. B lymphocytes: Lymphocytes formed in the bone marrow and processed there. When activated by an antigen and with the help of T4 cells they turn into larger *plasma cells*, which keep dividing forming a clone that makes large amounts of antibody to inactivate the antigen. Antibodies are poured into the blood and lymph.

2. Granulocyte series

a. Neutrophils (Figure 3-3a) These are the most common of the white cells and are usually the first to localize in an infected or wounded area of tissue. Neutrophils are attracted to sites of wounding or invasion by various chemical signals including products produced by bacteria, substances released by damaged tissues, and components of the

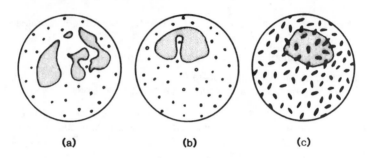

(a)   (b)   (c)

Figure 3-3 Cells of the granulocyte series

Representation of a) neutrophil, b) eosinophil and c) basophil.

complement system. They are highly motile and move like amoebas, surrounding and digesting (phagocytizing) bacteria and other particles. They contain peptides called *defensins* capable of killing bacteria, viruses, and fungi.

b. Eosinophils (Figure 3-3b) These cells are usually present in low concentrations in blood, 100 to 450 per cubic milliliter being the normal range. They are most numerous in the lining of the intestine, in the lungs, in the dermis of the skin, and in tissue of the external genitalia. They do not actively phagocytize but appear to be involved in tissue inflammation (anaphylactic) reactions, as they are numerous in tissues that are sites of allergic reactions and in the blood of persons with allergies. Hydrocortisone, which depresses allergic reactions, causes eosinophils to disappear from the blood.

c. Basophils (Figure 3-3c) These cells are quite rare and often difficult to find in blood smears. They have prominent granules which probably contain histamine and this is the primary initiator of an allergic or anaphylactic reaction. Antihistamines can neutralize their effect as can hydrocortisone and other steroids with similar activities.

3. Monocyte series

Monocytes migrate from the bone marrow into the tissues where they enlarge and become macrophages which can wander through most of the body. A form of macrophage which becomes fixed in the lymph nodes, spleen, or liver is termed a histiocyte. Macrophages are active in engulfing foreign invaders. They process the foreign proteins and then may pass some of the pieces to B cells or T cells which use them to become activated against the proteins from which the pieces were derived. They have a variety of other functions and may secrete various hormones and stimulants for other white cells.

The percentage range of white cell types in normal humans is given in Table 3-1.

Table 3-1 White cells in normal humans

Cell type	Percentage range
Neutrophils	40–80
Eosinophils	1–7
Basophils	0–1
Monocytes	2–11
Lymphocytes*	15–50

*70–90% of lymphocytes are T, the remainder, B. There may be 10 billion T lymphocytes in the body, one to three billion B lymphocytes.

Other cells derived from the stem cell in the marrow are red blood cells and megakarocytes, the latter are large cells which fragment to form platelets which are important to blood clotting.

Cell markers – the red cell

Although the human protein hemoglobin can be transferred safely from one human to any other human, red blood cells cannot be safely transferred from one person to any other. That is because red cells have markers on them. These markers are complex polysaccharides (sugars) termed A or B and one, both, or none, may be present. There are thus four major groups of red cells: A, B, AB, and O. Red cells or blood from a person with an A marker can be transfused only into a recipient with A cells, B cells into a recipient with B red cells, and so on. The immune system of each person recognizes its own markers and destroys any cells bearing others. Thus if B red cells are transfused into a person with A cells, the B cells will be rapidly destroyed. More seriously, the components of the immune system of the donor could possibly destroy large quantities of the red cells of the recipient, and there might be a serious anaphylactic reaction in addition. There are other red cell markers including the Rh factor which may be present or absent; Rh+ or Rh–.

Other cell markers – the major histocompatibility complex

All cells of the body except red cells have other cell markers on them, proteins called *histocompatibility antigens* (HLAs), which are unique for each individual. Each individual has four HLAs, two obtained from the mother and two from the father. HLAs are divided into two major classes.

Class I contains the genes A, B and C. There are many varieties (called alleles) of each gene, and their proteins are involved in interactions between cytotoxic T lymphocytes and target cells usually bearing a virus or tumor antigen. In addition to the foreign antigen against which the mature T lymphocyte is primed, the lymphocyte must also have presented to it the proper HLA it recognizes as "self." Class I antigen molecules are called classical transplantation antigens.

Class II contains the genes DP, DQ, and DR which are involved in interactions between helper T cells and antigen-presenting cells containing foreign protein. Class II antigen molecules are termed immune response (Ir) antigens.

Since each person has a different set of HLA antigens on the surface of every cell, they are like fingerprints that the immune system recognizes as self. The transplantation of tissue from one person to another – heart, kidney, liver, skin, and so on – is usually not possible because the foreign tissue has different HLAs which the immune system recognizes as foreign and destroys, primarily with cytotoxic killer T cells.

Tissue transplants can be made, however, under one of two conditions. First, if a close HLA match can be made between organ donor and recipient, there is a good chance the transplant will "take," that is, grow and function normally. Members of the same family often have one or more HLAs in common, and family members are the best organ donors. Second, if a match cannot be made, as is often the case in heart or liver transplants, then one must use what tissue is available and administer the drug cyclosporin a. This drug suppresses the immune system, particularly the T lymphocytes responsible for tissue rejection, and must be taken for life. Patients who take cyclosporin a continually are unfortunately put at greater risk of serious infection or cancer by virtue of the fact that their T cells are repressed. (Their condition is similar to that of an AIDS patient, only their immune systems are usually less severely repressed.)

HLAs and disease
The nature of HLAs may predispose a person to certain diseases or protect a person from others, including cancer. For example, different forms of arthritis are commonly associated with HLA, B27. While the combination A3, B7, DR2 predisposes one to (but does not assure that one will get) multiple sclerosis. Many suggestions have been offered to explain the relation between HLAs and disease. Perhaps the most simple one is that some viruses may use certain HLAs as receptors. A virus infection might then be responsible directly or indirectly for arthritis, multiple sclerosis, and so on.

Lymphokines Lymphokines are growth factors or hormones used by white cells and other cells and are important in fighting disease and in the functioning of nerve cells, intestinal cells, and others. They are often referred to as biological response modifiers. The major ones will be briefly described.

Interferons

alpha, 13 varieties;
beta, 5 varieties;
gamma, 1 form only

Interferons are small proteins produced by cells of the immune system, as well as all other cells, when they are infected by viruses or other microorganisms. Other substances such as double-stranded RNA and certain small organic molecules can also stimulate cells to produce interferons. They are excreted by the infected cells and taken up by uninfected cells in which they act as early warnings of an impending attack. The interferon-primed cell undergoes a complicated series of metabolic reactions that enable it to resist the infection and destroy the infecting agent should it enter the cell.

Interferons have proved to be useful in the treatment of certain diseases and also in the treatment of cancer, particularly hairy cell leukemia, osteosarcoma (bone cancer), bladder cancer, and other cancers, and also in AIDS. In AIDS interferon appears to inhibit the process of budding of the virus from the cell membrane, but it undoubtedly has other actions as well.

There are many different interferons with different properties and actions on cells. They all appear to exert toxic effects on the body, producing fever, aching joints, and loss of appetite and when injected in large amounts, they may give rise to mental symptoms. When one gets the flu, the symptoms are largely due to the production of interferons.

Interleukin I (IL-1). This substance is produced by activated macrophages, as well as by epidermal cells, astrocytes (brain cells), skin Langerhans cells (immune cells), kidney mesangial cells, and possibly B lymphocytes and others.

IL-1 appears to have many functions, including stimulation of thymocyte (early T-cell) proliferation, stimulation of fibroblast growth, and the release of prostaglandins (potent hormones with many effects) and collagenase (an enzyme capable of breaking down collagen) from synovial cells. There appear to be two different forms of IL-1.

Interleukin 2 (IL-2) This growth factor has been mentioned in the news quite frequently as a possible treatment for various forms of cancer and AIDS. It may be used alone or in combination with other substances. Some of its reported actions are as follows. It supports the long-term growth of T cells in culture (and in the body); it increases the generation of cytotoxic T lymphocytes; it enhances the activity of natural killer T cells; it stimulates lymphokine-activated killer cell activity; it restores, in part at least, the immune response in individuals whose immune system is weakened; it is involved in the induction of other lymphokines, particularly alpha-interferon and a B cell factor; and it plays a role in the stimulation of B cell growth.

This is a long list of important actions, and clearly IL-2 is an important cog in the immune machine. It is available for experimentation at present in large amounts and is made commercially by recombinant DNA technology.

Interleukin-3 (IL-3) This substance may be identical to multicolony-stimulating factor, which is capable of stimulating the formation of most of the blood cells derived from the stem cell. It has been shown experimentally that it can support the growth and long-term culture of several types of early B cells.

Tumor necrosis factor (TNF) This protein can be found in the serum of animals injected with immunostimulatory agents. When given to animals with various tumors, this serum causes necrosis (dissolution of the tumor cells) and occasionally complete regression of the tumors. TNF is also produced by activated macrophages and other white cells and does not appear to affect normal cells. It is available for clinical study and is being actively investigated as a treatment for many different kinds of tumors and for AIDS.

It is a highly toxic substance and when used, or naturally produced in large amounts by the body, may give rise to cachexia or severe wasting of the body. And it is possibly, in part at least, the cause of this wasting in AIDS, ARC, and cancer patients.

Colony stimulating factors (CSFs) Blood cells of all types are incapable of dividing in the absence of specific stimulants called regulatory proteins. In the presence of these proteins stem cells form clones of cells of one type or another, hence the name of the factors. In addition to stimulating progenitor cells to proliferate, these factors promote cell survival, commit cells to certain developmental pathways, and stimulate the final functional activity of cells. Some of these final activities are phagocytosis of bacteria or yeast; antibody cytotoxic killing of tumor cells by granulocytes; and synthesis of prostaglandin E, plasminogen activator, and other regulators by macrophages. Table 3-2 lists the colony stimulating factors.

Lymphotoxin. This lymphokine has tumor necrosis activity. It is produced by lymphocytes stimulated to divide and is active against certain types of tumor cells. Like tumor necrosis factor, it shows little activity against normal cells. The amino acid sequence has a small resemblance to that of TNF but lymphotoxin molecules are distinctly

Table 3-2 Colony stimulating factors

Name	Cells stimulated	Remarks
Granulocyte-macrophage colony stimulating factor GM-CSF	Granulocytes & Macrophages	Has proved very useful in treatment of AIDS (Chapt. 7)
Granulocyte colony stimulating factor G-CSF	Granulocytes	Prepared from mouse lung
Multipotential colony stimulating factor Multi-CSF	Most cells derived from stem cells	Amino acid sequence has been determined
Macrophage colony stimulating factor M-CSF		

different from TNF. Lymphotoxin, like most of the other factors described, is available for clinical testing. It will be years before all lymphokine combinations can be assessed for their curative effect on the many different clinical diseases that may benefit from such treatment.

Other factors New factors are coming to light every few months. Two that have recently been described are B-cell growth factor II (T-cell replacing factor) and B cell stimulating factor 2 (BSF-2), a growth substance that induces B lymphocytes to produce immunoglobulins (antibodies).

Activation of T cells

Most of the small T lymphocytes circulating in the blood or lymph are inactive but can undoubtedly be activated in several ways. One sequence that is fairly well established begins with a macrophage ingesting an antigen, for example, a virus protein. The macrophage partially digests the protein and then presents a small piece of it, probably about 15 to 20 amino acids long, to a T lymphocyte. The lymphocyte has a T cell receptor consisting of an immunoglobulin-like protein plus three other proteins. The immunoglobulin-like protein can probably be adjusted to recognize the antigen presented to it by the macrophage. Presentation of an antigen to a T lymphocyte activates it, and it begins to secrete interleukin-2. At the same time it forms interleukin-2 receptors on its cell surface. These interact with the interleukin-2 secreted, and the T cell begins to grow and multiply, forming a clone of the same kind of cells with the same specificity able to recognize the presented protein. When the cloned lymphocytes encounter this protein, for which they are primed, on a cell, they recognize it. They then need to recognize the HLAs or the cell surface as self, and if these HLAs are present, the lymphocytes will attack the cell and kill it. If the wrong HLAs are present, or there are no HLAs, the killer activity will not proceed. By this mechanism virus-infected cells, bacteria-infected cells, and tumor cells can be killed.

Formation of Antibodies to AIDS

Theoretically, each protein produced by an immunodeficiency virus can engender the formation of one or more antibodies against it from the infected human or animal. Usually these antibodies appear in the blood a few weeks to a few months after infection. However, it has been found recently that the period before which antibodies can be detected may be much longer – more than a year and possibly in a few cases, even longer. In view of the nature of the AIDS virus, particularly its slow spread in the body initially and its ability to lie dormant in the DNA of the host for years, this is not surprising.

This very long latent period is, however, disconcerting, for it means that testing procedures are surely missing some cases of AIDS virus infection (see Chapter 5). The principal author of the study which was reported in the British medical journal, *Lancet*, Dr. Kai Krohn of the University of Tampere in Finland, estimated on the basis of a small gay population that antibodies might not appear for as long as a year or more in 10 to 20% of a group infected by sexual contact. The group included 285 homosexual or bisexual men and 2 women. They were followed for up to 3 years with examinations for antibodies every 3 to 6 months, with storing of blood samples. Some of these individuals had AIDS virus in their blood long before antibodies could be detected. One did not have a positive antibody test 3 years after the virus was detected in his blood. Apparently the virus was able to hide in cells and remain inactive there before the immune system could react to it. Scientists, including Dr. Genoveffa Franchini of the U.S. National Cancer Institute, point out that the direct test for virus, while quite sensitive, is difficult to perform and, very expensive and so would not be practical for use on a large scale.

Failure of AIDS Virus Antibodies to Control Disease

Normally, after a virus or bacterial infection there is a large reservoir of antibodies against the invading organism which completely inactivate and destroy the invader or any cells bearing its foreign proteins. In AIDS, the disease appears to run its course despite the presence of antibodies, probably because cell-to-cell infection progresses in a way antibodies cannot detect. In fact, often contrary to what one would expect, the more antibodies present in the blood, the greater the severity of the disease. Patients who have low antibody levels may have no sign of the disease or at most mild symptoms such as swollen lymph glands. As the disease progresses, mostly out of reach of the antibodies that have been formed, and unchecked by helper T4 cells which have been largely destroyed, more virus proteins are made which cause the formation of more antibodies (from B lymphocytes). By this time, however, the immune system has collapsed and the patient gets worse.

HIV Proteins Causing Formation of Antibodies

As might be expected, the glycoproteins of HIV are highly immunogenic. They are two of the proteins manufactured in the largest amounts during active virus replication, and they reach the surface of the host cell where they can be easily detected by the immune system. All infected persons who have developed antibodies probably have antibodies to both proteins gp120 and gp42. A sensitive test for AIDS based on a piece of gp120 has been developed. The one-third of this protein ending in a carboxyl group, prepared by putting the gene for this piece in the bacterium *Escherichia coli*, is used. The test is a simple enzyme-linked immunoassay (see Chapter 5) which is claimed to be 99.9% sensitive.

Approximately 80% of all human sera with antibodies against HIV have antibodies that react with the reverse transcriptase of HIV. This was shown by a group headed by Dr. F. D. Marzo Veronese from Bionetics Research, Inc., in Bethesda, Maryland. These antibodies neutralize the enzyme activity essential for replication of the virus. As already mentioned, the reverse transcriptase would be a good candidate for making a vaccine against AIDS virus for this reason and also because it shows far less mutation (variation) than the coat proteins or glycoproteins.

A relationship has been found between antibodies to AIDS reverse transcriptase and disease progression. In patients who have antibodies to reverse transcriptase but no signs of the disease, these antibodies start to disappear and finally can no longer be detected as the disease appears and gets worse. This antibody therefore might be useful in predicting disease progression.

Antibodies to the two *gag* proteins or the two coat proteins of HIV have also been detected in the serum of individuals infected with the virus. In addition, several other antibodies have been detected, possibly directed against one or more of the gene products of the genes not yet mentioned, such as *tat III, trs, sor*, and *3'*-orf.

Classification of HIV As a Lentivirus

A National Cancer Institute publication of abstracts it produces on human retroviruses has a section entitled "AIDS and Other Lentiviruses." It is becoming generally accepted now that HIV is more closely related to lentiviruses than to HTLV-I or HTLV-II or other retroviral types. In a detailed study carried out by several cooperating laboratories, including the National Cancer Institute and the Johns Hopkins University School of Medicine and, headed by Dr. Matthew A. Gouda, HIV was compared to HTLV-I and -II and to visna virus, the lentivirus that attacks sheep and other hooved animals. There was a much greater resemblance of the RNA structure of HIV to that of visna virus than to that of any other virus. This resemblance extended through the whole genome and was particularly strong in the *gag* and *pol* genes. Electron photomicrographs of visna virus and HIV, taken of virus budding from cells, were practically identical. Other resemblances between HIV and lentiviruses are the ability of both to produce cell-killing effects and persistent debilitating diseases in their hosts. More recent studies suggest that HIV is more closely related to equine infectious anemia virus (Figure 3-4) than to visna virus.

Visna virus and equine infectious anemia virus readily induce neutralizing antibodies in infected animals. These viruses, like HIV, mutate rapidly in the *env* gene, and variants may be produced which can escape the immune system and produce a new cycle of disease. In contrast, it has been stated that caprine arthritis encephalitis virus does not induce the formation of neutralizing antibodies during natural or experimental infections. The reason for this has not been clarified other than to state that the animal is placed in a "hyporesponsive" state which can be broken by infecting it with the virus and some other antigen at the same time.

Nucleotide Sequence of HIV

Three different isolates of HIV have been used to determine the arrangement of nucleotides in the virus genome. This information is important to enable the researcher to determine the sequence of amino acids in the proteins made by the virus, to show the relationships of HIV to other retroviruses, and to find the variability of the virus genes in a single patient or from one patient to the next. These and many other useful pieces of information may be extracted from the virus code.

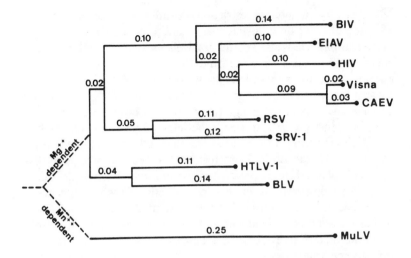

Figure 3-4 Relationships among various retroviruses based on *pol* genes. Reproduced with permission of *Nature* and Dr. Gouda from *Nature* 330, 388-391 (1987).

One group from Chiron Research Laboratories, Emoryville, California, found 9265 nucleotide bases in an isolate of HIV. A French group from the Pasteur Institute in Paris counted 9193 nucleotides in the virus, while a group from Genentech, Inc., San Francisco, California, and the Federal Centers for Disease Control, Atlanta, Georgia, determined that there were 9213 nucleotides in a sample of HIV. A fourth group consisting of 19 individuals from 5 different laboratories used 2 different isolates of HIV so comparisons could be made. This group found 9213 nucleotide bases with a 0.9% diversity of bases (approximately 1 in 100) in the coding regions and a 1.8% diversity (approximately 2 in 100) in the noncoding regions.

There were many differences besides this in various genes from the virus, these differences being an expression of the virus' ability to mutate and change continually while it is replicating in humans.

Dr. Flossie Wong-Staal and collaborators from the Laboratory of Tumor Cell Biology of the U.S. National Cancer Institute isolated virus from 18 individuals with AIDS or who were at risk for AIDS. Each of these isolates showed a different restriction enzyme pattern. (Restriction enzymes cut DNA where certain specific sequences of nucleotides occur.) The fact that restriction patterns differ indicates that there are significant differences in the nucleotide sequences of the

18 isolates. The number of restriction site differences ranged from 1 to 16. No particular disease state was found to be associated with any particular pattern. When 3 of the viral isolates were allowed to grow in cells in tissue culture for up to 9 months, no change in the restriction enzyme patterns was noted in any of the virus isolates. These results suggest that when the virus grows in humans, pressure is put on it by the immune system to change (to mutate) in order to escape destruction. Most patients appear to be infected with only one or two predominant forms of the virus at one time. Of the 18 studied only 2 showed some indication of 2 viral forms. This observation suggests that some type of interference process may occur in which, if a single isolate is established, growth of another isolate with different properties is prevented. Humans subjected to repeated infections from numerous sexual encounters or from the use of contaminated needles from different infected individuals do not appear to develop a large variety of different viruses.

Another question is, why do some individuals infected with HIV develop full-scale AIDS, others ARC, and some no disease at all? This could be related to the strain of virus and also to the host immune response, the hormonal balance, other infections, and a variety of other factors.

Genetic Variation in AIDS Virus in a Single Individual Over Time

An interesting study was done collaboratively by a group of laboratories and 10 investigators led by Dr. Beatrice H. Hahn. Four to 6 AIDS virus isolates were obtained at different points in a 1 or 2 year period from each of 3 different individuals persistently infected with HIV.

Changes were detected throughout the viral genomes, consisting of isolated or clustered mutations of a single nucleotide as well as short deletions of parts of the nucleotide chain or short insertions of new pieces of chain. Results from restriction enzyme mapping and nucleotide sequence comparison, showed that the viruses isolated sequentially had evolved in parallel from a common progenitor virus.

The rate of mutation for the *env* and *gag* genes was calculated to be at least a millionfold greater than that normally found in human DNA genes. In spite of this, virus isolates from any one person were much more closely related to each other than to viruses from another individual. These latter results also suggest some type of interference mechanism which may prevent infection by more than one major genotypic form of the virus. No direct evidence for this, however, has yet been obtained.

Genetic Variation in AIDS Virus from the United States and from Zaire

Another large group of scientists and laboratories led by Dr. Steven Benn has examined HIV from patients living in New York, Alabama, and Zaire. They found that some restriction sites (places where restriction enzymes cut the virus) were common to all the isolates, but that many were different, reflecting differences among the isolates. The African isolates as a group contained a greater number of distinctive restriction enzyme sites than the U.S. AIDS viruses. The variability found was concentrated within the *env* gene but could occur elsewhere. According to Dr. Flossie Wong-Staal, comparing the three most divergent isolates carried by her laboratory showed a difference of 10 to 20% in the amino acids of the *env* proteins. She was able to locate "hot spots," that is, places in the gene that are prone to mutation. The hot spots correspond to noncritical regions in the *env* glycoprotein. There are regions, however, of extreme conservation, such as that interacting with the T-cell receptor and those flanking the site for cleavage of the protein. If mutations take place at critical sites, as they may, the virus will not be able to reproduce and there will be no progeny to carry on the line.

Newly Discovered Relatives of AIDS Virus

The picture of the new AIDS viruses with respect to their origin, properties, relationships, and ability to produce disease is still very much in flux.

Dr. Phyllis Kanki and Dr. Max Essex of the Harvard School of Public Health and their colleagues have reported the isolation of a virus from apparently healthy individuals who live in the West African country of Senegal. Healthy prostitutes from Dakar, where AIDS is rare, have antibodies indicating they have been infected with a virus closely related to STLV-III (SIV) or simian T-lymphotropic virus III, which in some ways resembles HIV.

These investigators called the new virus HTLV-IV, although this name was later dropped and now Dr. Kanki believes this virus may be HIV-2 or a variant of it. Initially, this virus does not appear to be associated with illness. The virus appears to be spreading from Africa and has been detected in about 100 people in France, West Germany, and Britain, some of them AIDS patients. It has also been detected in Sao Paolo, Brazil, and in time, will probably work its way into the United States where, in fact, one case was recently reported.

The same two investigators, with many collaborators, published a detailed study of the distribution of the new virus in West Africa in *Science* in May 1987. They collected 4248 blood samples in 6 West African countries (Senegal, Guinea, Guinea Bissau, Mauritania, Burkina Faso, and Ivory Coast; see Figure 1-5 for the locations) from people listed as healthy controls, sexually active risks, or members of diseased populations. The mean age was about 30 years, and there were 80% more female samples than male.

The assays carried out were able to distinguish between HIV and the new virus. The healthy controls included pregnant women and patients hospitalized for other diseases. Sexually active individuals at risk included prostitutes and patients who visited or were in sexually transmitted disease clinics, while diseased patients had a variety of illnesses including tuberculosis. In Mauritania 0 of 184 samples tested positive for the new virus and in Guinea only 5 of 458 samples were positive. In the other four countries, positive tests ranged from 6.9 to 16%. Risk populations had a considerably higher prevalence of the new virus – 14.9 to 64% – than that found in healthy (control group) persons – 0.2% to 9.2%. In Senegal, Guinea, Guinea Bissau, and Mauritania, HIV prevalence was lower than the new virus while in Ivory Coast and Burkina Faso, HIV and the new virus occurred with about the same frequency.

Only 5 cases of *diagnosed* AIDS were found in the 4248 individuals examined. None of the patients who had the new virus showed any sign of disease. None of a group of prostitutes infected with it showed any sign of disease when followed for 2 years.

An interesting observation is that human cells in tissue culture infected with the new virus can be dually infected with HIV (super-infected). These cells form syncytia after 7 days, but the syncytia cells do not burst to release virus as is normally the case with HIV infected cells. It appears that the new virus interferes in some unknown way with the normal development and/or multiplication of HIV. Therefore this new virus might be an important candidate for a vaccine against HIV. Further studies are required to definitely prove that the new virus does not cause disease and that it can interfere with HIV replication in humans.

As already mentioned, HIV-2 resembles SIV which was originally found in captive Rhesus macaque monkeys with a disease similar to AIDS. The same virus, or one very much like it, also occurs in about 50% of healthy African green monkeys living in the jungle. The discovery of the similar virus HIV-2 in humans, lends support to the idea that AIDS viruses may have originated in monkeys and eventually been passed to humans. Initially and at present HIV-2 or a variant may not cause disease, or serious disease in humans, but then, through mutation, it may have changed to a virulent form HIV that spread from Central Africa.

Comparison of Gene Structure of SIV and HIV-2

Dr. G. Franchini and collaborators from three laboratories have compared the gene structure and nucleotide sequence of SIV, (STLV-III) and HIV-2. The gene arrangements are shown in Figure 3-5 which should also be compared to Figure 3-1 for HIV. SIV lacks 350 nucleotides shown by the dotted lines in the top genome of Figure 3-5 and there are other marked differences between SIV and HIV-2 located mostly in the nucleotides beginning at the end of the *sor* gene and running to the terminal LTR.

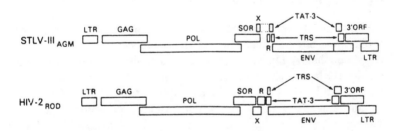

Figure 3-5 Gene arrangements of STLV-III, (SIV) and HIV-2. From G. Franchini and co-workers, *Nature,* 328, 539-543 (1987) with kind permission of the author and publisher.

Comparison of the amino acid homologies (percentage of amino acids that are identical) in the different genes indicates a close relationship between SIV and HIV-2, 82% in the *gag* gene, 76% in the *pol* gene and 70% in the *env* gene, and 72% over all. The relationship of SIV or HIV-2 to HIV is, however, much more distant, approximately 51% in the *gag* gene, 53% in the *pol* gene, 34% in the *env* gene, and 43% overall. Nevertheless, the authors believe the extent of similarity is such that all the viruses arose from a common ancestor.

Two additional reports appearing at the same time on sequence determination and properties of variants of SIV and HIV-2 confirm the results of Dr. Franchini and suggest the very complex situation that some of the isolates may cause immune deficiency while others may not or may be less efficient at inducing immune deficiency in humans.

Isolation of a New Virus in Patients with Lymph Gland Cancers

Dr. Robert C. Gallo's group has discovered a new virus in patients with a variety of disorders of the lymph glands. Two of the patients tested positive for AIDS virus, three tested negative for AIDS virus but had various lymphomas, and the sixth had acute lymphatic leukemia. The virus selectively infected freshly isolated B lymphocytes and converted them into much larger cells with inclusion bodies (material appearing dark under the microscope) in the nucleus of the cell, as well as outside the nucleus. The virus appears to be a herpes type but is unrelated to all the known human herpes viruses. As the virus was not found in 12 AIDS patients who did not have lymphoma, it is probably not of any consequence to AIDS. The virus is called human lymphotrophic B (cell) virus (HBLV).

Stability of AIDS Virus

AIDS virus has been pictured as a very fragile virus. In a report on AIDS by the Student Health Services for the University of Connecticut, it is stated that "AIDS is a very fragile virus. It dies in less than a second outside the body." This statement may be misleading, according to tests carried out by Dr. Lionel Resnick of Mount Sinai Medical Center of Miami Beach, Florida. At room temperature in a water solution of human blood cells the virus can live up to 15 days. When dried, complete inactivation of the virus in such a solution required 3 to 7 days. Virus concentrations in these solutions were thousands of times higher than those found in the blood of AIDS patients.

Although these findings do not mean the virus can be spread casually, by a toilet seat or by simple kissing, it suggests that anyone handling infected blood or other fluids containing virus should take proper precautions.

Suppressive Action of Semen on the Immune System

Semen is a complex mixture containing sperm, various hormones and other secretions, and considerable amounts of sodium glutamate

(MSG) and polyamines (chemicals with several amino groups). There are also fairly sizeable numbers of small lymphocytes of both the B and T variety and very likely some macrophages. It has not been sufficiently emphasized that these small lymphocytes and macrophages can pass through intact bowel tissue. They are naturally wandering cells capable of penetrating capillaries and other tissues of the body as well. If the cells are from a male with AIDS, there is a good chance that some or all of them are latently or actively infected with AIDS virus.

The passage of lymphocytes through intact rectal mucosa seems supported experimentally by the observation of antilymphocyte antibodies in healthy male rabbits in which semen was placed in the rectum or colon. And as many as 29 million small lymphocytes were found in a single human ejaculate.

In addition, many studies during recent years have shown that relatively small quantities of semen can inhibit the response of lymphocytes in tissue culture to a large variety of stimuli. Inhibitory effects have also been noted *in vivo*. Some of the impairment might be due to the inhibition of macrophages which participate in important interactions with lymphocytes. The response of granulocytes is also reduced by semen.

Seminal fluid has been shown to drastically inhibit the activity of natural killer T cells in tissue culture. The interference of semen with the functioning of the complement system has also been reported.

It has been suggested by Dr. J. D. Williamson, Division of Virology, St. Mary's Hospital Medical School, London, England, that the components responsible for immune inhibition by semen might be the polyamines spermine and spermidine. Small amounts of either component were strongly inhibitory to lymphocytes *in vitro*. Polyamines have also been reported to restore activity of suppressor T cells. Cytomegalovirus infection leads to greatly increased polyamine synthesis in cells, and since many AIDS patients have this infection, the increased polyamine synthesis can increase the suppressive activity of the suppressor T8 cells. This would explain the strong immunosuppressive activity of cytomegalovirus that is observed.

In another study Dr. Toby C. Rodman and co-workers at Cornell University Medical College found that most humans (99%) had antibodies that reacted to proteins in the cap region of human sperm. These same antibodies are absent or markedly deficient in the blood of AIDS patients. It is suggested that these antibodies play some balancing or regulatory role in the immune system, and that in their absence (e.g. in AIDS victims), control of the immune system is faulty. Obviously, further studies need to be done to define the exact role of these antibodies to sperm in the immune system. It appears possible that this is a natural defense mechanism designed to prevent any immune disturbance caused by sperm proteins that might enter the body through sexual intercourse. If a person has been promiscuous, depletion of these antibodies may have occurred.

Western blot readings have three possible interpretations

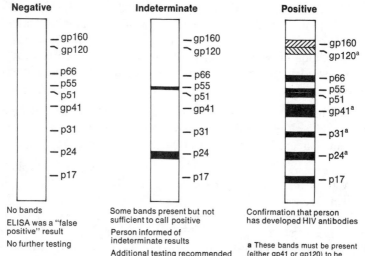

Negative

— gp160
⌒ gp120

— p66
— p55
⌒ p51
— gp41

— p31

— p24

— p17

No bands
ELISA was a "false positive" result
No further testing

Source: Du Pont

Indeterminate

— gp160
⌒ gp120

— p66
— p55
⌒ p51
— gp41

— p31

— p24

— p17

Some bands present but not sufficient to call positive
Person informed of indeterminate results
Additional testing recommended

Positive

— gp160
⌒ gp120[a]

— p66
— p55
⌒ p51
— gp41[a]

— p31[a]

— p24[a]

— p17

Confirmation that person has developed HIV antibodies

a These bands must be present (either gp41 or gp120) to be classified as positive in Du Pont's Western blot.

CHAPTER 4
TRANSMISSION AND SPREAD OF THE
AIDS VIRUS IN THE UNITED STATES

Introduction; Transmission among male homosexuals; Anal sex–very high risk; Oral sex–high risk; Mutual masturbation–risky; Passage of AIDS virus through exchange of saliva during kissing–some risk is involved; Living with a person with AIDS; Tears; Mother's milk; Semen for artificial insemination; Are health workers who treat AIDS victims safe?; Are research workers studying AIDS virus in danger?; Infection from contaminated needles; AIDS-related deaths among intravenous drug users in New York City; AIDS virus infection from blood transfusions; Transmission of AIDS by organ transplants; Heterosexual transmission of AIDS virus; Transmission from an AIDS virus-infected mother to child; Infection of hemophiliacs by blood and blood products; Can insects transmit AIDS virus to humans?; Can animals transmit the virus to humans?; Risk of infection from human bites and the risks to dental workers; Should two individuals with AIDS have sex; Probability of infection with AIDS after sexual contact; How rapidly is AIDS spreading in the United States?; Spread of AIDS virus among homosexuals in San Francisco; Results of U.S. Army testing for AIDS virus antibodies in blood; Spread of AIDS virus into the general heterosexual population; Canadian identified as playing a key role in spread of AIDS.

4

TRANSMISSION AND SPREAD OF THE AIDS VIRUS IN THE UNITED STATES

Introduction

My 10-year-old daughter came home from school the other day and said, "Daddy, did you know that AIDS can be transmitted by a mosquito bite?" "Where did you learn that?" I asked. "From the *Weekly Reader*," she said, "We were talking about it in school." "Well," I informed her, "You must know something I don't know. My studies have indicated that it cannot be transmitted by mosquitoes."

It is commendable that the *Weekly Reader* is talking about AIDS, but it is easy to see how wrong ideas are circulated. It is difficult even for an expert to state all the facts correctly. Our knowledge of AIDS is not only growing rapidly but is being refined — changing, so to speak — and in a way that establishes facts with more certainty. Just a short while ago we didn't believe AIDS could be transmitted by simple contact with blood or other fluids containing virus. Now we are pretty sure it can be under certain circumstances. In this chapter all the available evidence will be presented regarding AIDS virus transmission.

Transmission Among Male Homosexuals

There are three main types of homosexual sex: anal sex, oral sex, and mutual masturbation. In the past, one could probably divide homosexuals into different categories: Those who were highly promiscuous possibly with a new partner every night; those who were intermediate in their promiscuity with, perhaps, a partner every few weeks and those who had a single partner to whom they were strongly attached and remained faithful. It is expected that the chances of contracting AIDS are directly proportional to the number of sexual contacts a person has. However, many factors can modify this proportionality. No one knows what percentage of homosexuals test positive for AIDS virus antibodies, indicating that they may transmit the disease. Assuming it is 20% (although in San Francisco the figure 50% has been cited), then every sexual contact without the use of a condom presents 2 chances in 10 of contracting AIDS. After five contacts, on the average, one would have a high probability of catching the disease. With a single partner who is uninfected there is no chance of catching AIDS. These simple facts have made a striking change in the homosexual community, with single partners now much more common and certainly more faithful. For those homosexuals who do not favor this arrangement there has no doubt been a sizeable reduction in promiscuity, and when sexual contacts are made, all but the most foolhardy take precautions by using condoms and, possibly, spermicides that can kill AIDS virus.

Anal Sex—Very High Risk

Anal sex between homosexuals, bisexuals, and heterosexuals carries a very high risk. Initially it was believed that because rectal tissue is not very strong, it is a common occurrence for small tears to be made during sexual activity and that these lesions facilitate the entry of AIDS virus into the blood and its spread throughout the body. Undoubtedly this can and does occasionally occur, but it is not the only way and not a necessary way for the AIDS virus to spread. Semen contains large numbers of lymphocytes as well as some macrophages, both of which may be infected by AIDS virus. Both types of cells can easily pass through intact rectum or intestinal tissue. Although foreign cells are normally destroyed by the immune system of the body they invade, this might take several days, enough time for an infection to start.

With the use of a condom, the risk is materially reduced but by no means eliminated. There is the possibility of failure of the condom, which experts have said may vary from about 5 to 20% depending on a number of factors that will be discussed later (Chapter 5). The use of a spermicide plus a condom is still safer but, again, some risk remains. "Safe sex" is a myth; the only 100% safe sex is no sex, that is, abstinence or possibly self-masturbation.

Oral Sex — High Risk

It is clear that semen from an AIDS-positive person may contain intact virus particles as well as many cells that are virus- infected. Without a condom, oral sex is very risky. The major risk is from sores in the mouth or throat that facilitate entry of the virus. Even if there are no sores, it is probable that infected cells in the semen can penetrate intact mucous membrane that lines the mouth and throat. If any of the semen is swallowed there is a chance that the esophagus could be breached by infected cells. If the stomach is actively digesting food, its high acid content will probably destroy cells and virus alike. But if the stomach is resting, virus and/or infected cells might survive long enough to penetrate its mucous membrane.

The use of a condom for oral sex reduces but does not eliminate the risk. An uninfected participant has to be careful to avoid contact with semen, and there is always the possibility of a faulty condom, or improper use of one.

Mutual Masturbation — Risky

The hands are subject to daily trauma — scratches, bruises, cuts, and scrapes from everything imaginable. Many times we pay little attention to these injuries if they are slight. Another problem is chapped skin, particularly in the wintertime. Almost everyone can suffer from this. To use the hands, therefore, in mutual masturbation between two persons (two males, two females, or one male and one female), where one member of the pair might be infected with AIDS virus carries some risk. We have evidence now that transmission can occur through chapped skin and cuts or scrapes, and whether it is by infected cells or semen containing virus, or both, the end result is the same — AIDS. The use of rubber gloves for both males and females and condoms for males would probably reduce the risk to a low value. Unfortunately, those who most need to use these protectors probably will not read this book, and even if they do, probably will not want to use protectors.

Passage of AIDS Virus Through Exchange of Saliva During Kissing — Some Risk Is Involved

There have been at least two studies on the presence of AIDS virus in saliva. In one, about 70 patients with AIDS had their saliva checked for the presence of HIV. It was found in only several members of the group. In another study done cooperatively by several groups, 20 individuals were examined. Four had AIDS, 10 had ARC, and the remaining were 6 healthy homosexuals, 4 of whom tested positive for AIDS virus. HIV was isolated from the saliva of 4 of the ARC patients and 4 of the healthy homosexuals. It was also observed by electron microscopy in the saliva of 1 AIDS patient. The possibility that AIDS virus can be transmitted by kissing cannot be excluded. On a TV question-and-answer program on AIDS someone asked Surgeon General C. Everett Koop, "What about an intense kiss" (French, involving interplay of tongues)?" His reply was, "I won't say it is not possible for the disease to be transmitted by a kiss." The recent finding of a factor in saliva that prevents HIV infection reduces the risk of infection from this source.

Living With a Person With AIDS

Many families now have an AIDS victim living with them, or someone who does not have the disease but tests positive for virus antibodies. These family members share the same toilet, possibly share the same glassware and dishes, kiss each other, and so on. Can the uninfected catch AIDS? To my knowledge there has been no report of AIDS being transmitted by casual family contact. There have been, so far, thousands of instances of this type to draw on, but no positive report has been made as yet. It appears to be very safe to live with an AIDS patient, but the "as yet" was inserted in the last sentence to again allow for the possibility that infection could occur. It might have the same chance of occurring as one has of being hit by lightning or by a meteorite — not a zero chance, but one that is very, very slight. If you have a family member living with you, you should treat this person as you would any other family member and at the same time show him or her all the love and affection you can muster.

Tears

A body fluid that is not often considered a source of disease is tears. However, HIV has been shown to be present in tear fluid, on the conjunctival surface of the eye, in or on contact lenses worn by patients with AIDS, and even in these locations in those who are infected by the virus but show no symptoms.

Ophthalmologists need to be alerted to this and to establish guidelines for decontamination of instruments and protection of themselves and their patients from possible transmission of the disease. Although the chances of this occurring are slight, such chances should not be taken.

Dr. K. B. Moore of the Pennsylvania College of Optometry has studied the effects of various sterilization procedures on HIV and found that the common systems most often used to disinfect contact lenses, including heat, may not be adequate. Only hydrogen peroxide may be suitable. Bleach cannot be used, as it would injure the lenses.

Mother's Milk

If a woman with AIDS gives birth to a baby, the baby should not be nursed, as HIV may be found in the milk. Although ingested virus would undoubtedly be destroyed by the digestive system of the baby, there may be a few wandering infected white cells in the milk that could pass through the walls of the gastrointestinal tract.

Semen for Artificial Insemination

In the United States from 6000 to 10,000 births result each year from artificial insemination. The use of fresh sperm is hazardous unless it is obtained from the woman's own husband. Before sperm from an unknown donor is used, it should be tested for AIDS virus and possibly other infections such as herpes, gonorrhea, and hepatitis B. This takes several days, so the sperm should be frozen and then used only when it has received a clean bill of health.

Are Health Workers Who Treat AIDS Victims Safe?

Today thousands of nurses, physicians, and laboratory technicians work with AIDS patients. Thus far, the safety record for these individuals has been very good but not perfect. There is definitely a risk for them, a risk that can be minimized by using reasonable precautions in working with the patients, their blood and urine samples, and other items such as bed sheets and bedpans. These precautions are discussed in Chapter 5, but will be mentioned here as well.

Not long ago federal health officials described three cases of health care workers who became infected with AIDS virus after their skin was briefly exposed to blood from infected patients. These were the first instances that did not involve direct injection of infected blood into the body or prolonged exposure to body fluids. Six previously reported cases among health workers involved such injection or prolonged exposure.

In one of the three cases, a hospital worker was exposed to blood while she was pressing gauze against the arm of a patient who was bleeding. She was not wearing gloves and her hand was chapped. Hospital workers were trying to resuscitate a patient who was not breathing and had no heartbeat. The health care worker who became infected was exposed to the patient's blood for about 20 minutes as she applied pressure to gauze on the patient's arm. Interestingly, she became acutely ill 20 days after the incident (see "Shorter Survival Period for Women than for Men," Chapter 6) in an acute reaction to AIDS virus which sometimes occurs. Neither she nor the other two victims described below had any possibility of contracting the disease sexually.

In the second instance, blood splashed onto the face of a technician and into her mouth when a rubber stopper popped off a glass tube being filled with a syringe. This person had a history of acne but had no open sores on her face. Federal officials said the virus or infected cells might have penetrated the mucous membrane inside her mouth or possibly an inflamed area of her face.

In the third case, a health care worker was operating a centrifuge to separate blood components when blood spilled on her hands and forearms. She, also, was not wearing gloves. Skin on one of her ears had been inflamed, and she admitted she may have touched that area before washing the blood off her hands. Eight weeks after the incident, this worker became acutely ill with fever, diarrhea, and pain in the muscles due to another acute reaction. All three workers tested positive for AIDS virus antibodies.

Dr. James M. Hughes, an official of the Federal Centers for Disease Control, believes that these three cases emphasize the need for health care professionals to adhere strictly to federal guidelines for preventing infection with AIDS virus. These guidelines are stated in Chapter 5, and among other precautions, they advise always wearing rubber gloves and face masks when working with AIDS patients or their blood, as well as immediately washing and treating spills with a strong disinfectant such as bleaching liquid.

Are Research Workers Studying AIDS Virus in Danger?

Yes. Anyone carrying out research on any infectious agent must exert the utmost care and follow careful procedures designed to provide maximum safety. For highly infectious lethal agents, special laboratories may have to be built to minimize infection of workers or to prevent escape of the virus. These special laboratories, called BL-3 facilities, have not been required for AIDS researchers yet.

One worker in a research laboratory who became infected may not have been following accepted safety procedures for handling highly concentrated virus preparations. While he could not recall any apparent overt accident, he reported that the seals around the centrifuge rotor in which he was concentrating the virus had occasionally leaked. He had always worn gloves, but gloves may have tears or pinholes without the wearer being aware of them.

A second laboratory worker was infected while handling highly concentrated virus. Although wearing rubber gloves, the worker accidentally cut a hand, puncturing the glove while doing so. This person was contaminated in late 1985 and first demonstrated antibodies to AIDS virus in May 1986. However no signs of AIDS disease have developed in this individual.

Emmett Barkley, former director of the division of laboratory safety at the National Institutes of Health (NIH), believes that workers may not be properly educated concerning safety procedures. NIH safety inspectors are now visiting all facilities in the United States where concentrated quantities of HIV are produced. This includes companies making HIV antibody test kits. The bottom line is that any health or laboratory worker who may possibly be in contact with AIDS virus had best make certain that he or she knows all the rules and precautions. No one is allowed even one mistake because there is no second chance.

Infection From Contaminated Needles

Most people in this country do not have access to sterile needles and syringes. Physicians can buy them, as can hospitals and other medical institutions and any bona fide research center, and they are relatively cheap. One hundred sterile (plastic) 1-milliliter syringes with an attached needle cost $12 to $15, 12 cents to 15 cents apiece. Drug addicts do not have them and can obtain them only by theft. Consequently they use the few needles they have over and over. Although a used needle can be sterilized by boiling for a long period of time or by placing it in concentrated bleach for several hours and then rinsing it in tap water, for a group of drug addicts sharing a needle and syringe the time this requires would be inordinately long. Furthermore, although needles can resist the boiling process, syringes become deformed and useless as a result of heating or bleaching. Sterilizing the needle and not the syringe would be an exercise in futility. If any of the drug addicts using a shared needle are infected with HIV, soon they all will be. This is bad enough, but the sexual partners of the drug addicts will also soon become infected with the virus. This group has been a potent focus of infection for some time and continues to spread the disease without much diminution. Drug addicts are often sick, physically and mentally, and as a consequence they are less able to control their actions, being driven by their addiction. There are several approaches to the problem which shall only be mentioned here but discussed in more detail later (Chapter 5). These approaches are:

1. Stop the distribution of drugs. This seems unlikely to happen in the near future.

2. Make available an ample supply of free sterile needles and syringes to anyone who wants them. This appears to be a good idea but has not yet been adopted in this country although it is being discussed actively and will be tried by a private group.

3. Under careful supervision, bring *all addicts* into a program substituting methadone (which cures addictive craving) for other drugs. This proposal has merit, but there are problems—largely financial—in carrying it out.

AIDS-Related Deaths Among Intravenous Drug Users in New York City

New York City health officials report that a careful study of all drug-related deaths in the city from 1982 through 1986 found that an estimated 2520 AIDS related deaths were not officially included in the city's AIDS Surveillance Registry (Table 1-1).

If these deaths are added to the totals, it will make a very big change in the statistics, as illustrated in Figure 4-1.

In (2) the percentage of deaths of intravenous drug users is 57% compared to 37% in (1), thus surpassing by far, deaths from AIDS of homosexual and bisexual men (38%).

In light of the new statistics, Dr. Rand Stoneburner, a city health department epidemiologist, believes that a change is needed in the city's efforts to stem the epidemic. He says, "Attempts to stop the spread of AIDS among poor Hispanic and black New Yorkers through education and the use of condoms simply are not going to succeed."

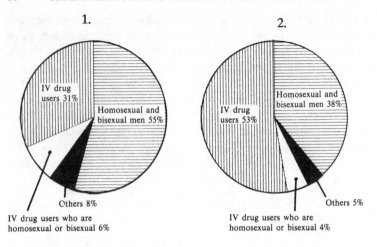

Figure 4-1 Revised profile of New York City's AIDS deaths.
(1) Distribution of deaths, Federal Centers for Disease Control.
(2) Distribution of deaths, New York City Department of Health.

The statistics in Figure 4-1 apply to New York City only, which appears to have the biggest problem with intravenous drug use. In San Francisco the majority of cases involve homosexuals, and intravenous drug use is much less prevalent than in New York City.

AIDS Virus Infection From Blood Transfusions

Testing of all blood donors for antibodies to AIDS virus began in 1985. Those that test positive are rejected as donors, and as a result, the blood supply for transfusion has been quite safe since the testing program began. Anyone who might need blood for an operation or to replace blood lost in an accident need not worry. It is true that an occasional blood donor may slip through the detection network by virtue of the very slow development of antibodies to AIDS (even though HIV is present in the blood), but it is estimated that this occurs with a very low frequency, perhaps 1 in 50,000 or 1 in 100,000 donors. Your chances of getting that blood are about as good as your chances of winning the lottery. You should not worry about AIDS, particularly if you are having a major operation, because there are many more possible complications to worry about.

It is estimated that, before 1985, upward of several thousand people contracted AIDS from blood contaminated with HIV. This number, whatever it is, includes many hemophiliacs who require frequent blood transfusions. Efforts have been made to contact persons who may have obtained contaminated blood. If you are having elective surgery some time in the future, it is possible to donate blood at intervals and have it stored for your use until the time of the operation. In this way you will be certain that the blood is not contaminated.

Transmission of AIDS by Organ Transplants

Although heart and liver transplants are very rare, about 5000 kidney transplants are performed every year in the United States. Lens transplants for cataracts are also fairly common. Anyone who is contemplating a transplant should be aware of the possibility of getting AIDS virus from blood or infected cells in the transplanted tissue. Of course, the blood of the donor, even though he may be dead, can be tested for AIDS virus antibodies. If the test is positive, the organs will not be used. A case has been described, however, in which organs from a donor were transplanted into two patients who subsequently developed AIDS. Apparently this donor had received massive blood transfusions before the testing for AIDS antibodies was done and these transfusions so diluted his blood that it tested negative. This is, hopefully, a rare occurrence that is not likely to happen often, but one that transplant recipients should be aware of.

Heterosexual Transmission of AIDS Virus

It is now clear that heterosexual transmission of AIDS virus can occur. Certainly anal or oral sex without protection of a condom can easily transmit the virus from an infected male to an uninfected female. Vaginal sex can bring about the same result. Although the virus will have greater difficulty finding a tear or lesion in the much sturdier vagina, infected cells might traverse it or other parts of the female reproductive tract and gain entry through mucous membranes. Thus the male may readily infect the female.

There has been some question about how easily a female may infect a male. Considering the need for a virus particle or infected cell to work backward against the flow of semen or urine into the tip of the urethra in the penis, it does not appear that infection can occur readily. Appearances are, however, sometimes deceiving. Many males, particularly if they are promiscuous, may have some type of venereal disease such as genital herpes, genital warts caused by a papilloma virus, or gonorrhea caused by a bacterium. All of these diseases can give rise to lesions on the penis, and these sores, which may sometimes be small and not readily visible, can nevertheless serve as easy entry points for cells or virus particles shown to reside in the vagina of infected women. Where statistics have been gathered on prostitutes, both in this country and elsewhere, the percentage who test positive for AIDS virus antibodies is quite high, somewhere in the range of 10 to 40% or more. All those who are infected are capable of transmitting the disease to a male partner. The use of a condom will, of course, offer a degree of protection from male to female and the reverse. Better protection can be obtained by the use of a condom *and* a spermicidal cream such as nonoxynol-9. Although this compound has been shown to kill the virus readily, I am not aware of tests having been done on infected macrophages or lymphocytes. However, since the action of the spermicide is to destroy the cell membranes, it is likely that the white cells are also destroyed.

The U.S. Army reported in 1985 that evaluation of the method of transmission of AIDS virus in 41 patients showed that 15 had become infected through contact with a member of the opposite sex. Ten of the 15 were men who apparently got it from women, and 5 were women who got it from men. These statistics should not be taken as indicative of the ease of transmission from male to female or the reverse. Thousands of cases would be needed to give an accurate picture of the relative ease of transmission of AIDS virus.

A year later a study in 21 women with AIDS revealed that all of them had AIDS virus in vaginal and cervical secretions. Nine of the women had been prostitutes, and several were pregnant. The presence of virus in the birth canal suggests that a pregnant woman might transmit AIDS virus to her baby as it passes through the canal at birth.

The New York City Health Commissioner, Dr. Stephen C. Joseph, has recently asked the state to add vaginal intercourse to the list of risky practices in commercial sex establishments. (This report is misleading because all sex for hire is illegal.) What is meant is that under the current rules, establishments that charge patrons money are not allowed to foster activities that have a high risk of transmitting AIDS on the premises. These activities now include anal intercourse and fellatio (oral sex), either homosexual or heterosexual. The establishments referred to are gay bathhouses and clubs catering to mate swapping, group sex, and sadomasochism. Massage parlors, in some cases, might be another source of sex for hire. Brothels should certainly be considered also, but they are illegal in most states and operate under cover. The prohibited activities, when they are carried out, for the most part are now done in small, closed rooms or cubicles. These rooms are presently off-limits for the inspectors who check these establishments. It seems futile to promulgate new laws which only have the effect of sending people into closed cubicles. Fortunately, the deadliness of AIDS has done far more than any laws could, and these practices among promiscuous persons of unknown AIDS status have been severely curtailed, except among those who don't care for either themselves or others.

Transmission From an AIDS Virus-Infected Mother to Child

The number of young children with AIDS is rapidly increasing as infected mothers give birth. The latent period of the virus in a child is considerably less than for an adult, being an average of about 2 years. This is probably because a young child's immune system is naive, not having been exposed to any diseases and is generally working overtime. If, as appears to be the case, stimulation of the immune system is what turns a latent AIDS virus infection into an active one, it is not surprising to find young children of AIDS virus-infected mothers coming down with the disease a few months to 1 or 2 years after birth.

If a child is about to be born to a mother actively infected with genital herpes, a caesarean section is always performed. This is done because, if the infant catches genital herpes from the mother, serious mental and other defects, or death of the baby can result. A caesarean birth bypassing the infected tissue can usually keep the baby safe. The obvious question is, does a caesarean birth protect a child of an AIDS virus-infected mother. I don't know the answer to this and am not aware of any discussion or study of this question. But I think the answer is no — no protection would be offered. I say this because AIDS virus is passed so easily from cell to cell. It seems more than likely that at least a few wandering macrophages or other white cells would have passed from mother to child. When born, the child may already be infected, and avoiding the birth canal would be of no further help. This question nevertheless deserves study and possibly a research effort.

A study completed in a statewide program involving every baby born in New York during a month-long period, 19,157, showed that in New York City 1 in 61 carried antibodies to AIDS virus. The prevalence varied from 1 in 43 for the Bronx to 1 in 749 for upstate New York.

The presence of antibodies does not necessarily mean that all the babies are infected. Usually from 30 to 50% of those that are HIV antibody positive are also infected with the virus and will probably develop AIDS. The remaining babies may have received only antibodies from their infected mothers but not the virus. These antibodies will eventually disappear, and the babies will not develop AIDS.

The total number infected, however, is disappointingly large, and it is estimated that as many as 1000 babies in New York State alone may be born with the AIDS virus in 1988.

Infection of Hemophiliacs by Blood and Blood Products

In Chapter 1, the plight of hemophiliacs was discussed. Many members of this group had frequent blood transfusions before blood donors were tested and thereby became infected from HIV-contaminated blood. This group apparently may develop the clinical symptoms of AIDS. Another large group of hemophiliacs received injections of a blood clotting factor, von Willebrand's factor or factor VIII, isolated from blood. Many of these individuals have subsequently tested positive for antibodies to HIV, but relatively few of them have developed clinical symptoms of AIDS. It has been suggested that the isolation procedures used in preparing the factor may alter the virus in some way so that it is less infective. Studies on this hemophiliac group are continuing.

Can Insects Transmit AIDS Virus to Humans?

There is no evidence at present that AIDS virus can be transmitted to humans by insects. However, in a letter written to *Chemical and Engineering News*, David F. Siemens, Jr., points out that if a mosquito or other blood-sucking insect is completing a meal, the blood in the gut will surely contain enough virus particles to infect. If the mosquito is swatted, the blood ingested may get on the skin, and the small puncture from the bite may be large enough for the AIDS virus to gain entry. The moral of this story is that when visiting an area where there is a high rate of AIDS infection, always apply insect repellant and never swat a feeding mosquito. The chances of becoming infected in this way, however, must be rated as vanishingly small.

Can Animals Transmit the Virus to Humans?

There is no evidence that any animal harboring an AIDS-like virus can transmit the disease to humans. This includes cats, bovine species, simian species, other hooved animals, and possibly other animals. Circumstantial evidence suggests that far back in the past a transfer from monkeys to humans may have occurred. If one is working with animals infected by AIDS-like diseases it nevertheless is advisable to take the same precautions one would in working with HIV or HIV-infected patients.

Risk of Infection From Human Bites and the Risks to Dental Workers

Several cases have already been described where a person was attacked and bitten by an AIDS infected individual. In one case a prison inmate bit two guards and later told a nurse that he hoped the guards would get AIDS. This statement, related at his trial, helped to convict him. When this individual was brought to trial, he was found guilty by a jury of purposely trying to infect another person. He faces up to 10 years additional time, but the case is being appealed by his lawyer who says that most of the evidence is a reflection of hysteria over the disease.

In a second case, a woman arrested as a prostitute was charged with attempted assault and reckless endangerment after she bit one of the arresting officers and then announced she had AIDS. She was charged with using her teeth and saliva as a "dangerous weapon." Several ethical questions are raised by this incident, for example, Does she really have AIDS? Can she be compelled to take a test for AIDS? What will be the consequences if she tests positive? The California Supreme Court has already supported a ruling that blood taken from a man who bit two police officers could not be tested for AIDS virus antibodies.

Since AIDS is not readily transmitted through saliva, the risk from a bite, even if the skin is broken and bleeds, is very small.

In the case of dentists and dental technicians, the risk of infection with AIDS virus is considerably higher. A dentist cannot be sure his or her patients do not have AIDS. Treatments involving the gums and dental surgery often involve copious bleeding. This is a different situation than a bite. The blood can be a source of AIDS virus and also virus-infected cells. The use of gloves by dentists and dental technicians at all times should be mandatory. Precautions should be taken with any item which has become bloody—instruments, cotton, gauze, and so on—and care should be taken not to have any droplets of blood blown into the air, as during drying, rinsing, or other operations. Many

use to treat known AIDS patients because they worry about
to maintain a sterile environment for all their patients.

eral Centers for Disease Control have issued guidelines for
medical and dental workers which are discussed in Chapter 5.

Should Two Individuals with AIDS Have Sex?

On moral grounds, no individual who knows or suspects that he or she
has AIDS should have sex of any kind, (even if protected with a
condom) with an uninfected person without the permission of that
person. That leaves only a known AIDS victim as a possible sex partner
for another AIDS victim. Is there any reason they should not have sex?

There are two reasons why there could be a problem if no condom
is used. First, it is quite possible that one or both of the two AIDS-
infected individuals is promiscuous to some degree. For this reason,
one or both members of the pair may very well have some other sexually
transmitted disease (STD). Acquiring a new STD would not be helpful
in the least, because it could complicate and make worse the course of
an active AIDS infection and could possibly activate an inactive AIDS
infection. The second reason is that the partners might each have a
significantly different strain of HIV. Infecting each other with a new
strain could have unforeseen consequences. While it is likely that any
new strain introduced would simply be excluded by the old strain, we
do not have enough information to be certain of this. There is always
the possibility that the two strains can recombine in different ways,
producing a faster multiplying or more virulent strain. This is a significant unknown, and because of this, such practices involve some risk.
Individuals with AIDS should be aware of these risks and make their
own decisions.

Probability of Infection with AIDS After Sexual Contact

Throughout the book a number of cases have been mentioned in which
wives of infected husbands did not invariably get AIDS but no definitive
study had been done before Dr. T. A. Peterman and co-workers
published an article in the *Journal of the American Medical Association*
in early 1988.

Peterman and coworkers utilized a pool of 55 infected men and 25
infected women and their uninfected spouses and took careful medical
and social histories from them as well as details of their sexual practices
and number of contacts. All family members were tested for HIV

antibodies. All the infections were obtained through blood transfusions and therefore were initially unknown to the spouses who were uninfected.

Dr. Peterman found that 2 of the 25 husbands of infected wives and 10 of the 55 wives of infected husbands were positive for HIV antibodies. When this was correlated with the number of sexual contacts the surprising conclusion was obtained that transmission probability is unrelated to the actual number of sexual contacts for partnerships ranging from one to several thousand contacts.

One might argue that using transfusion recipients who acquired AIDS does not give a correct picture of transmission probability but there is no evidence to support or contradict this argument. It is of course more reasonable to conclude that transmission probability depends on number of contacts, increasing as the number of contacts increases.

The average transmission probability for this experiment, 0.1 for female to male and 0.2 male to female, is consistent with other estimates (not counting sexual contacts).

About the only safe conclusion to be obtained from this study is that not every sexual contact results in the transmission of AIDS from an infected partner and the transmission may occur on the first contact or after 1000 contacts. Obviously this is no help whatsoever for the heterosexual worrying about catching AIDS from a casual sex encounter.

In another study published in the *Journal of the American Medical Association* of April 22, 1988 by Dr. Norman Hurst and Dr. Stephen B. Hulley and entitled "Preventing the Heterosexual Spread of AIDS, Are we giving our patients the best advice?" the authors made estimates for the risk of HIV infection for heterosexual intercourse in the United States.

Estimates were made for infection rates with or without use of a condom, for one or 500 sexual encounters and assumptions were made for the prevalence of HIV infection in various risk groups, the infectivity and, when condoms/spermacide were used the failure rate was assumed to be 10%.

The estimated risk of infection for individuals not in any risk group and of unknown HIV status was 1 in 50 million for one sexual encounter using condoms or 1 in 5 million not using condoms. For 500 sexual encounters under the same conditions the odds become 1 in 110,000 and 1 in 16,000, respectively with and without condoms/spermacide.

With a HIV infected partner the risks are with condoms 1 in 5000 for a single sexual encounter and without condoms 1 in 500. For 500 encounters this becomes 1 in 11 and 2 in 3 respectively for encounters with and without condoms.

It would appear that casual sex between heterosexuals not in any risk group would be relatively safe especially if condoms are used. I would hope, however, that everyone would feel as uneasy about these figures as I do. First of all keep in mind, that whatever the odds you could win the lottery the first time you try it. Secondly, the assumptions about the prevalence of HIV infection and infectivity of the various groups are not well supported and finally, the whole thesis of this article rests on your knowing your partner well enough to determine his or her risk status with absolute assurance.

I doubt this absolute assurance could be obtained in most cases.

How Rapidly is AIDS Spreading in the United States?

This question is, of course, a very important one because its answer will determine whether the AIDS epidemic will reach a plateau and then taper off, or whether it will continue to increase, possibly at a slower rate, but nevertheless to increase.

Various efforts have been and are now being made to obtain an estimate of the rate of spread and also the prevalence of the disease. The Army, for example, has recently completed testing its entire personnel. Persons testing positive are not allowed to have overseas assignments, and they are closely watched medically. The State of New York intends to randomly test 100,000 persons in various groups to determine the extent of the disease and the federal government is carrying out testing that will comprise some 400,000 samples of blood. These state and federal tests are being made anonymously so that even those who contribute blood samples will not be given the results.

The government has changed its ideas on how best to make this survey. Officials state that they hope to conduct a "family of surveys" in the 20 top metropolitan areas containing 25% of the population and 75% of the reported AIDS cases. It also intends to test in ten cities with moderate to low incidences of AIDS cases. When all such surveys are operational in May 1988, about 1.6 million different people will have their blood tested every year. Samples will have no identification by name – just by age, sex, race, and area of residence. It will be impossible to notify those who test positive.

Studies will also be conducted in at least three cities to determine whether a valid nationwide survey can be conducted using a random sampling of households. Health experts fear that individuals most likely to be infected will not cooperate, thereby causing a large under-estimation of the incidence of infection.

Special studies already underway will also test the blood of blood donors, military personnel, college students, hospital emergency rooms, and so on. By 1988 approximately 7.7 million blood samples are expected to be tested annually.

Spread of AIDS Virus Among Homosexuals in San Francisco

According to the preliminary results of a blood-testing program con-ducted by the federal government, the spread of AIDS virus has slowed dramatically among this group. The San Francisco homosexual group has always been a very coherent, well-informed one with good com-munication among its members. Their lifestyle has changed radically resulting in safer sexual practices. According to Walter R. Dowdle, deputy director of the Federal Centers for Disease Control, months have gone by with no record of new infections by the virus in some groups of gay men and also in a group of bisexual men. Other studies have found, unfortunately, that over half of the members of these groups have already been infected. The study in San Francisco is being expanded to 20 other cities in which large numbers of persons have the virus and the results will be ready early in 1988. The blood of hospital patients and persons visiting clinics for STD, tuberculosis, and family planning was used, as well as that from some prisons and colleges. A study planned for New York State will use blood samples from similar groups.

Results of U.S. Army Testing for AIDS Virus Antibodies in Blood

By September 1987, the Pentagon had tested more than 3 million individuals. They identified 3085 people in the military and 1766 recruit applicants for a total of 4801 positives. The overall rate is roughly 1.6 per 1000 persons tested, and there is only a slight difference in rate between army personnel and recruits. This rate appears to be lower than that believed to be present in the general population, which is somewhere in the neighborhood of 1 to 2 million cases and is 4 to 5 times the rate of 1.6 per 1000. Some interesting statistics were obtained somewhat earlier from tests on 305,747 U.S. recruit applicants. Infected applicants showed a sex ratio of 2.5 men to 1 woman, much lower than the 13 to 1 sex ratio for AIDS cases in the general population. In New York City, the recruit applicant ratio for those with AIDS antibodies was 1.2 men to 0.9 women.

Dr. Donald S. Burke, senior author of the Pentagon report, suggested that these figures indicate a considerable amount of hidden AIDS virus infection. The exact meaning of this study is difficult to interpret, however.

Spread of AIDS Virus into the General Heterosexual Population

The rate and extent of this spread is one of the least known facts in the epidemiology of AIDS. There are several factors that appear to prevent rapid spread into the heterosexual population. First, education programs are taking hold. There has been so much media coverage in the last 2 years that it is likely that nearly everyone is now aware of the menace of AIDS and the high probability that it will result in death. Second, a large percentage of the heterosexual population is married and thus likely to have safe sex partners. Of course, extramarital sex does take place, but probably less so in the married population over 50, and only to a certain small percentage in those under 50. The fear of AIDS has perhaps reduced extra-marital sex to a low level in any case.

We have no indication that HIV is spreading unchecked into the general population. Initially there was a very rapid spread among homosexuals, drug abusers, bisexuals, hemophiliacs, and probably prostitutes. Now, except for drug abusers, this rapid spread has been checked, and the rate at which new cases of AIDS are being initiated may be so slow that the number of cases may begin to fall off in a few years and decline to a low, probably constant, value. We should know in several years if this is the case.

Dr. Harold W. Jaffee, chief AIDS epidemiologist at the Federal Centers for Disease Control, believes there are still no signs of a significant viral outbreak in the general heterosexual population. He notes that neither he nor several other epidemiologists expect a large outbreak in this group. There may, of course, be a slow gradual increase, and it is especially important to continue with educational and prevention campaigns to minimize this increase.

Studies on several groups of heterosexual patients who had visited clinics for other sexually transmitted diseases have provided some reassuring data. All of the groups (three), including one in Denver (1000 patients), one in Seattle (300 patients), and one in Queens, New York (300 patients), had only one or no patients who also carried the AIDS virus. Although there are few AIDS cases in Denver or Seattle, New York has been one of the most highly infected areas for 7 to 8 years, and finding only one case of AIDS in 300 heterosexual patients who did not belong to any risk group reinforced the view that AIDS is not spreading rapidly in this population.

However, it should be mentioned that there is a school of thought, exemplified by A. M. Rosenthal, an editorial writer for the *New York Times*, that believes it is madness to think that heterosexuals are not at risk. He says, "AIDS specialists in Europe to whom I have talked see this refusal to recognize at least the possibility of heterosexual transmission on a large scale outside Africa as incomprehensibly stupid."

In March 1988 Dr. William H. Masters and Virginia E. Johnson, the well known sex therapists, and Dr. Robert C. Kolodny published a book "CRISIS: Heterosexual Behavior in the Age of AIDS" (Grove Press) in which they claimed AIDS virus *is* breaking out of traditional risk groups and is infecting heterosexuals not belonging to any risk groups at a rapid rate. These conclusions were reached by drawing on already published data and on an unpublished study carried out by the authors. The study utilized 800 men and women between the ages of 21 and 40. The group was divided into those who were strictly monogamous and others who had at least six heterosexual partners annually.

Only one of the approximately 400 monogamous subjects tested positive for antibodies to HIV. In the remaining subjects, none of whom were in special risk groups such as homosexuals or intravenous drug users, seven percent of the women and five percent of the men tested positive. This infection rate is considerably higher than any other study has found outside the high risk groups.

Other conclusions they published.

● Three million Americans are currently infected with AIDS virus. This is twice the number suggested by the Federal Centers for Disease Control.

● Two hundred thousand heterosexuals are infected. This estimate is nearly seven times higher than the estimate made by the Federal Centers for Disease Control.

- ●The authors believe that as many as 1600 contaminated blood samples may be escaping detection each year with almost as many transfusion recipients getting infected as before strict blood testing programs were mandated.
- ●The authors assert that a critical tool in controlling the epidemic would be mandatory testing for HIV antibodies for married couples seeking a license, pregnant women, convicted prostitutes and all hospital patients between the ages of 15 and 60.

The authors of "Crisis" are of course, entitled to air their views. One can argue that even if they are wrong, what they have said will prevent officials from getting complacent about progress in the fight against AIDS. In effect, they have thrown out a challenge: "Prove us to be wrong" they proposed.

The storm of criticism the book has aroused is immense. Almost all the experts in the field of AIDS research disagree with the conclusions and believe they are too extreme. In all truthfulness, however, the experts who disagree do not have the hard facts as yet to refute any of the estimates of the authors. We do not know the total number of U.S. citizens infected; we do not know how many heterosexuals are infected; we do not know how many donations of HIV infected blood are getting past the screening procedure.

I think the book will have a salutary effect on those who read it. I would suggest reading it with the understanding that there is a large body of critical comment against some of the authors' estimates. I also think it is probably better to err on the side of too much preventive effort against transmission of AIDS than not enough. The book will certainly give pause to some heterosexuals who may think they are not at risk for acquiring HIV from a casual sexual encounter.

Belle Glade, Florida and the Spread of AIDS

A few years ago the small town of Belle Glade, which is just south of Lake Okeechobee and about 40 miles west of Palm Beach, Florida, achieved unenviable notoriety. It became a place with one of the highest incidences of AIDS in the country. Epidemiologists flocked there expecting to find something of interest to explain this high incidence. Mosquitoes were blamed because the place abounded with them, but this theory was soon dismissed as untenable. Several scientists claimed that a herd of sick pigs had African swine fever, which these scientists associated with AIDS, but this was soon shown not to be true. In 1986, 79 cases of the disease had been confirmed, for an incidence of 295 per 100,000 people, which is comparable to San Francisco and New York City.

Careful study of these patients showed that the reasons for the high number of cases were no different than for any other locality—sex and contaminated needles. The distribution of the cases was somewhat different, however, from the patterns in larger cities. Intravenous drug use and sexual transmission among heterosexuals accounted for a much higher proportion of the cases, namely, 30.4 and 34.2%, respectively, compared to the national average of 16.8 and 3.7%, respectively, in 1986.

About 959 blood samples from residents of Belle Glade were tested for antibodies to HIV. The highest rates were found in persons aged 18 to 29 (8.9%), but no children under the age of 11 or persons over the age of 60 had positive tests. The high rate of heterosexual transmission is unusual but can probably be explained on the basis of the high incidence of intravenous drug-related AIDS and males passing the disease to their spouses or other female partners. The town is very poor and run down and has a large number of economically disadvantaged people, many of whom may have other sexually transmitted diseases which could facilitate the spread of AIDS.

Canadian Identified as Playing a Key Role in Spread of AIDS

In a book published by St. Martins Press, *And the Band Played On: People, Politics and the AIDS Epidemic*, by Randy Shilts, a Canadian airline steward is identified as possibly the first person to bring AIDS to the United States on a large scale.

This individual, Gaetan Dugas, who died in 1984, is suspected of having contracted the disease in Europe through sexual contacts with Africans. Studies by federal medical detectives implicated him in the initial spread of the virus in California in the late 1970s before AIDS was identified as a disease. He traveled throughout North America, going from Canada to New York to Toronto to San Francisco.

Of the first 19 cases of AIDS reported in Los Angeles, 4 had had sexual relations with Dugas, and 4 others had had sexual relations with one of his partners. New York's first 2 known cases in 1979 were his sexual partners. According to Shilts, at least 40 of the first 248 AIDS patients reported in the United States by April 1982 had had sexual relations with Dugas or with one of his sex partners.

In July 1981, Dugas told doctors trying to track down the origin of the disease that he had averaged 250 sexual liaisons every year for the last decade. According to the book, he refused to believe that his "gay cancer," as he called it, could be spread sexually and asserted his right to do what he wanted with his body.

This 5 February 1988 issue of *Science*, an important science publication in the United States features an extensive series of review articles on AIDS. With permission of the editors of *Science*. Design by Sharon Wolfgang.

CHAPTER 5
TESTING FOR AIDS AND PREVENTION MEASURES

5

TESTING FOR AIDS AND PREVENTION MEASURES

Introduction

Our society has not required very much of its citizens in the way of testing for disease. Some states mandate a test for syphilis in order to apply for a marriage license, and blood banks have screened donors for hepatitis B for some time now. But people with tuberculosis, herpes, papilloma, cytomegalovirus infections, and a large variety of other diseases can be blood donors and also are usually never asked by prospective employers to prove that they are disease-free, even in the food preparation industries.

The advent of AIDS has changed this. The apparently universally fatal nature of the disease, thus far, has made it imperative not only to design accurate tests for the presence of infection but also to consider ways of testing different groups of people in order to find out who is infected. If it is known who has AIDS, society can then take measures designed to prevent its spread. This opens up a very large range of problems, all of which involve knotty moral and ethical issues. Testing, in addition, can infringe on the freedom of individuals. As yet, no consensus of opinion has emerged on these issues, which have been addressed only superficially by state legislators. There has been little or no leadership from the federal government, although President Reagan has recommended that certain groups of persons be tested. These groups, however, represent only a small portion of the population and include none of the groups that are most at risk for infection with AIDS virus.

How AIDS Testing is Done

In testing for AIDS there are two possibilities. First, one can test directly for the presence of AIDS virus. There are several ways to do this, and the methods are usually fairly difficult and expensive to carry out. These tests can be designed to be extremely specific. At present, tests for the virus are not routinely carried out when large scale screening for AIDS is done. However, new and simpler tests for the virus are being developed. For example, Oncor, Inc., a biotechnology company in Gaithersburg, Maryland, is marketing a blood test for detecting AIDS virus. It uses a piece of RNA that will bind to a unique complementary segment of the virus RNA. The RNA probe is labeled with radioactive sulfur[35]. A patient's white cells are placed on a slide and then treated with a chemical to make the cell membranes permeable so they will allow the labeled RNA probe to pass through. The probe enters the cells and attaches to any virus particles that are present. The slides are coated with a photographic emulsion, stored for 2 days, and then developed. The virus location is revealed by black dots where radiation from the sulfur[35] exposed the emulsion (Figure 5-1).

The Oncor test is based on work published in 1987 by Robert C. Gallo and Flossie Wong-Staal of the National Cancer Institute. Two other companies are evaluating tests based on similar methods: both

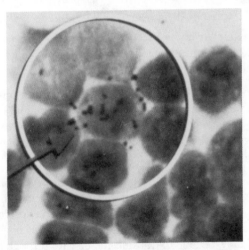

Figure 5-1 Results in Oncor test reveals the presence of HIV as small black dots. The larger bodies are stained nuclei of white blood cells obtained from a patient.

Enzo Biochem of New York City and Cetus Corporation of Emeryville, California, use a DNA probe, but this probe is not radioactive.

The Oncor test may be simple and inexpensive enough to use routinely in place of antibody tests which tell only if a person's immune system has responded to the virus and are often misleading or insensitive.

Second, testing can be done for the *presence of antibodies against the AIDS virus* in blood or tissues. This is the technique presently used all over the world for testing blood donors, immigrants, army personnel, army recruits, organ donors, and others, for example, volunteers who visit free testing stations set up in large cities. Testing for antibodies is a simple, inexpensive, rapid procedure easily carried out by the average medical laboratory. The test is referred to as an ELISA, for *enzyme-linked immunosorbent assay*. There are presently seven different kits available from as many different companies for performing ELISA. These kits supply all the materials and chemicals for performing the test. In principle, AIDS virus proteins fixed to a support of plastic or paper are treated with a blood sample. After a period of incubation to allow combination between the virus proteins and the sample's antibodies, if they are present, the support is washed free of blood and a chemical reagent is added which will develop a color if antibodies have combined with the virus protein. There are some problems, however, when ELISA testing for antibodies is performed:

1. There is a relatively high frequency of nonspecific reactions. That is, a positive test may be obtained, at a frequency ranging from 1 to 5% in individuals who do not have antibodies to AIDS virus.

2. Antibodies are often developed very slowly after infection, anywhere from several months to several years after initial contact with the virus, so if a person comes in for a test during this period, he or she may test negative even though there are virus particles in the blood or cells.

It should be emphasized that a positive test for AIDS antibodies is *not diagnostic* for the disease. It simply means a person has been exposed to the disease and may or may not have virus in the blood or cells. An individual that tests positive for AIDS antibodies may very likely, but not certainly, be able to transmit the disease through body fluids. *All persons testing positive in the first ELISA test should have a second confirmatory test performed.*

Since a positive diagnosis for AIDS results in extreme mental trauma and carries a harsh stigma as well, no mistakes should be made. All those who test positive in two ELISA tests should be retested, preferably by a different method. One of these methods is called the Western blot technique and specifically identifies antibodies to the *gag* gene proteins p18, p24, and their precursor p55. Also identified is the glycoprotein that traverses the membrane of the infected cell, gp42, and possibly other virus proteins. The Western blot procedure as developed by Dr. Victor Tsang of the Federal Centers for Disease Control, encompasses the following steps:

1. Antigens from HIV (obtained by treating virus with detergent) are placed in a polyacrylamide gel slab and caused to migrate by an electric field (electrophoresis).

2. The separated antigens are transferred to a nitrocellulose sheet by blotting.

3. Patient serum specimens and a control specimen from an uninfected person are incubated with the sheet, and antibody-antigen complexes are detected with an enzyme immune assay (ELISA) carried out on the strips. The results obtained from this procedure are shown in Figure 5-2.

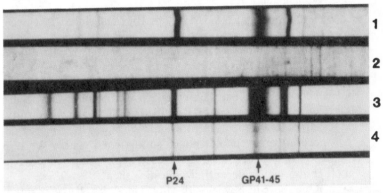

P24   GP41-45

Figure 5-2 A Western blot assay for AIDS antibodies; 1 and 3 indicate a positive reaction, 2 is a negative reaction and 4 indicates a weak reaction. The core protein (P24) and what are thought to be coat proteins (GP 41-45) are the protein bands that are diagnostic for AIDS. Photo courtesy Dr. Victor Tsang, Federal Centers for Disease Control.

The Western blot assay is highly specific for AIDS virus proteins, and it is roughly quantitative, allowing measurement of the amounts of different antibodies. It is not fail-safe, however, and the method of interpreting the results has not been standardized. Different laboratories can interpret a weak reaction, as in Figure 5-4, in different ways.

Some people may have negative or unusual Western blot activity patterns but still have detectable virus in their blood. To get around this difficulty a new test, the Envacor test, can supplement the Western blot test. It is described below.

Other Tests for AIDS

Many other tests for AIDS, either for the virus or for antibodies, are being assessed and proposed all the time. A few of these, called second-generation tests, are worth mentioning.

- *The dot enzyme immunoassay (dot EIA)* This test was developed at the University of California at Davis. It detects antibody to gp42, the glycoprotein that spans the outer membrane of HIV. A drop of serum is placed on gp42 protein on a plastic card. If anti-gp42 antibody is present, it binds to the gp42. Detection reagents are applied, and bound antibody causes the appearance of a blue dot. No color is obtained if there is no antibody. The assay is claimed to be 99% accurate, takes only about 30 minutes to perform compared to 2 to 4 hours for an ELISA, and costs only 25 cents per assay versus $1 to $4 for ELISA kits. It appears to be a valuable assay for use in developing countries.

- *Latex reagent test* This test was developed by Cambridge BioScience, Worcester, Massachusetts, and is based on Recombigen, a recombinant antigen that binds antibodies to both gp42 and gp120. Again a drop of blood serum is mixed with a drop of latex reagent on a plastic card. If antibodies are present in the sample, the tiny latex beads will clump together. The test takes only 5 minutes, and if there is no clumping, there are no HIV antibodies. The test has been used on sera from 2000 patients in Africa and is claimed to be more than 99% accurate and reliable enough so that confirmatory Western blot tests are not needed. It can be used in physician's offices and at other low-volume decentralized testing sites.
Both of the above tests work with whole blood as well as with serum and therefore have the potential to be over-the-counter or home test kits. This, in view of the nature of the problems arising from a positive result, could be a risky business.

- *Envacor* This test, produced by Abbott Laboratories, is a backup or replacement for the Western blot test. It detects core protein p24, as well as gp42, envelope protein. The procedure is easier to perform than the Western blot test because it is in an ELISA format and gives a numeric reading of results, thus avoiding the subjective interpretations of the Western blot test. It is also quicker, but it does require overnight incubation. The specificity is claimed to be 99.9%, and the test has been in use in Europe for more than a year.

● *Tests for antibodies to HTLV-I.* As already mentioned, HTLV-I produces a fatal leukemia after a long lag period in a small percentage (about 0.1 to 1.0%) of individuals who carry the virus. It is estimated that about 5% of those infected with HIV also have HTLV-I. Several companies are gearing up to test for this virus in patients and in the blood supply.

Tests for Different AIDS Viruses

There is a need for tests that will distinguish between HIV, HIV-2, and STLV-III. Dr. Erling Norrby of the Department of Virology, Karolinska Institute, Stockholm, has led a joint program involving several laboratories to develop what they call "site-directed serology", which will distinguish between HIV and HIV-2. They have developed an ELISA test which reacts positively to an antibody directed against a 22-amino-acid peptide from the glycoprotein gp41 from STLV-III, which closely resembles HIV-2. Similarly, they have developed a peptide ELISA specific for the same region in HIV. A person with HIV reacts negatively to the HIV-2 ELISA, and the reverse is also true. Therefore, by running the two ELISAs it is a simple matter to tell if a person has HIV infection, HIV-2 infection, or possibly a dual infection with both, in which case a positive reaction with both ELISAs will be obtained. The scientists involved pointed out that these tests, which are simple to run, would be very useful in developing countries.

Testing the Blood Supply

All donated blood is tested three times by the ELISA technique. If these repeated blood tests are positive, a Western blot procedure may be run. If this test is positive, the blood is discarded and the person's name is placed in a registry indicating that he or she is probably infected and should not be used as a donor. Blood banks and other collecting agencies that identify donors who are positive by ELISA and Western blot procedures notify them that they are probably infected with AIDS virus. It is recommended that such persons be enlisted in a counseling program advising them what to do about their infection and their sexual contacts and urging them not to donate blood or share needles. If the person is a woman, she should be informed about the risk of transmitting the disease to a child if she becomes pregnant.

For donors who test positive on three ELISA tests but negative on the Western blot test, current procedures differ. Although probably not infected with AIDS virus, persons in this category still have their names placed in a deferral registry, and if they donate blood, no blood bank will use it. Many blood-collecting centers do not tell such individuals that their blood is being discarded.

In a consensus statement from a National Institutes of Health meeting on protecting the blood supply from AIDS virus held in July 1986, it was considered inappropriate to enter a person's identity into such a registry without his or her knowledge and without sharing the possible meaning of the tests.

The present test program screening for AIDS virus in donated blood is good but not perfect by any means. The principal problem, as already pointed out repeatedly, is that recently infected persons may not have developed antibodies by the time they make a blood donation but may still have virus in their blood, blood cells, and semen. Also, some people develop antibodies very slowly, taking from months to years to do so. These individuals may have virus in their blood and cells, and there is still a chance that donated blood will be contaminated. The risk is probably small — a reasonable guess is 1 in 10,000 to 1 in 100,000. But every time you drive your car, you probably take that much of a risk of being involved in an accident. If you need blood, don't hesitate to accept it.

For some time now, many open-heart procedures have used a patient's own blood for transfusions. Storing the blood for long periods of time, as for emergencies that might occur in the future, is generally not practical, largely because stored blood does not last more than a few years.

One further problem with blood banks and manufacturers of blood products is that they have been exempted by legislation in most states from any liability due to accidental contamination. This, of course, weakens their incentive to raise product quality. Even though patients are relatively safe from AIDS virus, it is estimated that each day many Americans still contract hepatitis of one form or another from transfusions.

The Government's View on Testing for AIDS Virus

Thousands of persons may be involved in a single facet of the health services of the United States, such as the Public Health Services. The leaders of these organizations can express all shades of opinion from strongly in favor of to strongly against an issue. As leader of the government, President Reagan usually expresses the consensus of the views of his advisors, modified to some extent by his own personal opinions.

During 1986 and 1987 there was a very widespread public debate on testing for AIDS, and many groups were represented. From this debate, which has been discussed in detail by the media, certain facts stand out.

The Reagan administration has initiated a policy of mandatory testing for military personnel, military recruits, State Department and other federal service officers, federal prisoners, and immigrants. Some advisors want tests on those entering Veterans Administration hospitals. All mandatory testing is opposed, however, by Surgeon General C. Everett Koop. The government is still considering whether other groups, particularly nonfederal prisoners, hospital patients, and applicants for marriage licenses, should be included in the mandatory test groups.

Historical precedent is on the side of mandatory testing. In the past, national decisions have been made to test for tuberculosis and syphilis. In both cases the testing began before there was a cure for the disease, and this is the same situation that exists for AIDS at present. The State Department has decreed mandatory testing for all its personnel and foreign assignments are usually not given to anyone testing positive.

The Public's View on Testing for AIDS Virus

In a Gallup poll reported in July 1987, most Americans favored widespread testing for infection with AIDS virus. Of the respondents, 90% favored testing immigrants applying for permanent residence, 88% favored testing inmates in federal prisons, 83% favored testing members of the armed forces, 80% favored testing couples applying for marriage licenses, and 66% favored testing visitors from foreign countries.

The opinions of the participants varied according to their education. For example, 58% of college graduates were against all-inclusive testing, and only 39% were in favor of it. Respondents without high school diplomas, however, approved of such testing, with 64% for it and 34% against it. Approximately 1000 persons were questioned with a sampling error of about 4%. Similar results on the testing of applicants for marriage licenses were obtained in a *Wall Street Journal*/NBC poll of 2204 adults. This poll asked if employers should test new employees to see if they had AIDS virus. Opinion was fairly evenly divided here, with 42% answering yes and 48% no.

Arguments in Favor of Testing for AIDS Virus

Both sides advance several cogent reasons supporting their viewpoints. The most common arguments for testing are the following.

- Advocates assert that wider testing is the only reliable way to see how AIDS is spreading beyond the groups hit hardest so far. Dr. Robert Redfield, a physician at Walter Reed Army Medical Center who helped run the U.S. Army AIDS testing program says, "We have to change our focus in this country from AIDS to the virus." By concentrating on the disease, he contends, the country is dealing with infections that began years ago. By testing we can try to prevent cases in individuals still unborn. After finding those who carry the virus we can try to counsel and educate them and possibly prevent further spread of AIDS, he says.

- Proponents of testing believe it is wise to test low-risk groups, for example, marriage license applicants. In the only study undertaken so far, in Oakland, California, 8 of every 1000 applicants were positive for exposure to AIDS virus. If the positive applicants know this and still want to go through with the marriage, with the use of condoms they can probably prevent spread of the virus to the uninfected partner.

- Those who test positive for AIDS virus can be offered treatment to prolong their lives. They can take medication to prevent infection by *Pneumocystis carinii* and other organisms that often are the cause of death. They can also guard against other diseases such as herpes and hepatitis that may activate a dormant AIDS infection.

- Prominent AIDS researcher Dr. Robert C. Gallo says, "I'd want to know," if infected with the virus. "I'd want a chance for not passing it to my wife. I'd want to be near a good doctor and I'd want the latest and best medicines available or a vaccine, if there is one."

- Knowing who has AIDS is important in case a drug is found that can prevent or delay the onset of clinical symptoms by preventing or inhibiting virus activation. Once the disease has a good start it will be much harder to treat or cure if a cure becomes available.

- A very important point made by testing advocates is that most people who test positive for an AIDS virus are likely to take precautions against spreading the disease to others.

- It is possible for the spouse or lover of a carrier to be saved from infection if a test for the virus is made soon enough. Dr. Redfield has stated that among married AIDS patients he has treated in the military program, only about half have already infected their spouses.

  Testing advocates assert that the partners of infected persons have a right to know that their lovers or spouses are infected. Medical professionals who treat AIDS victims — dentists, physicians, and surgeons — also have a right to know. It can be argued, however, that they should always assume the possibility of infection and take the proper precautions anyway.

- Proponents of testing say that expanding the program along proposed lines would be relatively cheap and cost-effective in the long run, if it did nothing more than to slow the spread of the disease. Costs of tests are moderate, are decreasing, and will do so even further as the number of tests performed increases.

  Testing proponents argue that AIDS test results can be kept confidential in the same way the medical community keeps other medical information secret. However, the information should not be kept confidential from doctors and nurses, who take care of those who are infected, or spouses.

Costs of AIDS Tests

Government officials state that the initial tests cost only a few dollars per person. The confirming Western blot procedure is more expensive, now running about $45 per test. This procedure has to be done only in a small percentage of those individuals tested, who test positive in ELISA — about 1 to 2% or less of the general population. Of course, if testing is done in one of the high-risk groups, for example, intravenous drug users, the confirming Western blot test might have to be run in 50% or more of those tested, since a large proportion of intravenous drug users would test positive with the ELISA test. For the 3 million tests the Army has done, the average cost was less than $5 per person, and this is what could be expected for large-scale tests of the general population, for example, those applying for marriage licenses.

Finally, the cost of testing to stop the spread of AIDS in such places as hospitals and federal prisons is far less than the $100,000 or more it now takes to treat each victim of the disease.

Arguments Against Testing for AIDS Virus

●A forceful argument against testing is that any voluntary program or even a routine or mandatory program in which a person has the right to refuse the test will scare a lot of people away. These individuals are the ones who probably most need to be tested and counseled if they test positive. They are the sexually promiscuous, homosexuals, teen-agers, intravenous drug users, Haitians, and others at high risk. Many of these people fear discrimination in jobs, housing, and insurance, and social ostracism.

●Opponents of testing fear the danger of careless record keeping and subsequent disclosure. Government records have been breached before and are accessible to law enforcement agencies.

●Critics of testing also worry that many influential testing advocates actually favor some sort of quarantine for AIDS carriers. On a television panel show, former Secretary of Education, William Bennett suggested that some AIDS virus-infected prisoners might have to be kept confined even after they finish their prison terms. Senator Jesse Helms has said, "Somewhere along the line we are going to have to quarantine if we are really going to contain this disease."

●In addition, opponents to testing believe that the administration and others advocating mandatory testing have not thought about all the implications of their plans. For example, what will be done with the information collected? What efforts will be made to notify former sex partners? How will prison officials go about isolating AIDS virus-infected prisoners? In states like New York, California, and Texas, where there may be hundreds of prisoners who test positive, this would be a difficult problem to solve.

AIDS testing of low-risk groups, such as marriage license applicants, on a wide scale will be expensive and will result in a large number of false positives if only the ELISA test is used. Palmer Jones, executive vice-president of the New Hampshire Medical Society, points out that of 22,000 applicants who apply for a marriage license in New Hampshire, about 220 (1%) would test positive in the initial screening. Follow-up testing would probably show that only 1 or 2 of those were true positives. If each applicant pays $10 for the fee for testing, or $20 for the pair, that would work out to $110,000 to detect each of two AIDS carriers. The Federal Centers for Disease Control have estimated a somewhat lower cost for detecting each AIDS carrier in a group of low-risk individuals at about $20,000. This is still a formidable cost, and the critics of testing claim that widespread programs will cost far more than the proponents of such programs claim.

- Furthermore, critics claim that the funds could be better used to expand voluntary testing and counseling at existing AIDS testing sites, drug and sexually transmitted disease clinics, and family planning clinics. Opponents of mandatory wide-scale testing also point out that in many cities there are waiting times of 3 to 6 weeks for testing and that many family planning clinics have no AIDS testing at all. They assert, however, that it is especially important to have all pregnant women tested in order to try to cut down on the number of children who become infected before or during birth.

Persons who test falsely negative, and many may, might celebrate this fact by becoming wildly promiscuous, feeling they can do so safely. This can result in further spread of the disease. To be really safe, a testing program, particularly of moderate or high-risk individuals, should repeat negative tests every 6 months. This would greatly increase the costs and difficulty of administering the program.

Those against mandatory testing understand the need to have more information on the spread of AIDS, but they believe this can be obtained with anonymous testing. In fact, the Federal Centers for Disease Control have an expanding network of hospitals that routinely tests blood samples collected anonymously. It is not clear how the centers expect to handle the data. Surely they must intend to inform those who test positive (including ELISA and Western blot test results).

- If AZT or some other drug is effective in preventing activation of virus in those infected with AIDS virus but showing no sign of the disease, this whole argument about testing may become moot. AZT is presently undergoing tests for this very purpose (Chapter 7). If it does prove useful, then survival of those who are infected may depend on their knowing early that they are infected, and it would be in the best interests of anyone who might possibly be infected to come forward for voluntary testing.

Testing for Those at High Risk of Contracting AIDS

Dr. Walter W. Dowdle, AIDS coordinator for the Public Health Service, recommends that every person in a high-risk group come forward and be tested at 6-month intervals. He calls for utmost confidentiality in the keeping of records. Those most at risk are considered to be

- Homosexual and bisexual men and female partners of bisexual men
- Present or past intravenous drug users and their sex partners
- People with mild symptoms compatible with AIDS, for example, swollen glands and a mild fever
- People of Haitian or African birth
- Male and female prostitutes
- Hemophiliacs and their spouses
- Newborn children of AIDS virus-infected mothers.

American Medical Association Support for AIDS Testing of Two Groups

In June 1987 the American Medical Association endorsed mandatory testing of prisoners and would-be immigrants for AIDS virus. They do not favor mandatory testing for other groups but do favor "routine" testing of patients at clinics that treat drug users and people afflicted with other sexually transmitted diseases unless a patient objects to the test. They also call for more federal financing for AIDS treatment, testing, and research, stating that the $1 billion planned for 1988 is not enough.

The National Medical Association, a group of black physicians, endorses mandatory AIDS virus tests for donors of blood, organs, and tissue and for military personnel and immigrants seeking long-term residence.

Testing in Individual States

According to Table 5-1 New York State has the highest incidence of AIDS, with most of the cases in New York City. The state has set up a $3.4 million program to test 100,000 blood samples, selected randomly from routine specimens taken at state hospitals, for antibodies to HIV. The samples will be numbered and assigned to groups such as intravenous drug users, homosexuals, heterosexuals, and so on. Those tested will not be informed of the results, and testing is expected to take 6 months to a year. The purpose of this testing program is to give the state a basis for estimating future needs for hospital care, determining the direction of educational programs and the like. It is also hoped that information will be obtained on how AIDS virus has spread through different population groups and different regions of the state and how it is communicated. Descriptive information about the patient will

Table 5-1 Cases of AIDS in some states[a]

State	Total cases	Cases per capita
Highest numbers of cases		
New York	12,981	1:1,369
California	10,761	1:2,507
Florida	3,477	1:3,358
Texas	3,272	1:5,098
New Jersey	3,088	1:2,468
Lowest numbers of cases		
South Dakota	5	1:141,600
North Dakota	7	1:97,000
Wyoming	7	1:72,429
Montana	8	1:77,154
Idaho	13	1:77,154

[a]Data courtesy of Federal Centers for Disease Control.

accompany each sample, including age, sex, ethnic background, alcohol and drug use, income level, and so on.

There is some question about the authenticity of the results that might be obtained, since the hospital population is heavily skewed toward older age groups which are sparsely infected with HIV. Also, there is additional doubt about the ethical problems arising from not telling someone who tests positive for AIDS virus about the results, even though a health department spokesman Peter Slocum says the study would be unethical only if there were an effective long-term treatment or cure for AIDS and the state did not share it with those who were infected. What about AZT? It may very well be an effective long-term treatment, at least for some patients.

The same doubts could be raised with regard to a similar study being run by the federal government on 45,000 blood samples to be collected voluntarily and anonymously. The Federal Centers for Disease Control are running the tests and hope to enlist 15 hospitals in the study.

Passage of AIDS testing bills in Illinois
Governor James R. Thompson has signed a package of AIDS testing bills designed to fight the transmission of AIDS virus. These bills provide

- Mandatory AIDS testing for sex crime offenders
- Financial incentives for nursing homes to accept AIDS patients

- That all marriage license applicants must show proof they have been tested for AIDS, although they do not have to show the results
- Mandatory AIDS education in public schools from grade 6 through grade 12
- Strict confidentiality for test results.

The measures passed were more reasonable than those initially presented, which included tests for all prison inmates and hospital patients 13 to 55 years old, as well as requiring the state public health department to seek out sex partners of AIDS victims for the past 7 years. Initial results with the test required for marriage license applicants have proved vexing. Present free testing stations are swamped with the demand and a large percentage of couples getting married are going to neighboring states to avoid the test.

How North Dakota has responded

North Dakota, at least, is not complacent or smug about having only seven cases. Dr. Robert Wentz, the state health officer, describes AIDS as "the greatest threat to North Dakota public health since tobacco use became commonplace." He has urged the state legislators to begin an earnest campaign to build public awareness of its dangers and to support state financing for preventive and education measures that will keep North Dakota's incidence of AIDS low.

North Dakota has many small towns and a proportionately high farm population. To most of its citizens AIDS is a very remote, unlikely occurrence. Nevertheless, the state health department has prepared a 131 page report, "AIDS and North Dakota: A Plan for Action," which outlines a broad legislative program. The program includes comprehensive health education on AIDS in all public schools and mandatory blood testing of prison inmates, prostitutes, and all applicants for marriage licenses. Tough new laws are included to guard patient confidentiality and forbid discrimination. The governor, George Sinner, supports this program. He was confronted by a teacher who heard there were two children with AIDS in school and demanded that teachers be told who they were. The governor answered that it was of no value to know the two names if the teacher did not know who might be infected in his own class. "Why should we make just those two children pariahs?" the governor asked.

North Dakota is fortunate in having a relatively homogeneous population with a high social and religious ethic. There are few intravenous drug users, and male homosexuals cannot find much in the way of support groups, even in the larger cities. The biggest risks are to heterosexuals and young adults who think AIDS just doesn't exist in the state.

Passage of a new AIDS law in Colorado

A law passed late in 1987 requires the reporting of names of patients with AIDS virus to the Colorado Department of Health. It imposes a fine of $300 on doctors, laboratories for testing blood, clinics, and other health officials who do not report a name, but at the same time a fine of $5000 for any state official who does not keep the information confidential.

The law has been met with considerable protest, and Dennis Brinn, an attorney who represents a coalition of homosexual and civil rights groups, says it will keep homosexuals, intravenous drug users, and other high-risk persons away from the testing sites, to the detriment of themselves and others to whom they might transmit HIV.

The law also permits, with court approval, state health officials to quarantine for 48 hours any AIDS carrier considered a threat to public health.

As of April 30, 1987 Colorado has reported 370 cases of AIDS, mostly in Denver, and the number of individuals carrying the virus is not known.

The new law's provisions for confidentiality are actually very strong. Health records may not be examined at any hearing – judicial, legislative, executive, or otherwise – and they may not be released upon subpoena, discovery proceeding or search warrant.

A Law Prohibiting Deportation of Certain Illegal Aliens with AIDS

A landmark immigration law granting amnesty to certain illegal aliens who have resided in this country since 1982 was passed in 1986. This law specifically prohibits deportation of illegal aliens residing in the United States based on any information, including the results of an AIDS test, provided to the government as part of an application for U.S. citizenship.

In May 1987, however, the Public Health Service recommended mandatory AIDS testing for the more than 530,000 immigrants who each year seek permanent residence in this country. If an immigrant tests positive he or she will be denied entry. This proposal has been approved by the Reagan government. It apparently does not need congressional action, despite the above provision of the 1986 law which appears to protect those *already* tested but not those *not yet* tested. Since the amnesty law ran out in May 1988 it appears that all those who seek to become U.S. citizens will be required to have an AIDS test.

Jim Brown, a spokesman for the Public Health Service, says the agency wants to add HIV virus to the list of dangerous infectious diseases used to prevent infected aliens from gaining permanent resident status. The list includes leprosy, tuberculosis, syphilis, and gonorrhea. If this proposal becomes final, everyone who wants permanent status will have to undergo an AIDS test and a physical and mental examination.

AIDS Testing by Sports Teams

The Dallas Cowboys, Houston Oilers, and at least 3 other teams of the 28 in the National Football League offer free, confidential AIDS virus tests to players, coaches, and staff members at their training camps.

Shortly after these tests were announced, spokespersons for the major league baseball and basketball associations stated that there were no plans at present to offer such tests but that the education of players about the risks of AIDS was being encouraged.

According to Rich Levin, a spokesman for the baseball office, pamphlets on AIDS prevention prepared by the American Red Cross have been circulated to major league teams.

The program of the NFL clubs includes the mandatory use of rubber gloves by trainers and other personnel dealing with open cuts and bloody uniforms. Team physicians have voted to urge all NFL clubs to adopt such programs.

Robert E. Stein, president of Environmental Mediation International, a group that advises both business and government on AIDS-related policy issues, believes some good can come from these programs. He points out, however, that the ramifications of this policy are very complicated and difficult to address: How will confidentiality really be maintained? What action should a team take when a player tests positive? Antidiscrimination laws in many states prevent a team from firing a player solely for testing HIV-positive unless it can be demonstrated that his condition makes him unfit to work. If he is fired, will that conflict with his confidentiality rights? Could players refuse to practice or play with a teammate if the management knows one member has tested positive? Could a team require that all members of an opposing team test negative before they play?

Some countries require negative AIDS tests for visitors. What if Canada or the United States required persons to test negative before they issued a work permit? Would a voluntary program encourage players to come forward for a test if they fear a positive result would interfere with their careers?

Many professional athletes are very newsworthy, and if their participation in and support for voluntary testing and other AIDS programs gains extensive media coverage, which is likely, this may have a positive effect on Congress and encourage the public to promote and participate in voluntary testing.

Barring of an AIDS Test for Health Insurance in New York State

Insurance companies have double trouble as far as AIDS is concerned. First, they are faced with a large excess of deaths they otherwise would not have had. This number is now about 25,000, but could rise considerably. And it may be too low also because many AIDS deaths are reported as due to other causes to avoid the stigma that is attached.

Second, health insurance is a very expensive item for many insurance companies. It has been mentioned that a single AIDS case may cost as much as $100,000 to $150,000 to treat. This estimate may be too conservative, particularly now that AZT is apparently prolonging the lives of many AIDS victims.

Insurance companies would like to require a test for AIDS antibodies for all potential health insurance customers. Connecticut and New Jersey now allow such tests, but they have been barred by New York and California, which together account for more than half of the total number of AIDS cases. In New York, this regulation, issued by New York State Superintendent of Insurance James P. Corcoran, was sought by Governor Mario Cuomo and civil rights and homosexual groups who contend that a blood test would deny insurance to thousands of people who are suspected of being homosexuals or whose blood tests positive for HIV. It is probable that many more states will take a stand on one side of this question or the other. For the present I believe that everyone is entitled to a reasonable amount of health and life insurance regardless of the state of his or her health. At present many states have programs that insure motorists who for one reason or another are unable to obtain liability insurance for their cars. Perhaps the same sort of program should be set up for health and life insurance at the state or federal level. Governor Michael Dukakis has already proposed a state health program for Massachusetts which was passed in 1988.

Army Policies on AIDS Testing

As mentioned in Chapter 4, the U.S. Army has tested over 3 million individuals. At present any personnel who acknowledge the use of intravenous drugs or that they engage in homosexual acts are given honorable discharges on the grounds of either medical disability or "for the convenience of the government," which is a general term used in cases where it is not desirable to state the real reason. This guarantee, however, does not apply to partners of homosexuals identified in AIDS screening, as a Pentagon spokesman, Lieutenant Colonel Pete Wyro has noted.

Those found to have AIDS will be given medical treatment, counseling, and medical discharges under honorable conditions, and AIDS will not be identified on the discharge certificate. Those who test positive for AIDS but show no signs of the disease will be retained in the service, possibly with restricted duties and restrictions on geographical location.

Homosexuals and drug users whose conduct is discovered outside the AIDS screening program could possibly receive a dishonorable discharge and, rarely, might be court-martialed, depending on the circumstances. The Army plans AIDS screening for all personnel on active duty once every 2 years. No soldier receiving a transfer to a post outside the United States may go unless he or she has had an AIDS test within the past 6 months. The 6-month standard will also be used for all soldiers forming special units, such as Ranger and Operations Command.

Testing in Other Countries

Japan
In Japan AIDS is a notifiable disease according to new laws. Doctors must report the age, sex, and source of infection of those with AIDS to the local government within 7 days. If a doctor believes a patient may ignore his instructions, the doctor must immediately report the name

and address of the patient to the authorities. Governors are empowered to order AIDS tests and medical checkups for people who are infected or suspected of being infected with AIDS. A maximum fine of 100,000 yen ($670) can be imposed on those who refuse. Foreigners with AIDS are not allowed into Japan. Many groups have objected to the tests as an infringement of human rights.

West Germany
An international symposium held at the University of Munich in 1987 concluded that voluntary testing for AIDS should be offered to all pregnant mothers. A pilot program of testing pregnant women has already begun in the university hospitals in Munich. The results are confidential between patient and physician, and virtually no one has refused to be tested thus far.

Bavaria
Despite strong criticism, Bavaria began testing, in May 1987, all prostitutes, intravenous drug users, and other suspected AIDS virus carriers. It proposes measures for the isolation of AIDS virus carriers who behave in an unreasonable way, for example, prostitutes who do not use condoms. Also to be tested are applicants for public service jobs and immigrants. Prostitutes must report for quarterly AIDS tests, but how the condom measure will be enforced is not clear. The West German government has criticized the measures as giving a false sense of security. About 1000 cases of AIDS have been reported in West Germany, and it is estimated there are 50,000 to 100,000 carriers of the virus.

China
Stringent measures are being used to prevent the introduction of AIDS into China. Blood tests are required for all foreigners who wish to enter the country to work or visit and for all Chinese who return from abroad. The police have been instructed to prevent casual sexual contacts between foreigners and Chinese, particularly Chinese prostitutes who are becoming more common in the larger cities.

In the years 1986 and 1987 only 11 cases of AIDS were discovered in China. Four of these involved Chinese citizens, the rest foreigners. Chinese officials say that the four Chinese victims had received blood or blood products from the United States.

Foreigners have resisted blood tests because they claim that the sanitary standards in Chinese hospitals are low and there is a risk of contracting hepatitis and other diseases from poorly sterilized needles.

Canada has warned its citizens not to have acupuncture in China because it believes that a Canadian woman who died from AIDS and had no other risk factors but an acupuncture treatment in China may have contracted the disease from unsterile needles. The Chinese, of course, vigorously deny this, claim that the needles are carefully sterilized and, furthermore, that the curative properties of acupuncture treatment inhibit AIDS and can in fact totally cure the disease.

The import of all foreign blood products has been banned by China, and in many Chinese cities, including Beijing, foreigners cannot enter dance halls or discotheques.

South Korea
South Korea demands an AIDS test for foreigners seeking long-term residency.

Saudi Arabia
Saudi Arabia requires an AIDS test for long-term visitors and those seeking work permits.

Belgium and India
Belgium and India require AIDS tests for those applying for student visas.

The Soviet Union
All foreigners who intend to stay in the country more than 3 months are now tested for AIDS virus. The Soviet requirement for tests has made some people uneasy because they believe that Soviet hospital standards do not measure up to those in the United States. A group of students from England, while not objecting to the tests, wondered how the confidentiality of the results could be maintained if they were sent home because they tested positive. The Soviets admit to 102 cases of positive tests but claim that 80 of them involve foreigners.

France
France is faced with the prospect of 10 to 15 thousand cases of AIDS in 1989. Consequently it is stepping up its educational programs and providing more facilities for AIDS sufferers. France makes available hypodermic syringes without prescription. In addition to 11 existing AIDS clinics and advice centers a further 11 are to be opened, two in French colonies.

Asia
Dr. John Dwyer, director of the AIDS Treatment and Research Institute at Prince Henry Hospital in Sydney, Australia, describes AIDS as a time bomb for Asia. He points out that if an international conference

had been held in Africa 10 years ago, something might have been done about the disease running rampant there. He believes that when the epidemic does strike the region, it is more likely to reflect the experience of Africa where it has spread mainly through the heterosexual population.

So far, according to figures made public by the World Health Organization, just 208 cases of AIDS have been reported in 18 Asian nations. One wonders, of course, at the accuracy and completeness of these reports, and there is not even an estimate of how many Asians are carrying the virus.

Italy
Italy has a major problem with intravenous drug abusers, and about 1500 cases of AIDS had been reported by the end of 1987. Heroin users account for about 62% of these cases, more than two times the national average for the United States (about 30% of cases) from this source. The highest concentration of heroin use and cases is in Milan. The situation is a difficult one because about 80% of drug addicts test positive for AIDS virus. This uniquely high infection rate precludes any education program, because it will probably reach 100% before the program can get started. As already mentioned, the program must nevertheless begin and be vigorously pursued in schools to reduce the number of drug users in the future. Economic factors also have to be improved so youngsters will not be driven to drugs by despair and frustration.

The Catholic Church has been carrying out a large effort to rehabilitate heroin addicts with considerable success. Reverend Gino Rigoldi, who treats one group of addicts, works slowly and with small groups teaching new trades like landscaping and animal husbandry. His "community" has been able to help more than half its graduates remain free of drugs for 5 years after they leave.

There is concern among these clergy who devote their efforts to drug rehabilitation that when it becomes generally known that all of these former users of intravenous drugs have AIDS, they will be rejected on this basis and turn to drugs again in frustration.

Great Britain
In England only about 1250 cases of AIDS disease have been reported. Noting how AIDS has spread in the United States, the government has started a strong nationwide educational program, passing out leaflets to every household. It hopes to avoid the rapid spread of the disease

that took place in the United States before most people were aware of the menace of AIDS.

Cuba
It has been reported that Cuba has begun mandatory isolation for all those with AIDS virus. This may be possible only during the early stages of its spread, because the number of cases may eventually overwhelm the facilities set aside for victims.

Brazil
Brazil now has the second highest total number of AIDS cases after the United States, 2102 as of September 1987. At that time a prominent sociologist, Herbert de Souza, publicly announced that he and his two younger brothers were carriers of AIDS virus.

This announcement, which also pointed out that all three brothers were hemophiliacs and had been infected by blood transfusions that had not been tested for AIDS antibodies, brought the discussion and debate about AIDS into the open. Mr. de Souza, as president of the Brazilian Interdisciplinary AIDS Association, greatly improved his credibility, expanded his audience and directly confronted the Health Ministry which had initially refused to allow the importation of AZT. His public denouncement of this action caused the Health Ministry to reverse itself, but there are still bureaucratic obstacles to importation of the drug and it is too expensive for all but well-to-do patients.

Mr. de Souza also criticized the government for its failure to properly test blood and for haphazard procedures at blood banks, many of which fail to carry out the tests. In Brazil as many as 14% of AIDS virus infections are due to contaminated blood.

The Netherlands
The Dutch are noted for their willingness to perform voluntary euthanasia (injection of drugs to painlessly terminate life in patients suffering unbearable pain and with no hope of recovery). About 5000 cases of voluntary euthanasia occur each year, and lately some of them have involved AIDS patients. Officials are worried that permissiveness toward mercy killing will attract large numbers of AIDS patients from around the world, but thus far this does not appear to be happening.

The Dutch have always been quite tolerant of homosexuals and intravenous drug users. There is a large homosexual population estimated to be about 250,000, and the number of drug addicts is estimated at 8000. Four hundred thousand sterile hypodermic syringes and needles are expected to be distributed free in 1988. An active education program is being conducted by the authorities and they hasten to point out that euthanasia is allowed only in extreme cases and then with very careful regulation and the consent of at least two physicians.

AIDS Testing Bills Before Congress

There are eight different bills before the House of Representatives that address the issue of AIDS testing. A bill introduced by Henry Waxman (Democrat, California) seems to have the most support. It would give the Department of Health and Human Services $400 million a year for the next 3 years to establish centers for voluntary testing for HIV antibodies. The bill would require testing centers to offer counseling both before and after the test is given when the results are known. There are strict confidentiality provisions, with fines for violation of privacy. The new act would also prohibit discrimination against those who test positive for HIV, although it is not clear how this latter provision would be enforced.

William Dannemeyer (Republican, California) has a greatly different view. Several bills he has introduced call for mandatory tests for couples seeking marriage licenses, prostitutes, and hospital patients. He also favors disclosing the status of HIV-infected individuals to their sexual partners. These issues are discussed in Chapter 9.

The House of Representatives has passed a bill authorizing the creation of a National Commission on AIDS. This 15-member group would have at least 8 members from the scientific and medical communities who would be charged with advising Congress and the President on priorities in research, public health, and education. This bill was introduced in response to widespread public criticism of the President's commission which was established late in July 1987. The House bill must be passed by the Senate and signed by the President before it becomes law, two hurdles which may not be jumped.

Senator Edward Kennedy has introduced legislation to launch a major new initiative against AIDS. The bill (S 1220) offers a four point plan which would:

1. Educate all Americans about AIDS risks and enable them to make informed choices to protect themselves

2. Develop care and treatment networks for people with AIDS that are more economical and appropriate

3. Accelerate the search for AIDS vaccines and cures by putting federal funds to work faster; and

4. Assure that all Americans have access to voluntary and confidential AIDS testing and counseling and are protected against discrimination.

Senator Kennedy chairs the Senate Labor and Human Resources Committee which would have jurisdiction over the measure.

Prevention of AIDS

Every case of AIDS prevented represents a life and a very large sum of money saved, and an incredible amount of mental and physical pain and trauma averted. Everyone asks the same question, over and over, How can I protect myself from AIDS? Or if they are the parent of a teen-ager, How can I protect my children from AIDS? Or if they are an infected pregnant mother, How can I protect my unborn child from AIDS? The answers usually given to these questions are not always as accurate or complete as they might be, and sometimes they are over-simplified. In answering many of the questions that often arise in this area, I will try to be as direct, honest, and thorough as present information on AIDS will allow.

Can one be absolutely certain not to catch AIDS?
The only way to be *absolutely certain is to not have sex with another person and never to use an unsterile needle.*

Even this fairly direct answer requires additional comments. You should avoid working with AIDS virus in a laboratory or with AIDS patients in a hospital or other medical institution. You should avoid blood transfusions except with your own blood, or the use of any blood products made from blood or serum. You should avoid organ transplants unless careful testing for AIDS virus has been done on blood of the donor and it is certain that he or she was not heavily trans-fused with blood before donating the tissue. You should never use a semen donation that has not been tested for AIDS virus. Even then there is a risk of AIDS, as many AIDS tests can give a false negative.

"Well," you might ask. "Isn't it safe to have sex with a virgin?" The answer is no. It is not safe. Many youngsters use intravenous drugs. And how do you know the person is a virgin? Do you take their word for it. No SEX! But how about a couple who has been happily married for 25 years? Okay, provided neither member of the pair has strayed, uses intravenous drugs, or has been subjected to any of the other risk conditions.

As a single person you say, "What is left for me if I want to be certain?" The answer is — only self-masturbation. It is far better than nothing.

"All right," you reply, "I will be careful. I'll use a condom, and if I am a female I will always carry condoms with me and insist my partner use them." My answer to that is "Fine," but you will still run a much reduced risk. Condoms can be defective or fail or be used improperly.

Having sex today with a partner of unknown background without a condom is like playing Russian roulette. Sooner or later there will be a bullet in the chamber — a live AIDS virus particle. One live virus particle may be enough — we don't know how many virions are needed to transmit the disease.

Since you have mentioned condoms, let us consider their use in more detail.

Safer Sex with Condoms

You will notice that I do not use the term "safe sex." There is essentially no safe sex except, as I mentioned, that involving faithful partners who have not had sexual relations with anyone else (or used intravenous drugs).

The use of condoms will protect partners to a considerable degree from sexually transmitted diseases and, of course, pregnancy, but neither protection is absolute. Condoms now have a new aura of respectability because of AIDS, after having been thought of as "dirty" and inappropriate for sex with wives or nice women.

Condoms have been used for hundreds of years. Casanova is credited with devising a prophylactic made of sheep intestine to avoid disease and pregnancy. By 1840 the vulcanization of rubber allowed rubber condoms to be made easily and cheaply. The use of latex, which began in 1930, improved the strength and durability of condoms, and the ones in use today have not changed significantly for 50 years. Condoms are readily available in drug stores and in most other stores that sell drugs, for example, supermarkets. They are now mentioned frequently on the radio and on TV and discussed in detail by magazines and newspapers, whereas a few years ago even the mention of them was taboo. In 1977 the Supreme Court declared unconstitutional all laws restricting in any way use of condoms or their sale.

Effectiveness of Condoms

Condoms should be used consistently for anal, oral or, vaginal sex. A person in a situation leading to some type of sexual encounter might forget to bring a condom and think that one time without one probably won't matter. Nothing could be further from the truth. That one time might be the time that AIDS virus is transferred. Anyone who is sexually active, male or female, should always have a supply.

All viruses, bacteria, or protozoan organisms are prevented from passing through a condom. If the sheath is not fitted all the way up the shaft of the penis, as far as it will go, it is possible some fluid might be forced out through the opening, resulting in failure to contain the disease.

Some venereal diseases may still be transmitted even if a condom is worn. For example, herpes sores may be present on the scrotum (the covering of the testicles) or in the pubic hair. Contact with these sores, which are outside the condom, may transmit herpes and also, possibly, papilloma (a wart and cancer-causing virus). Additional protection can be obtained by applying germicidal sponges, jellies, and creams to these areas and also to the vagina. Nonoxynol-9 is the best and it will kill the AIDS virus and other viruses and microorganisms.

With the most careful and consistent use of condoms, infection rates can probably be reduced to a low value of a few percent. Mistakes occasionally happen: the condom can slip off during vigorous action, or it can be faulty. Latex condoms have a finite shelf life. With increased aging the rubber tends to become brittle and to be more easily cracked or torn. One should purchase condoms in a store where there is likely to be rapid turnover. Condoms that have knobs or ridges on them (to increase the pleasurable feeling) are obviously more subject to failure or slippage and a plain latex condom is usually best. A small space should be left at the bottom to allow room for the ejaculate. Without this, there will be great pressure forcing the ejaculate out the open end of the condom. Some condoms are made with a little blip on the end to contain the ejaculate, and these are the best kind.

With a worst case scenario the failure rate using a condom can be as high as 25%. With moderate care it should be less than 5%. Fortunately, every sexual act does not invariably mean that the disease will be transmitted, but one must always reckon with the possibility of failure and a disastrous transfer of the virus or infected cells.

Proper use of condoms

In addition to latex condoms, condoms made from animal intestines, usually sheep, are also available. They are said to give better sensations than latex condoms, but do not stretch, which may be a disadvantage in terms of fit. There is no absolute proof that AIDS virus cannot penetrate such condoms, since we know it is likely that virus and virus-infected cells can penetrate intact human intestine. In addition, these condoms are more likely to have defects, and they are more expensive.

To prevent disease transmission or pregnancy, the condom should be placed on the penis before any contact with the partner is made, whether with the genitalia, mouth, rectum, or hand. Often, during erection or foreplay, the penis may exude fluids, clear liquid from Cowper's gland or sperm in small quantities. These fluids can contain virus particles or virus-infected cells if the male is infected.

After ejaculation the penis becomes limp and smaller. Care must be taken to hold the base of the condom tightly against the penis so the condom does not slip off and spill its contents during withdrawal.

The whole process of withdrawal and removing the condom is fraught with danger. Suppose you are a male and it is possible that your female (or male) partner is infected. The exterior of the condom will be covered with vaginal or anal secretions which may contain virus or virus-infected cells. If your hands have any cuts or bruises or are chapped, you will be at risk. It would be best, but admittedly impractical, to use rubber gloves. The next best thing is to wash your hands immediately with hot water and soap.

A way around this difficulty is to use a spermicide or lubricant containing nonoxynol-9 which will kill AIDS virus. This will help with the sexual process also, since condoms do not slide easily and usually need some kind of lubrication. Do not use petroleum-based lubricants such as petroleum jelly, however, since they may weaken the condom.

Condoms come in different thicknesses. While the ultrathin types may give one better sensation, they are obviously more liable to failure.

Why do so few married U.S. couples use condoms?

Most married couples don't worry about AIDS or other venereal diseases. If a couple is trying to avert pregnancy a pill is easier to use. Condoms have two major drawbacks: First, they make spontaneity in sex impossible. There must be forethought to obtain them, careful preparation with spermicides and lubricants, and they must be placed on the penis—all of which ruins any chance for spontaneity. Second, sensation is significantly reduced. This could be helpful in many cases, since males often achieve orgasm ahead of their female partners and the damped-down sensation would tend to prolong the time to ejaculation. In reality, married couples do not need to use condoms unless the female has problems with the pill.

Nevertheless, the use of condoms by married couples is much higher in other cultures, being estimated at about 65% in Japan and probably equally high in Sweden and other Scandinavian countries.

The use of a condom with all the above-mentioned precautions should be mandatory for anyone, male or female, who tests positive for AIDS, has any sexually transmissible disease, or is sexually active with partners of unknown background.

Does the use of condoms create a false sense of security?
Dr. C. Everett Koop, the Surgeon General of the United States, has repeatedly endorsed condoms as the best line of defense against AIDS. Many health officials fear that campaigns encouraging condom use may create a false sense of security in people whose behavior may put them in danger.

Surgeon General Koop has also advised against any sexual contact at all with carriers of the virus, even with condom use. It is still unknown just how much protection condoms really give. There have been no thorough studies on the efficacy of their use in preventing AIDS or, for that matter, any other sexually transmitted disease. A campaign for condom use to prevent the spread of gonorrhea in Sweden has worked very well, reducing the incidence of the disease by 80% in several years. Sweden is a highly developed, technologically oriented country with good communication and universal literacy. What appears to work well in Sweden may not work as well in a less developed or less literate country, however.

Some of the facts to keep in mind when using condoms are the following.

- Studies have shown that condoms fail to prevent pregnancy for 1 out of 10 couples who have relied on the method for a year. The reason for this is unknown.

●Latex condoms deteriorate rapidly when exposed to heat, light, or oil-based lubricants.

●Dr. Marcus Conant, chairman of the task force on AIDS for the California Department of Health, estimates the failure rate for condoms at 10% per user over the course of a year.

●The Food and Drug Administration recently required three leading manufacturers to recall 100,000 condoms because a spot check had found that an excessive number leaked.

●The uninfected partner in 2 of 12 sexually active couples who said they regularly used condoms became infected. No details of the study were given, so there is no proof that the condoms were to blame.

The important conclusion is that you just can't tell people it's all right to do whatever they want as long as they wear a condom.

AIDS Protection for Medical and Health Workers

The Federal Centers for Disease Control have suggested precautions and guidelines for all health care personnel to take while on the job. Individual professional societies such as the American Medical Association, the American Dental Society, and nurses' organizations have also issued directives for their members on how to minimize the risk of getting AIDS. The guidelines are essentially the same for all groups and are what common sense would tell one to do when undergoing the risk of contracting a communicable disease.

The Following Precautions Should Be Taken by Health Personnel:

1. Wear protective clothing, preferably a type of uniform which can be immediately exchanged for a clean, sterile set if blood is spilled on it or it is otherwise soiled with body fluids. The uniform should be laundered at the end of the day's work with hot water, detergent, and a disinfectant like bleaching liquid.

2. Use rubber gloves whenever handling patients in surgery, hospital wards, or elsewhere. If a glove is pierced or cut with a sharp instrument, immediately remove it, wash the hands thoroughly with soap and hot water, and apply a strong disinfectant to the pricked or cut area.

3. Surgical masks should be worn in the presence of patients and whenever handling any material which may contain virus, such as sputum, blood, urine, or fecal samples.

4. Bandages, cotton, swabs, or other materials which may have come in contact with an AIDS patient should be placed in a plastic bag and incinerated at the end of the day.

5. Gowns or clothing worn by AIDS patients should be carefully segregated and washed as described under item 1.

6. All instruments, toothbrushes, tableware, and so on, used by AIDS patients should be carefully sterilized or disposed of. Disposable paper and plastic tableware is preferred to permanent tableware.

7. Protective goggles should be used when handling the blood of AIDS patients. Glasses with flat lenses can be used.

These guidelines should go a long way toward protecting health professionals. They are not foolproof, and carelessness, or forget-fulness in applying them can be highly detrimental. For those who work in laboratories with AIDS virus preparations, especially concentrated preparations, special precautions are needed. It is essential to have absolute protection against aerosols (very fine droplets) containing virus particles. All work should be done in a hood with a gentle inward flow of air. Precautions 1 through 7 are, of course, to be followed as well.

Guarding Against AIDS in Student Laboratories

Students studying biology, physiology, medicine, and other courses often do experiments using their own or blood bank-supplied blood. Recently my university circulated a two-page set of guidelines to all professors and students in such courses. The guidelines are very thorough, emphasizing the use of gloves, precautions when drawing blood, that a person should work only on his or her own blood, what to do about spillage or accidents, and so forth. Complying with these guidelines will certainly make life more difficult for students and instructors, but will also make life safer, which is their function. These guidelines are given in full in the appendices.

Providing School Workers with Disposable Gloves

The New York City Board of Education has distributed 1.5 million pairs of disposable gloves to all city schools in an effort to protect teachers and other school workers from AIDS. The chief reason for this is to have the gloves available if there is a significant blood spill. In such cases, school nurses would be particularly vulnerable. Although only 10 or 20 children in the school system are known to have AIDS, a much larger number may be infected by the virus and be symptomless.

Police officers are also warned to be aware of the possibility of contracting the disease from blood. Most police departments have begun intensive educational programs. They also provide all officers who walk beats or drive patrol cars with disposable rubber gloves and face masks and advise them to take other precautions when coming in contact with a person who might be infected with AIDS virus.

Officers who administer cardiopulmonary resuscitation (CPR) have a problem with mouth-to-mouth contact. For this purpose special CPR masks are available which prevent exchange of saliva during this procedure.

Firefighters are often officially required to use lifesaving procedures, and they should of course be provided with protective equipment.

Masturbation — A Good Way to Protect Yourself From AIDS

In the past, masturbation has been the least discussed of the widely used sexual practices. Recent studies on the prevalence of masturbation have revealed that a large majority of both sexes of all ages now practice and approve of it.

Children appear to have a natural tendency to masturbate from the earliest age. Undoubtedly, this is the result of accidental touching which creates pleasurable stimulation. This accident can lead to purposeful fondling of the genitals at various occasions as the child grows older.

During the first half or more of the twentieth century, before the sexual revolution, many parents considered the practice to be morally repugnant and probably physically harmful. The child was admonished severely and told that he or she would be punished if the practice continued. Later it was said that masturbation could destroy the health and cause insanity. It was also suggested that warts and pimples could arise from such behavior, and that normal sexual response to a partner would become impossible.

Nowadays we have a much more tolerant attitude, due in part to the extensive writings of sex therapists, psychologists, and psychiatrists who point out that it is natural behavior and in most instances causes no physical or mental harm. It is a way of exploring one's body and sexual responses and often has a useful effect in relieving tension which builds up in both males and females over time.

In males, sexual maturity is generally measured by the ability to reach orgasm and ejaculate sperm. This may occur between the ages of 13 and 15. The period of roughly 15 to 20 years is the one in which a male generally has the greatest potency and a tremendous sexual drive. During this period, however, the male is very often too young or otherwise unable to find a responsive sex partner, leaving only masturbation as a way of obtaining sexual relief.

In females, orgasm may be achieved before sexual maturity, which is usually taken as the menarch or first menstruation, occurring on the average between 12 and 14 years of age. Females growing up have the same pressures and needs as males and it is therefore not surprising to find that a large proportion of them masturbate. Studies carried out by Dr. Philip M. Sassel and Lorna J. Sassel, co-directors of the Yale Sex Counseling Service which periodically surveys students, have found about 70 to 80% of college women say they masturbate. For males five out of six are masturbating by the time they enter college.

Parents are warned today by sex therapists not to punish children or frighten them about masturbating. This can cause strong feelings of guilt which may in later life produce the feeling that sex is wrong or unhealthy, giving rise to sexual problems in adulthood. At most, the child should be asked to conduct such activities in private.

In general, sex therapists recommend masturbation for the following reasons:

It is one of the best ways to learn about one's sexual responses.

It is helpful in both men and women in reaching orgasm.

It can relieve tension safely without the fear of an unwanted pregnancy.

Adolescents who masturbate seem less likely to develop sexual problems as adults.

It can play a significant role in the lovemaking process and can be mutually satisfying.

Like anything else, masturbation can be used as a refuge for persons unable or unwilling to face the need for interpersonal relationships. If it interferes with social development and causes withdrawal, for whatever reason, it is not good.

Although most persons prefer sex with another person, it is interesting to note that quite a few specialists in sex have said that orgasms achieved during masturbation are usually more intense.

A few words of caution are needed. The remarks about masturbation and its safety apply to self-masturbation. The risks of mutual masturbation with someone infected by AIDS or by some other venereal disease were discussed in Chapter 4. Also, clean hands are important. Infections of bacterial or yeast origin, while difficult for the male to catch are possible and much easier for the female to contract.

Naturally, there are those who because of religious or moral scruples, as well as for other reasons, are very much against masturbation. Everyone is entitled to his or her viewpoint. For those who want to be absolutely safe from AIDS, self-masturbation is one way out of the dilemma of obtaining sexual relief without compromising safety.

Prevention of AIDS Through Education

All public health officials and other specialists who deal with AIDS agree on the importance of educating everyone about the disease — from school children to senior citizens. With this in mind, it is rather surprising to find that in the United States, one of the countries hardest hit by the epidemic and one having knowledge of its existence for 6 years, a major educational program was begun only in October 1987. And this program has been severely criticized by many. The United Kingdom and Australia, nations that have only a scant number of cases compared to the United States started an intensive educational program more than a year before.

The title of the program, "America Responds to AIDS," is fine, but the big question is whether its vigor and forthrightness will be strong enough to slow the spread of AIDS by the methods being advertised.

One of the largest advertising agents in the country, Ogilvy and Mather, is handling the program. In slick Madison Avenue style, they have designed television and radio spots lasting no more than a minute presenting "vivid stories about the dangers of being uninformed about AIDS." There are messages specifically aimed at blacks and Hispanics.

The criticisms that may be made of these messages relate to their content and dissemination:

Content: Few specifics about how AIDS virus is transmitted are given or how one might protect oneself from contracting the disease. People are urged to call a toll-free number to get the facts.

Dissemination: *No money has been budgeted for broadcast time.* Reliance is instead on public service announcements that broadcasters are expected to present in the public interest.

Some of these commercials are rather bland and really don't tell one anything, only to call a national toll-free number. Instead of showing rather well-fed persons of different ethnic groups, they should show a cadaver-like AIDS victim obliterated by tubes in a hospital or a closeup of the ravages of Kaposi's sarcoma or the disfigured face of a patient suffering from AIDS-related psoriasis. Scare tactics? Yes, but what can serve better as scare tactics than to have a loved one die of AIDS? If that doesn't change one's habits, nothing will.

Some care will have to be taken not to show such harrowing scenes at times when small children might be watching. They are easily scared and may experience nightmares. A campaign in Australia which featured the Grim Reaper as the symbol of AIDS death was too shocking. The Grim Reaper, a rotting corpse carrying a bowling ball, aims it at a group of ordinary Australians set up as tenpins. Nine of them are knocked dead. The tenth, a little girl holding a doll and crying, is sent flying by the next ball for a spare. There have been other criticisms of the Australian campaign to educate, namely, that no clear information is provided on how AIDS virus is transmitted and that exaggerated figures are used concerning the number of people probably infected with the virus.

The U.S. government is getting more than it deserves. Some networks are showing these commercials during prime time, which can cost upward of $100,000 a minute if one had to pay for it.

Although about 45 million copies of an informative brochure will be distributed to accompany the TV and radio spots, there is some question whether this campaign will reach those most in need of its message. Even if it does reach them, will it change their behavior? That too is questionable. For several years now the gay community has been keeping itself well informed about prevention and treatment through good communication. Unfortunately, many gay people were infected before their communication network was established. On the other hand, intravenous drug users have continued along their destructive path and are not likely to change much.

AIDS 101

Last winter at the University of California at Los Angeles a geneticist decided to teach an undergraduate class on AIDS, a course that would not only visit such areas as virology and etiology, but would travel the entire cultural, political, and ethical landscape surrounding the deadly virus. Designed for 10 students, the professor squeezed in 14 paying customers.

This winter UCLA is giving Richard Siegel the use of Room 100 in Moore Hall, the largest auditorium on campus. "it holds something like 479 seats, but the fire marshal will let us set up some chairs in the aisles," says Siegel. Enrollment in Biology 40, "AIDS and Other Sexually Transmitted Diseases: The Modern Plague," is expected to top 500. Colleagues have suggested Siegel prepare a waiting list.

"The right of a country to call itself civilized might be decided by how we react to AIDS," says Siegel, a man who considers himself more of an educator now than a scientist. "Discussion of AIDS is the way to educate students about such a wide range of ideas. The topic grabs them. It hooks them in. It makes them think. Because the epidemic is something very real to kids on campus."

Siegel takes an interdisciplinary tack. Readings are as likely to come from the scientific literature as from Shakespeare, the Bible, or *Moby Dick*. Historical context may be gleaned from the plague of the Egyptians, . . .

With the kind permission of the editors of *Science* and William Booth from *Science* **238**, 477(1987).

Whom Should the Educational Message Reach?

The best place to put any message across is in the schools. Youngsters approaching sexual maturity are the most likely targets for a good educational campaign. If they know how to prevent AIDS and practice what they know, one can expect that, denied this new pool of individuals, the AIDS epidemic will begin to die out. It is of utmost importance to introduce good programs of instruction about AIDS in a timely fashion in all American schools. Can this be done without offending the legitimate sensibilities of parents who may worry about such programs stimulating precocious sexual activity in their youngsters? I feel confident it can be done in a tactful, yet informative way.

There is no need to worry children about AIDS in the early grades of elementary school. Here the emphasis with regard to AIDS should be on how to handle strangers or even family members who may approach the children with the aim of sexual molestation or abuse.

When a child is approximately 10 years old, facts about AIDS can be included in the health curriculum: What it is, what it does to the immune system, and the general aspects of how it is transmitted. By the time children are 12 years old, they have picked up from TV, movies, and their peers, a surprising amount of information on sex, much of it incomplete or wrong. More detailed information should be given to youngsters, not only about sex but about the disease — how it is transmitted and how one can protect oneself. I would put strong emphasis on abstinence but be realistic enough to realize that this approach will not always work. By the time children are sexually mature, the major facts about transmission and prevention contained in this book should have been explained to them. This knowledge should be reinforced and extended through the high school years. If the program is effective, AIDS 101 will not have as many applicants. By the time students are 18 to 22 years old and in college, it is too late to protect those who might have become sexually active at the age of 15 or earlier.

Fortunately, most inner city disadvantaged youngsters continue school until about 16. By this time they should be well informed about AIDS and how to prevent it.

National Education on AIDS

In addition to the TV programs already mentioned, Surgeon General Dr. C. Everett Koop has prepared a 36-page report on AIDS which is available to members of Congress to send to their constituents. Over 3 million copies of this report have been requested, but the coverage obtained is bound to be spotty. Some members of Congress, for example, Gerry E. Studds, Democrat of Massachusetts, has requested copies for all 268,000 households in his district. However, the majority of congressmen may not send out any copies at all. An updated report is being prepared.

It appears that if the booklet is worthwhile, and Surgeon General Koop is certainly one to inspire confidence that it is, it should be sent out in a national mailing. Public health officials say they are contemplating a national mailing but with a smaller booklet, called "Understanding AIDS" and it is being widely distributed in the U.S. See page 138.

Meanwhile, the administration of President Reagan has not been acting forcibly in dealing with the question of education. Its members behave as if the problem is mainly one for gay and drug-using communities, and they appear reluctant to make a costly all-out effort to provide education about AIDS. Thus it is being done piecemeal, by the armed services, by states and cities, by special interest groups, and by the media.

An angry and highly critical book by Randy Shilts, a gay San Franciscan, has achieved a high place on the bestseller list. In one telling statement in *And the Band Played On: Politics, People and the AIDS Epidemic*, he points out that when President Reagan gave his first national talk on AIDS, more than 36,000 persons had already received a diagnosis for the disease and over 21,000 had died from it. It is a compelling story but not a measured one. Some of the criticism in it is overdrawn. There were people who recognized the gravity of the situation, but it is true that few recognized the danger for the first 3 or 4 years of its spread. Such books provide a national educational experience, and other, more temperate accounts are bound to follow.

Statewide Education on AIDS

Some of the big states, such as New York, California, and Texas where the AIDS problem is pressing, have begun intensive educational programs. New York City, which has the highest number of cases, has been particularly active. Some of its activities are described below

The New York City Department of Health has begun a program called "Let's Fight AIDS Together," with health fairs at 13 of the city's larger health centers. Also, there will be seminars for health care workers, church and community leaders, and civic groups.

The Board of Regents of New York State has approved an instructional guide for teachers of AIDS education in New York State public and private elementary and secondary schools. The inclusion of instruction about AIDS is now a mandatory part of the health education program for all schools in New York State. The content is very much along the lines suggested earlier. Elementary school pupils will be taught a sense of self-worth, respect for their bodies, and how to develop good health habits. In junior high schools and senior high schools, a separate half-year AIDS course will be taught by certified health teachers. By the time they have finished sixth grade, students will have been told about the nature of AIDS, its methods of transmission, and methods of prevention. The course will stress abstinence. No student will be required to receive instruction about prevention methods if his or her parents file a written request with the school principal and provide assurance that appropriate instruction will be given at home. The use of a condom during sexual intercourse will be considered "extremely high-risk behavior." On the face of it, this statement is misleading and incorrect. It has been strongly criticized by New York City's health commissioner, Dr. Stephen C. Joseph.

It is important for language to be precise. What should be said is, "Condoms will give protection against venereal diseases including AIDS, but they do have a significant failure rate with regard to protection, possibly from 5 to 20%. They will not protect well against diseases like herpes, genital warts, and possibly *chlamydia*. The best protection is abstinence from interpersonal sex before marriage and intravenous injection of drugs."

The New York City Board of Education has purchased copies of a 20-minute videotape, "Sex, Drugs, and AIDS," and shows it to high school students, including all graduating high school seniors. The film is quite explicit.

Mayor Koch of New York City has directed health officials to prepare a new advertising campaign telling people that the safest way to avoid AIDS is to abstain from sexual relations. He says, "It is a misnomer, a fraud to try to convey to people that if they use condoms they're absolutely safe from contracting AIDS. Just as it is a fraud to say that if you use condoms there's no danger of pregnancy. So you must use the phrase 'safer sex,' not 'safe sex.' "

Earlier ads that were aimed at heterosexual women and promoted the use of condoms met with a very cool reception from local television stations.

The College Campus Against AIDS

At the college level, most institutions have by now implemented a program informing students of the major facts concerning AIDS. An example of one such effort, from the University of Connecticut, is given in the appendices. Although this booklet leaves many questions unanswered, there are counseling services available on campus, as well as professors with a good knowledge of AIDS. The library has a good supply of informative, up-to-date books, seminars are commonly promoted and articles appear in the campus paper.

In Connecticut the state legislature recently appropriated $2 million to establish two endowed chairs devoted to the study of AIDS. One is at the university's Health Center, and the other is at the School of

Law. The mission, as stated in the legislation, is to gather the latest day-by-day news-breaking information, disseminate that information, and put the disease under a legal microscope to diagnose, prescribe, and prognosticate its effect on civil justice. The bill establishing the chairs also sets aside funds for the Department of Health Services to be used for research and to educate the public. A major educational program will involve distribution of the Surgeon General's report to every household in the state.

How Well Informed are College Students About AIDS?

With the current information barrage on AIDS in the media one might expect even first-year college students to be moderately well informed. Dr. Jeffrey Fisher, head of the University of Connecticut's social psychology program, is studying how well students are informed and several other questions on student practices and beliefs about the disease.

Surprisingly, among students sampled on campus, Fisher found discouragingly low levels of knowledge and only moderate levels of fear—a slight improvement over the previous year. He says that as a group college students are at high risk for AIDS, display little knowledge of it, and engage in minimal preventive behavior. They have, however, a much better knowledge about the practical aspects of prevention.

Dr. Fisher has found that young people, more than their elders, cling to "an illusion of invulnerability." It's always the other person rather than themselves who is more likely to experience injury or illnesses.

Cathy Kodama, coordinator of the AIDS education program at the University of California at Berkeley, says, "You need to insure that there are ongoing services" in order to counter students' tendency to respond to threats by denying they are at risk. One brochure on awareness day is not going to do the job.

Hollywood Trends Toward Safer Sex

With about half the families in the United States now possessing tape-playing video equipment, the movies are setting the trends more than ever. Fortunately they are moving in the right direction.

Some may recall the scene in "Dragnet" in which Tom Hanks rolls over in bed, looks lustfully at his blond companion, and reaches for a box of condoms. He finds it empty, tosses it away with a disgusted look, and gives up the idea of a good time before going to work. This is certainly good promotion for AIDS prevention.

In another movie, *The Living Daylights*, instead of having his usual three women in bed at various times, James Bond has three liaisons with the same woman. Richard Maibaum, who wrote 13 Bond movies including this one, says, "You must take the new sex mores into account when you write a picture now. With AIDS you can't have James Bond alley-catting around anymore."

In general, producers are aware of the new situation created by AIDS. It doesn't always come up, as in *Fatal Attraction*, in which the male lead has a wild weekend with a woman he meets at a party. AIDS is not mentioned, but the woman turns out to be a manic psychotic who almost kills him and his wife. In real life, however, he might have died of AIDS.

The president of Universal Pictures, Sean Daniel, points out that the movies have always been a place where fantasies are played out. "People meeting and falling into bed almost immediately has always been fantasy," he explains, "but now with the advent of AIDS it is sheer fantasy."

The movies have not yet been affected as much as the legitimate theater in New York City. With the death of many prominent actors and associated artists, New York City is very conscious of AIDS, and there have been several plays built around the subject.

Evaluation of the Effectiveness of Educational Programs

It's one thing to start an intensive educational program, but quite another to determine whether the program is reaching those it was designed to educate and, if it is reaching them, whether it is effective in changing attitudes and habits.

A large number of educational programs are being instituted in the United States for the general public and for special groups such as intravenous drug users, school children, certain ethnic groups, and others. How does one evaluate the results?

Three centers in the United States are being funded by the National Institute of Mental Health and the National Institute of Drug Abuse. One of the largest centers, the Center for AIDS Prevention Studies, is at the University of California, San Francisco, and is headed by Stephen

B. Hulley. This center works collaboratively with the university, the San Francisco Department of Public Health, and Multicultural Inquiry and Research on AIDS, formed by a group of researchers who study the impact of AIDS on minorities. The center has so far received $10 million. Its 50 investigators will concentrate on intravenous drug users and their families, gay and bisexual men, and ethnic minorities. The center is also studying high-risk behavior in Rwanda, Africa.

A second center is at Columbia University in New York City, the HIV Center for Clinical and Behavioral Studies. The New York Psychiatric Institute and Columbia Presbyterian Hospital are partners in this endeavor funded recently with a $19 million grant. Three of the five studies proposed by the center will analyze the effectiveness of AIDS preventative education, with an emphasis on how best to reach adolescents.

A third center is at the University of Miami School of Medicine — the Biopsychosocial Center for the Study of AIDS — and it is focusing on the development of AIDS dementia and how social and psychologic factors influence the course of HIV infection.

Understanding
AIDS

A Message From The Surgeon General

This brochure has been sent to you by the Government of the United States. In preparing it, we have consulted with the top health experts in the country.

I feel it is important that you have the best information now available for fighting the AIDS virus, a health problem that the President has called "Public Enemy Number One."

Stopping AIDS is up to you, your family and your loved ones.

Some of the issues involved in this brochure may not be things you are used to discussing openly. I can easily understand that. But now you must discuss them. We all must know about AIDS. Read this brochure and talk about it with those you love. Get involved. Many schools, churches, synagogues, and community groups offer AIDS education activities.

I encourage you to practice responsible behavior based on understanding and strong personal values. This is what you can do to stop AIDS.

C. Everett Koop, M.D., Sc.D.
Surgeon General

Este folleto sobre el SIDA se publica en Español.
Para solicitar una copia, llame al 1-800-344-SIDA.

HHS Publication No. (CDC) HHS-88-8404. Reproduction of the contents of this brochure is encouraged.

CHAPTER 6
SYMPTOMS OF AIDS AND CARE FOR AIDS PATIENTS

Introduction; time of appearance of AIDS symptoms; Why do some infected men stay healthy?; An early symptom of AIDS: generalized lymphadenopathy syndrome; Acute AIDS infection; Symptoms of AIDS-related complex; Symptoms of AIDS; Survival; Shorter survival period for women than for men; Kaposi's sarcoma; Cytomegalovirus infections; Mental symptoms in apparently well patients; Reiter's syndrome and psoriasis as a sign of AIDS infection; Brain damage caused by AIDS virus; AIDS and the rise in tuberculosis cases; AIDS and syphilis; Caring for AIDS patients at home; You can't go home again?

6

SYMPTOMS OF AIDS AND CARE FOR AIDS PATIENTS

Introduction

AIDS is an exceedingly complex disease for a number of reasons:

- AIDS virus not only attacks the immune system but can directly or indirectly attack brain cells, intestinal cells, heart cells, spinal cord cells, and many others.
- AIDS can result in cancers of the lymph glands, skin, and other organs (Kaposi's sarcoma), as well as leukemia and lung cancer.
- When an immune system is weakened, almost any organism that gets into the body — viral, bacterial, or protozoan — can cause a devastating disease.
- AIDS virus and/or imbalances in the immune or hormone system that are caused by it can bring on arthritis, psoriasis, and probably many other afflictions seemingly unrelated to AIDS.

It is not surprising, therefore, that there is a very large variety of symptoms associated with AIDS. The disease may follow very different courses in different people, and the symptoms may also vary widely from one person to the next and between males and females. The presence of other existing venereal diseases may alter the course of the disease and the nature of the symptoms when a person becomes infected with AIDS virus.

Time of Appearance of AIDS Symptoms

In women, as will be discussed later in this chapter, the appearance of the disease seems to be more rapid, the disease progresses faster, and survival is shorter than in men. In men, symptoms of the disease may be long delayed after infection with AIDS virus. The average time before the appearance of symptoms, as already mentioned, is about 5 years, but this figure is not well established and is subject to change. There is also great variability in the length of time before symptoms appear in men. In some it may take only a year or two. In others, no sign of the disease may have occurred after 8 or 9 years. There is even the possibility that in a few persons the disease may be permanently repressed, according to the results of a study on a group of 4955 male homosexuals. The group was tested for AIDS viral antigens in the blood at intervals for a period of several years. Five men were found who initially tested positive but at a later date showed a negative test. Interpreting these results is difficult, however, and several possibilities exist:

The five were able to permanently destroy all the virus. (This seems unlikely.)

The antibodies initially formed decreased to such low levels that they were below the amount needed to give a positive test. Virus may still have been present in the blood or cells. (This appears to be a reasonable interpretation.)

The virus changed (mutated) in these individuals to an extent that its proteins no longer gave a positive test with the ELISA method. (This is possible, but a Western blot test should have picked them up.)

Several years may have to pass, with continuous observation of these five individuals, to solve this mystery. Tests for AIDS virus in white cells or in blood, or for the presence of virus DNA in cell DNA, might give an answer more quickly.

Why Do Some Infected Men Stay Healthy?

This is an important question because if the reasons can be determined, factors that keep the virus in check could perhaps be bolstered in other infected persons and the debilitating and lethal effects of the infection averted.

Thirteen homosexuals who are infected with AIDS virus and have shown no signs of disease for nearly 10 years are now being studied. The 13 all appear to have completely normal immune systems. Although there is no hard evidence to help physicians point to a specific item, they can postulate several likely factors protecting the long-term survivors:

1. Genetic background: Dr. Anthony J. Pinching and his collaborators, from St. Mary's Hospital and Medical School in London, have suggested that differences in an inherited blood protein called Gc may modify susceptibility to AIDS. Scientists from the National Cancer Institute also have found that another inherited blood protein may be important. At present, other groups have not confirmed these results. Generally speaking, it is true that the effectiveness of an individual's immune system is a product of inheritance. Some people have very strong, efficient immune systems. Others may have systems with different degrees of strength and efficiency ranging from high to low. Those with excellent immune systems might be protected from other infectious diseases which could trigger the activation of AIDS virus.

2. Virulence: Different strains of AIDS virus may have different degrees of virulence. Little is known about this except that HIV-2 seems to be considerably less virulent than HIV. Even among different strains of HIV, however, there may be differences in virulence. This could be studied in the laboratory with cells grown in tissue culture.

3. Life style. Anything in a person's life style can affect the virus and/or the immune system. Diet, exercise, use of drugs, and stress avoidance are some of the important factors. A good diet can strengthen the immune system, and it is well known that regular exercise does the same. Drugs may adversely affect the immune system but, depending on the drug, may help or hinder the development and growth of AIDS virus. Stress is generally bad for the immune system, as it leads to increased secretion of glucocorticoid hormones which have been shown to be harmful to the thymus and to suppress many activities of white cells.

All of the above factors may therefore influence whether one does or does not get the disease. Long-term studies will be required to assess the importance of known factors, and there may be other unknown factors affecting the course of the disease.

An Early Symptom of AIDS: Generalized Lymphadenopathy Syndrome

One of the earliest symptoms of AIDS is a swelling of the lymph glands, most prominently on either side of the throat. There are hundreds of lymph glands in the body, most of them not readily visible or subject to access by palpation (feeling). This may be the only symptom present, and it may last for a long time without the appearance of other symptoms.

In a low-risk individual the swelling of lymph glands does not necessarily mean AIDS is on the way. Almost any infection may cause a swelling of the lymph glands, and this swelling usually declines and disappears in a week or two as the person recovers. Occasionally, a swollen lymph gland may become calcified and remain more or less permanently enlarged. Again, this does not mean one has AIDS or is likely to get it.

In a high-risk individual—a homosexual, an intravenous drug user, or a prostitute or other sexually promiscuous (or even sexually active) person—the appearance of swollen lymph glands is at best troubling. It should lead one to have a test for AIDS antibodies immediately. One does not want to deny the possibility, because if the swollen glands are due to AIDS, it is important to know as soon as possible. Then the fullest advantage can be taken of prophylactic (preventative) treatments for AIDS or for an opportunistic infection such as *P.carinii* (Chapter 7).

Several studies have been done to determine the prognosis of men with generalized lymphadenopathy syndrome. In one, 93 homosexual men were followed for from 3 to 17 months after diagnosis. Of these, 11 developed AIDS. Undoubtedly, as the test continues others will develop the clinical disease, and eventually all of them may, although it is apparent that the delay may be lengthy in some cases.

Acute AIDS Infection

Mention has been made of some persons who upon becoming infected may experience a flu-like reaction within a few weeks after exposure. Symptoms may include fever, enlarged lymph nodes, skin rash, malaise, sore muscles, loss of appetite, and diarrhea. The symptoms do not last long and may disappear after another week or two. That this acute infection is caused by AIDS virus is supported by the isolation of virus particles from the blood and cells of these patients.

Some patients who have the acute infection go on to develop AIDS, while many others do not. The significance of these early symptoms, which may not occur in many who become infected with HIV, is not known.

In a rare individual, there may be a transient neurological seizure or disorientation. However, this can occur also in diseases as simple as the flu.

Symptoms of AIDS-Related Complex

About the only major difference between AIDS and ARC is that ARC is not accompanied by an opportunistic infection. ARC is no longer considered as a separate disease from AIDS.

The symptoms of ARC are weight loss (many ARC patients look exceedingly gaunt), enlarged lymph nodes, fever, sore throat, diarrhea, and lethargy possibly caused by weakness. Any of these symptoms or all of them may also be present in AIDS. ARC is almost always accompanied by some form of neurological disturbance ranging from mild to severe. The symptoms are collectively referred to as dementia and include loss of memory, disorientation, loss of locomotor control resulting in a jerky gait and jerky motions in general, and inability to carry out higher mental functions such as computation and logical thinking.

ARC patients may have mild infections which could account for some of the symptoms listed above. They may also have oral thrush, a fungal disease of the mucous membranes of the mouth, which is characterized by the appearance of whitish spots or areas.

Symptoms of AIDS

AIDS patients may have any of the symptoms discussed so far and, in addition, one or more of four or five opportunistic infections or cancers of which the most common are

1. *Pneumocystis carinii*: A protozoan infection of the lung producing a pneumonia-like disease. About the only symptoms are cough, fever and shortness of breath. By the time these symptoms appear the disease is well established.

2. *Cytomegalovirus infection*: A rather diffuse viral infection producing a variety of symptoms.

3. *Kaposi's sarcoma*: A skin cancer which can also spread to internal organs. This disease is discussed in detail shortly.

4. *Lymphoma*: Cancer of the white cells in the lymph glands

5. *Lung cancer*

6. *Mental symptoms*: Which range from mild to severe.

Patients with clinical AIDS disease may also have:

A decreased number of helper T4 lymphocytes

An increased number of suppressor T8 lymphocytes

A low level of antibodies to AIDS virus

A high level of antibodies to cytomegalovirus

A history of sex with someone in whom AIDS
has already developed.

Night sweats can be a common symptom in anyone infected with AIDS virus. Again, night sweats in themselves are not diagnostic of anything because they can occur with a bad cold and many other infections. Pervasive diarrhea not helped by most drugs may occur and persist through the course of the disease.

Survival

We are led to believe that once a person starts manifesting the symptoms of AIDS the decline is inexorable and continues to a fatal termination. This picture is not correct. First of all, statistics do not support it and, second, the widespread use of AZT has prolonged the life of many victims for a time that not yet been determined but apparently may be as long as several years.

An analysis of 5833 patients with AIDS disease in New York City indicated that 15% survived at least 5 years. This is not 5 years after infection with the virus but 5 years after overt symptoms of the disease occurred. Dr. Richard Rothenberg, who reported this data says that a few patients do well but the major portion does badly. Half of all patients died within the first year after their disease was diagnosed, with black and Hispanic drug users dying more quickly than gay men.

One man has lived for 9 years, so it is perhaps too early to categorically state that AIDS is universally fatal. The statistics as published in the *New England Journal of Medicine* are shown in Table 6-1.

Interestingly, those with the best survival rate were gay white men who had Kaposi's sarcoma but none of the other serious infections that AIDS patients commonly get. In this group 72% survived at least a year and 30.0% were alive 5 years later.

Those who fared worst were women, blacks, and Hispanics. Black women who were intravenous drug users survived only an average of 206 days after diagnosis. Patients in the age group 30 to 35 tended to survive the longest, with those older and younger faring worse.

Some of these differences might reflect differences in health care and how early a person's disease is diagnosed. In addition, present

Table 6-1 Survival of AIDS patients.
**Study of 5,833 New York City patients diagnosed from 1981
through 1985.**

Patient group	No. in group	Average survival in days
SEX		
Men	5281	374
Women	552	298
ETHNIC GROUP		
White	2753	411
Black	1769	325
Hispanic	1281	320
RISK GROUP		
Homosexual activity only	3400	400
Homosexuality and intravenous drug use	335	348
Intravenous drug use only	1660	318
Other risk factor	438	312
DISEASE AT DIAGNOSIS		
Kaposi's sarcoma alone	994	568
Kaposi's sarcoma and *P. carinii* pneumonia	337	424
Kaposi's sarcoma and another disease	194	376
P. carinii pneumonia alone	2541	317
P. carinii pneumonia and another disease	719	338
One other disease alone	814	293
Two other diseases alone	219	306

methods using improved treatments for *P. carinii* pneumonia are helping patients with this disease survive longer. In 1981 only 18% of New
York City's AIDS patients with this opportunistic infection survived a
year, in 1985 48% survived a year, and today this figure is probably
considerably higher.

If this study were to be redone with patients with diagnoses dating
from 1987 to 1991, the average survival in days would undoubtedly be
much higher for each group.

Shorter Survival Period for Women Than for Men

Although women at present comprise only a small percentage of AIDS
patients, this percentage is rising and may continue to do so for some
time.

A dramatic difference has been found in the intensity of the disease and the rate at which it kills women compared to men. In general, women get much sicker more quickly and die much sooner. The most shocking data come from California and involve 7704 people who received an AIDS diagnosis before December 31, 1986. There were 128 women in the study who lived an average of only 40 days, while the 6946 males lived an average of more than a year and many were still alive when the study was completed.

Other figures were not so striking. The Federal Centers for Disease Control found that its sample of women with AIDS lived an average of 6.6 months after diagnosis, while men survived an average of 12 to 14 months.

Dr. Margaret Fischl at the University of Miami, Florida, reported that in Miami women not only died sooner but were much sicker. Nearly one third had several infections at diagnosis, whereas most men had only one.

Nonbiological reasons could account for these differences and must not be ruled out. For example, the women could have been mostly intravenous drug users, who are known to have other diseases or infections that can make their condition worse when they get AIDS. In a comparison with a gay male group, whose members generally take good care of themselves, this could account for the more rapid decline of the women.

One biological possibility could involve hormones — female sex hormones might facilitate the spread and growth of HIV. A second possibility is a difference in the immune systems of men and women, with women less able to respond to HIV infection. No such difference is presently known, but the effect, if real, could open up useful avenues of research.

Kaposi's Sarcoma

This formerly rare cancer, once seen only in a few elderly African men, is one of the great enigmas of AIDS. Why it has suddenly changed its nature in AIDS patients and become a rapidly spreading virulent cancer, not only of the skin but of internal organs as well, is entirely unknown. During the early period of the AIDS epidemic it affected as many as 40% of the victims, mostly male homosexuals. This value has dropped off significantly over the past 6 years, and the cancer is now seen in only about 14% of AIDS patients. The reason for the decrease is also completely unknown.

Physicians' experiences with this cancer in Africa have been startling. Dr. Anne C. Bayley, a surgeon who has worked in Africa for the last 16 years and is an internationally recognized authority on the disease, describes the changes that occurred: "It was like coming home from work and finding your spaniel had changed into a wolf. It was horrifying. Here was a disease I was comfortable with because I could treat it and suddenly I could not treat it."

Before this, Dr. Bayley says, a combination of two anticancer drugs, actinomycin D and vincristine, were effective in controlling the cancer. But in AIDS patients they were ineffective, and the victims, usually young, were dead in 6 months despite treatment with the same drugs.

Thus far, one can make the easy deduction that a well-functioning immune system, probably helper T4 cells is especially important in controlling Kaposi's sarcoma. With this part of the immune system gone, the disease runs rampant. But why Kaposi's sarcoma, of all cancers?

Again for unknown reasons, more than 90% of Kaposi's sarcoma cases in the United States have involved homosexual men, and it rarely occurs among users of intravenously administered drugs, hemophiliacs, and children who have developed AIDS. In Africa, where as many women have AIDS as men, Kaposi's sarcoma still primarily affects men. There is an old and rare form of the Kaposi's sarcoma that kills children in Africa, but children with AIDS seldom have it and African children with Kaposi's sarcoma usually do not have AIDS — another puzzle.

Often the first symptom of Kaposi's sarcoma is a swelling of the feet and legs, followed by the appearance of purple, red, or brownish nodules in the same area. There may be smooth patches of purplish-colored skin scattered about, ranging from pea-sized to several inches in diameter. The lesions can also form on the scalp and in the mouth, voice box, stomach, intestines, and, less commonly, eyes. In rare cases the nodules disappear spontaneously but may return months or years later. They can grow and ulcerate and become badly infected. The most persistent symptom of the classic form of the disease is a feeling of tension and pain in the hands and feet. Also, a burning and itching sensation occurs.

The above paragraph depicts a classical form of the disease that is rarely fatal. In the new form of Kaposi's sarcoma associated with AIDS, lesions tend to develop on the face and the tip of the nose. Patches commonly occur behind the ears and on the arms and trunk, areas not often affected in the old form. Sometimes the lesions grow in the lungs and lead to an accumulation of fluid that may cause breathing difficulties. In some cases of Kaposi's sarcoma the patches may be so light in color that they escape discovery. Or there may be no patches at all. The cancer may occur as small groups of cells within a lymph node and be detectable only on careful examination by a pathologist.

One way in which Kaposi's sarcoma differs from most cancers is that it appears initially as multiple lesions. Most cancers arise from a single cancerous cell which may multiply and grow into a tumor. This tumor may or may not spread, or metastasize, throughout the body. Kaposi's sarcoma apparently has multiple foci, as if it were caused by a large number of cells becoming cancerous at once. This observation has led to the theory that an infectious agent of some kind, probably a virus, might accompany AIDS virus, in some cases, during sexual transmission of the disease. Sexual transmission is required, as intravenous drug users seldom get Kaposi's sarcoma. Although members of this group of course indulge in sex, many of them are rendered impotent by the drugs they use or at least lose their sex drive.

Another unexplained development was the finding of an unusual number of Kaposi's sarcoma cases among kidney transplant recipients maintained on large doses of cyclosporin a, a drug that suppresses the immune system. The cancer develops about 16 months after a transplant is performed. If the drug dose is lowered, the tumors may disappear. This finding suggests that if there is a virus causative agent, it is something a lot of people have. Herpes and chicken pox virus, which remain in the body for life, are likely candidates. The fact that AIDS infection may bring on shingles, a painful disease of the nerve endings caused by chicken pox virus (*Varicellar zoster*), appears to support this theory, which is favored by several physician researchers studying Kaposi's sarcoma.

Dr. Harold W. Jaffe, an AIDS epidemiologist at the Federal Centers for Disease Control, says that interviews are planned for nonhomosexual AIDS patients with Kaposi's sarcoma, to see if some common factor can be found that predisposes one to the disease or brings it on.

A likely approach is to look for something in semen that may be related. Undoubtedly there has been a big decline in anal sex without the protection of a condom, and this decline is coincident with the decline in Kaposi's sarcoma cases.

Obviously, continuing research is necessary to answer the many puzzling questions that surround this unique cancer and its strange association with AIDS.

Cytomegalovirus Infections

Most people harbor this herpes-type virus in their systems. Dr. Douglas Dietrich of the New York University School of Medicine has estimated that up to 75% of New Yorkers are infected with it. On first exposure, persons with a normal immune system might have either no symptoms or perhaps mild flu-like symptoms with a brief fever. The virus then goes underground lying latent in white cells and possibly other body cells. Generally, no further harm results, unless the immune system is somehow compromised by, for example, AIDS virus infection, the use of immunosuppressant drugs like cyclosporin a, or other infections which may weaken it. Under these conditions the cytomegalovirus infection may erupt and become very virulent and life-threatening. Some of the organs infected by it are the eyes, brain, mouth, esophagus, stomach, colon, rectum, and lungs. On autopsy almost all AIDS patients are found to be highly infected with cytomegalovirus, and it works, together with other infections, to kill the victim. Particularly troubling are infections of the retina by cytomegalovirus, which can lead to blindness.

There is an experimental drug, ganciclovir, which appears to be helpful in treatment of the eye and possibly other infected sites. Unfortunately, ganciclovir is a bone marrow suppressant, and in patients who are taking AZT, also a bone marrow suppressant, ganciclovir cannot be used. The suppression becomes so powerful that it can kill the patient. Ganciclovir has not yet been approved by the FDA, but it is being taken by several thousand patients on an experimental basis. Untreated cytomegalovirus infections of the retina never get better, but the infection is halted in at least half of all patients who take the drug. It must be given intravenously for the life of the patient.

Almost all patients who have had to choose between AZT for possible lengthening of life and ganciclovir for saving eyesight, have chosen ganciclovir.

Cytomegalovirus is a vicious killer. It causes ulcers in the esophagus so painful that the victim often cannot eat. It also causes ulcers in the small or large intestine that may perforate these organs. It can cause colitis, leading to diarrhea and wasting, it can infect the brain, leading to dementia, and it can infect the lungs, causing pneumonia.

Another opportunistic infection in AIDS patients is produced by *Cryptosporidium*, a parasite that causes uncontrollable watery diarrhea. Patients can easily die of dehydration and malnutrition resulting from this loss of fluids. There is essentially no effective treatment except intravenous feeding and restoration of fluids and salts.

Mental Symptoms in Apparently Well Patients

A troubling development has been the finding that in some AIDS carriers who show no overt signs of the disease, measurements of various types of mental functions show some impairment. Dr. Edmund C. Tramont, director of the chemical research program on AIDS at the Walter Reed Army Medical Center in Washington, reports that the symptoms might be memory loss and deterioration in attentiveness, inability to concentrate, and reduced hand-eye coordination. Although the changes are subtle, Dr. Tramont recommends that people infected with the virus be taken out of sensitive or stressful positions in the Army where they could be harmful to themselves, to other persons, or to the mission of their military unit. He states, "If a person's brain is not functioning correctly you do not want him flying high performance aircraft, decoding sensitive messages for the President or driving tanks in combat." Officials of the Defense Department have agreed to comply with the recommendations.

Civil rights advocates have criticized this military policy on the grounds that it stigmatizes an entire group rather than focusing on probably a minority of individuals who experience a decline in mental function. Although measurements of these functions are not difficult to make, they are time-consuming and therefore costly. Obviously, the same problems exist with respect to civilian carriers of AIDS. No one would want an individual who works in an atomic power plant, is an engineer for a train, or is a physician to work at these jobs if he or she has impaired mental function. This finding needs to be quantitated in terms of the number of otherwise symptom-free AIDS carriers who might have decreased mental function and the range of this decrease that is encountered.

A study reported in the *Annals of Internal Medicine* found neuro-psychological abnormalities in 7 of 16 persons who had positive AIDS tests but no symptoms of disease. However, the number in this test is much too small to provide any firm conclusions.

Dr. Anthony S. Fauci, a top government expert on AIDS, has cautioned against hasty measures to require mandatory testing of persons in sensitive positions. He believes that the anger, fear, depression, and panic people feel on learning that they test positive for AIDS might account for, or at least contribute to, the low scores they obtain on tests of neuropsychologic performance.

An international conference of medical experts held in March 1988 announced that it had found no evidence that people infected with HIV were likely to suffer mental disturbances before suffering from the disease itself. However, the conference members did not present evidence to support their statement. In view of the opposed opinions on whether AIDS infected individuals without symptoms may undergo minor mental impairment, only further careful research will be able to resolve this question.

Reiter's Syndrome and Psoriasis as a Sign of AIDS Infection

Reiter's syndrome is a very severe form of arthritis affecting the bones of the feet, legs, and spine. It often fuses the latter bones, either ramrod straight or bent forever. It also affects sites where tendons are attached to bones, making it extremely painful to move.

The disease occurs almost exclusively in people with certain histocompatibility genes inherited by only about 2% of the population. Various diseases bring it on, for example, shigella and salmonella or dysentery. AIDS is apparently an additional disease that has the same effect even though the full symptoms of AIDS have not appeared in the patient.

Psoriasis is more common than Reiter's disease. In mild cases itchy, scaly patches form on the skin, particularly on the knees, elbows, and scalp. They can progress to include the face, leading to sores and lesions. In AIDS patients the disease may become severe leaving the skin over large portions of the body ravaged almost indescribably. Interestingly, psoriasis in these patients tends to merge into a disease like Reiter's syndrome, with the same kind of lesions in both diseases and signs of arthritis in both as well. This suggests that the two conditions have a similar origin and that this origin may be some imbalance in the immune system caused by AIDS or other infections. The focus now is on suppressor lymphocytes or T8 (CD8) T lymphocytes which are unaffected by the AIDS virus and come to dominate the immune system after the destruction of helper T4 cells by AIDS virus.

Both Reiter's syndrome and psoriasis have commonly been treated with drugs that suppress the immune system. The paradox is that AIDS, which cripples the immune system, brings on these diseases, but neither

AIDS nor the drugs destroy or suppress the entire immune system, so this apparent paradox is not so puzzling. Dr. Gary Solomon of the Hospital for Joint Diseases in New York City has tried cyclosporin a for treating Reiter's syndrome, but only in one patient. Cyclosporin a suppresses T4 and T8 cells and was helpful to this patient but in Chapter 7 it is pointed out that cyclosporin a is doomed to failure in treating AIDS and probably also in the long-term treatment of both Reiter's syndrome and psoriasis. Researchers will have to determine more exactly what goes wrong in the immune system to bring on these diseases, and once this is done it will be possible to devise a more rational and undoubtedly helpful treatment.

Brain Damage Caused by AIDS Virus

The damage done to the brain by AIDS virus is considerable, and many laboratories all over the world are actively researching this area. To summarize what has been said so far, the following observations appear to be true:

1. A large part of the detectable virus in brain is found in macrophages and monocytes (young macrophages), and infected macrophages may secrete substances harmful to brain cells.

2. Several other brain cell types may be directly infected by virus. These include, at least, astrocytes, glial cells, and capillary endothelial cells.

3. The higher central nervous functions are particularly affected — frontal white matter and hippocampus gray matter.

4. The virus glycoprotein gp120 can combine with and block neuroleukin receptors on brain cells, interfering with the natural functions of neuroleukin.

5. Actual structural damage to the brain is minor.

Eventually, between 50 and 70% of AIDS patients will develop some mental symptoms. These can range from mild confusion and poor coordination to profound dementia and an inability to control movement.

Recent studies by Dr. Jay Levy and his colleagues at the University of California Medical School in San Francisco appear to support the idea that both glioma cells (cancerous glial cells) and human fetal brain cells can be directly infected in tissue culture. Astrocytes contained in these cultures can also be infected. Brain macrophages, astrocytes, and endothelial cells do not need the T4 (CD4) receptor to be infected. Further support of the view of direct infection is provided by new data from Dr. Joseph Melnick and his coworkers at Baylor College of Medicine in Houston. They found AIDS virus in both astrocytes and oligodendrocytes in fresh brain tissue obtained from deceased AIDS patients.

Some investigators have noticed that it is often difficult to find evidence of viral infection in the brains of patients with neurological symptoms. Only about one-third of the time can they be detected. It is possible that techniques are not sensitive enough or that only a few cells in widely scattered areas are affected. A more likely possibility is that there are indirect methods by which the virus interferes with cells, for example, by the blocking of neuroleukin receptors with gp120 from the virus. Another possibility suggested by Dr. Candace Pert and her colleagues is that the T4 receptor, when present on brain cells normally binds a small neuropeptide necessary for functioning of the cell. If virus blocks the T4 receptor, then the cell cannot function. The most likely possibility is that there are several ways AIDS virus can interfere with brain cells — direct infection, blocking of receptors, and cell-to-cell infection.

Often overlooked is concomitant infection of the brain with other viruses. Cytomegalovirus is particularly common and is being found in the brain of an increasing percentage of AIDS victims (now up to 67%).

Fortunately, AZT seems to slow or reverse these neurological symptoms, but even here the results are quite preliminary and it is not clear to what extent this damage can be reversed and whether the reversal is permanent or short-term.

AIDS and the Rise in Tuberculosis Cases

The Federal Centers for Disease Control report that tuberculosis cases increased 2.6% in 1986 compared to 1985, with 22,768 and 22,201 cases, respectively. This is the first substantial increase since the reporting system was initiated in 1953.

The increase has been linked to the spread of AIDS virus and its immunity-weakening effects. Many individuals have dormant tuberculosis which normally presents no problem and often cannot even be detected. But when the number of helper T4 cells drops to a low value, as it does in active AIDS infection, the dormant cells are able to grow and multiply.

A study reported early in 1987 found that 5% of New York City's AIDS patients also had tuberculosis. The percentage was even higher in Florida, with 10% of the state's first 1044 patients also reported as having the disease. Put another way, of 58 male tuberculosis patients in New York City, 31 tested positive for infection with HIV.

Other factors, including larger numbers of high-risk patients from Asia, may have contributed to the increase. Also, through December 26, 1987, only 21,093 cases had been reported compared to 21,625 cases at the same point a year ago. The explanation for this is not known.

AIDS and Syphilis

In New York City syphilis had been declining steadily for 20 years, but starting in February 1987 reports of cases began pouring in and by the end of 6 months a surprising increase of 105% had been reached. Whereas in 1986 72% of the cases were in men, in 1987 women made up 50% of the cases, marking a 150% increase over 1986 for women. In 1986 there were 2000 cases of syphilis reported in New York City, and by October 1987 there were more than 4000.

Syphilis, like AIDS, is a very complicated disease. Normally there are four stages. The first is the formation of chancres or sores in genital or oral areas of the body. If untreated the disease proceeds to the second stage within 6 to 12 weeks, causing an array of vague symptoms including hair loss, sore joints, rashes, swollen lymph nodes, and weight loss. All of these symptoms can occur in other diseases, so syphilis is often misdiagnosed at this stage.

The cause of syphilis is a bacterium called *Treponema pallidum*, a spirochete or spiral organism. This organism may enter the eye and the brain in the second stage, or even in the first stage if the infection is treated inadequately or not at all. The bacteria may then enter a latent period, only to erupt years later in tertiary syphilis which can seriously affect vision, the heart, and the brain. The final stage of syphilis leads to death.

Many new cases of syphilis appeared to be more intense then those previously encountered, and a possible reason for this is the finding that 20% of the men and women infected with syphilis were also found to be infected with AIDS virus. Certainly, the existence of syphilis can facilitate the transmission of AIDS between sexual partners. Conversely, an immune system damaged by AIDS can lead to an unbridled infection by syphilis organisms.

With the occurrence of both AIDS and syphilis in the same patient it soon became clear that the standard treatment for syphilis, injection of a single dose of 2.4 million units of benzathine penicillin, was inadequate. What might be adequate is not known.

Doctors have been left wondering whether HIV infection activates latent syphilis and sometimes accelerates the course of the disease. The question has also been raised, Was the condition referred to as AIDS dementia actually syphilis infection of the brain? In fact, it is very likely that a great many cases of syphilis have been masked in HIV infected patients since both diseases affect much the same populations and are largely transmitted in the same way. Also, it can take years for an infected person to manifest the symptoms of syphilis, and its course varies dramatically from person to person, as does that of AIDS.

Only a maverick would then ask the question, What if AIDS is simply a new manifestation of syphilis? But there are quite a few mavericks around. What is the evidence?

- The only cells on which AIDS will grow in tissue culture are cells from a leukemia patient — someone who is already seriously immunosuppressed. There is no evidence that HIV can infect healthy T cells without extraordinary laboratory manipulation, according to Joan McKenna, research physiologist and information scientist in Berkeley, California. She believes that HIV is a byproduct of AIDS rather than the cause.

- She has found articles in old volumes on sexually transmitted disease relating both *P. carinii* pneumonia and Kaposi's sarcoma to syphilis. Dr. Kaposi first identified the lesions in syphilis patients.

- There have been reports of successful treatment of Kaposi's sarcoma with high doses of penicillin.

- The literature suggests that syphilitic patients are prone to opportunistic infections. Syphilis suppresses the immune system in the latent (second) and third stages.

- Twenty-one out of 24 AIDS patients with documented syphilis infection tested negative for syphilis antibodies.

Two doctors in Germany treated six AIDS and ARC patients, 5 of whom tested positive for syphilis, with massive doses of penicillin — 40 million units per day for 21 days. All the patients who had dementia and other neurological symptoms are now well, 6 months to several years after treatment.

The German doctors offer considerable additional evidence for their thesis that syphilis is really the cause of the symptoms of AIDS. The situation is in reality quite complex, because syphilis is a complex disease and the results produced by treatment with penicillin depend in part on the stage of the infection.

What do experts on AIDS think of the idea? They are highly skeptical and admit only that immunosuppression by AIDS virus may cause a flare-up of syphilis symptoms, many of which resemble those of AIDS.

The final comment is always, "What we need is a careful experiment using adequate numbers of patients." Since in the absence of allergy reactions penicillin is not usually toxic even at the high doses used, why not give it a try?

Finally, it should be mentioned that Dr. Peter H. Duesberg, a molecular biologist from the University of California at Berkeley, has published an article in the highly prestigious journal *Cancer Research* in which he advances the theory that HIV is not the primary cause of AIDS. He has marshaled considerable evidence to support his thesis, however, virtually all the workers in the field of AIDS research believe he is wrong.

Caring for AIDS Patients at Home

Caring for an AIDS patient in a municipal hospital costs about $800 per day, according to James M. Foster, a member of the San Francisco Health Commission. A program operated by the Visiting Nurse Service of New York City, on the other hand, calculates its cost per patient as $81 per day.

Most insurance plans are set up only to pay for hospital care, and this is unfortunate because many AIDS patients can be treated adequately at home, with perhaps an occasional visit from a nurse. This would not only save enormous sums of money and prevent overcrowding of hospitals, but would generally put the patient in a more felicitous environment.

Not all AIDS patients can be treated at home, and most require hospitalization at some point in their illness. Dr. John C. Bartlett, director of AIDS Care Service at Johns Hopkins Hospital in Baltimore, says AIDS patients require hospitalization an average of 2.4 times a year, the average length of stay being 13.4 days per visit. He believes that the availability of chronic care facilities could reduce this period considerably.

Caring for a person at home is a difficult labor of love and should not be undertaken lightly. The amount of time required is formidable, and anyone with a full-time work schedule should probably not undertake such a task. But a considerable reward is obtained in knowing that the loved person is getting the kind of support and affection so necessary in keeping up his or her morale. Although it is not likely that home care will change the course of the disease or even prolong life for the patient, certainly the quality of life for the person afflicted with AIDS will be as good as possible.

There are books available to help anyone who wants to care for an AIDS patient. One is by L.J. Martelli, F.D. Peltz, and W. Messina: *When Someone You Know Has AIDS: A Practical Guide.* (Crown Publishers, paperback, $9.95). Another is *AIDS: A Self Care Manual,* edited by Betty Clare Moffatt, Judith Spiegel, Steve Parrish, and Michael Helquist (IBS Press, paperback, $12.95).

What to do directions are based on common sense:

- Keep the patient busy doing as many things he or she enjoys. Have a good color TV available and a VCR. Watch comedies and generally happy movies and TV shows, staying away from unhappy endings, psychological dramas, and somber subjects. If the patient likes music, provide the types most enjoyed. Again, try to keep it light and cheerful; songs about loss or parting are taboo.

- Invite people over whom you know well and like, particularly anyone with a good sense of humor.

- If the patient will read, provide books, from the library if necessary, as well as magazines and newspapers.

- Treat the patient as a normal person, not a sick one. Do not deny the disease or the possibility of a fatal outcome, but remember that it is very important to maintain hope. Mention any positive information that comes up in the news — such as a new drug or the testing of a vaccine, which might be available soon. Keep stressing the long-term survival of some patients with AIDS.

- Ask a visiting home nurse to make regular calls.

- Enlist a support network including good friends and relatives who will relieve you and give you and the patient emotional support.

- Try to get the patient out or up and around as much as possible. Weather permitting, short walks are good or visits to any activity the patient can tolerate. Movies, libraries, museums, restaurants, and religious services are some of the possibilities.

● Provide simple foods that the patient likes and can tolerate. Do not cook elaborate meals which the AIDS victim may not be able to eat. Chicken soup will not cure AIDS, but it's a good food. Have nutritious snacks available and juices.

● Tender loving care (TLC) is always helpful. Do not be afraid to touch or hug the patient. Massages are also very relaxing.

Precautions to avoid becoming infected and to avoid infecting the AIDS patient

It is probably a good idea to keep small children from physical contact with the patient because youngsters are always picking up a cold or a 24-hour virus. Older children can certainly visit and give support. If you or any other visitor has a cold, use a simple mask which can be obtained at the drugstore.

Wash your hands often, particularly before and after ministering to the patient, handling food, and when disposing of body fluids. Disposable gloves should be used if your hands are scratched, cut, or chapped in any way. Consider the possibility that urine, feces, saliva, and tears might contain virus particles. Many AIDS patients may become incontinent. Disposable bed pads can be used, and adult diapers for men or women are available in drug stores. When cleaning soiled bedding, wear a washable full-body rubber apron and disposable gloves. Carefully place all soiled disposable material in a plastic bag and wash all tableware and anything else, such as clothing, in hot, soapy water containing 1 part chlorine bleach in 10 parts water.

An electric razor is better than a blade, and a soft toothbrush should be used. If a patient cannot stand or sit in the shower, use a sponge bath with mild soap. No one should use the patient's towels, soap, or razor, even if electric.

Pets should be kept away from an AIDS patient.

An egg carton mattress can help prevent bed sores.

Remember, as the disease progresses, the patient may show increasing signs of dementia, for example, forgetfulness, lack of understanding, disorientation, and even striking personality changes — irritability and downright hostility. This is all a part of the disease and must be endured by the caretaker with patience.

The American Red Cross of Greater New York offers a free six-session course for families and friends of AIDS patients who provide home care. This course may be offered in other large cities as well. In New York, call 212-787-1000, extension 8200.

You Can't Go Home Again?

(Excerpted from *The New York Times* article, "Coming Home With AIDS to a Small Town" by Dirk Johnson, Nov. 2, 1987. With the kind permission of the editors.)

The gay young person with AIDS often faces a double stigma. Many people are intolerant of homosexuals, and the occurrence of AIDS, even in a person who is not gay, is often reason enough for violent ostracism of the sufferer.

It is small wonder that a young gay person with AIDS looks with great trepidation on the possibility of going back home. How will his parents, who might not have known he was a homosexual, react? How will friends and neighbors react, and how will the townspeople behave? Will his home be picketed and demands made that he leave town or at least not show up in public?

The alternative to going home is even more bleak: a possibly friend-less existence in a single-room occupancy (SRO) building with no one to care for or comfort him and an unlamented and unnoticed death.

Fortunately, attitudes toward AIDS are improving as the general population learns more about transmission of the disease. Often you can go home again, as one young man who lives in Waseca, Minnesota, found out. Dean Lechner, who lived most of his adult life in San Francisco, where he had worked most recently as assistant to the president of a political fund-raising company, decided to go home. Thirty-four years old, he had grown up in a small town of 8000 in the farm country of southern Minnesota in a nineteenth century white clap-board on a country road. He had attended public school there from kindergarten through high school, graduating with membership in Arista, the National Honor Society. His homosexual leanings were al-ready present and apparently known to his peers, who hounded him mercilessly.

In May of 1987 he caught a cold marked by persistent coughing and wheezing. A doctor in town, where he was visiting at the time, diag-nosed his illiness as bronchitis. But he continued downhill, so weak that he stayed in bed for 2 weeks. Then he became really sick with *P. carinii* pneumonia and was taken by ambulance to the Mayo Clinic where diagnosis of AIDS was made.

Lechner told his family he would return to San Francisco after the pneumonia cleared up. He did not want to put them through the pain and trouble that was in store for him. However, his family rallied to his side and insisted that he come home. His sister Barbara, who had seen sickness before, with a brother who had had polio, said, "Dogs go off to die," and his mother continued, "You're a son, you're a brother. And you are loved."

The family members decided they would take turns caring for him. When her son first came home, Mrs. Lechner did not sleep for 7 days. Now she brings him coffee every morning and cooks him nourishing meals. And when she cries, which is often, she goes into her bedroom and shuts the door. She does not want him to worry.

Lechner has been taking AZT and is considerably better. His weight is back to 165 pounds, and he does not look like an AIDS victim now. But the town knows about it. A banner headline in the local newspaper proclaiming that fact greeted him when he moved back into town. He had worried about what would happen because the town had had no experience with anyone who was openly gay and had AIDS. The answer came from the townspeople. The owner of a hair salon he had stopped going to, for fear he would scare away customers, met him downtown, threw her arms around him, and said, "We miss you."

The 57-year-old owner of the Busy Bee Cafe said, "Who are we to judge?" She does not throw away his dishes, but washes them with the rest.

Dave Condon, owner of a feed service for farmers, said, "You don't kick a guy when he's down." Nearly 200 cards of support were mailed to Lechner, as well as books, poems, prayers, and money. Flowers are continually sent to him.

It has not been all roses, however. A classmate he had known since kindergarten called on behalf of the high school reunion organizing committee and told him not to come. "If you do," she said, "people will leave." For the first time since the AIDS diagnosis he sat down and cried. Fortunately, however, there is a happy ending to this story. It turned out that the reunion committee had not voted to exclude him. The woman who called, worried about AIDS, had made up the story. Several people invited Lechner to go to the reunion with them. He went, and no one left. Later he met the woman who had told him not to come. He raised a champagne glass to her and said, "I understand." She turned and walked away.

We should remember that it's rough to be gay in a world that is often prejudiced, and it's doubly rough to have AIDS in a world that is not well informed about it and fearful. But there are a lot of good people in the world, many more, I believe, than those who are prejudiced and/or ignorant. It is this that makes living life to the very end among people — friends and relatives — worth while.

CHAPTER 7
TREATMENT OF AIDS

Introduction; U.S. decision to relax rules on experimental drugs; Passage of an AIDS drug testing law in California; AIDS victims' search for a cure; Chemical antiviral agents or drugs; New drugs not yet being clinically tested; Treatment of *Pneumocystis carinii*; Some general thoughts on drug therapy; Biological (immune) response modifiers; Vaccines as a cure for AIDS; AIDS vaccine workshop; Use of viral protein pieces to make an AIDS vaccine; Anti-idiotype vaccines; Anti-thymosin antibodies; Protection of volunteers who test AIDS virus vaccines; Use of substances that block the entry of AIDS into cells; Prospects for treatment of AIDS – chemicals and immune stimulants.

7

TREATMENT OF AIDS

Introduction

Theoretically there are a number of different ways AIDS could be treated:

1. Use of a chemical antiviral agent or agents.

2. Use of natural protein agents – biological (immune) response modifiers which are produced by the immune system to fight a disease

   a. Different interferons (alpha, beta and gamma), as well as some modifications of these compounds that are now available

   b. Colony-stimulating factors that stimulate the growth and replication of different white cells, for example, macrophages

   c. Interleukins-1, -2, -3, and -4 which are growth factors for B and T lymphocytes – all-important for immune defense against viruses and bacteria

   d. Tumor necrosis factor

   e. Leukotoxin.

3. Use of vaccines directed against the virus or parts of the virus

4. Use of substances that can block the entry of HIV into cells, for example, chemicals or proteins that can bind to the receptors on white cells which normally bind AIDS virus. If these receptors are blocked, the white cell cannot bind the virus and the virus cannot gain entry into the cell.

5. General supportive care such as use of antibiotics to control opportunistic infections that attack AIDS patients. Use of anticancer drugs such as cytoxan to control Kaposi's sarcoma or other cancers that may strike AIDS victims. Treatment with vitamins and a good diet to build up patients.

6. Use of general immune stimulants which strengthen the immune system. There are many of these, including BCG (a bacterial product), tuftsin, a small chemical called a peptide obtained from the breakdown of antibodies, which are natural proteins produced by the immune system to fight disease.

7. Monoclonal antibodies against AIDS. In theory it is possible to make monoclonal antibodies that will attach to and inactivate specific HIV proteins. However, there has not been much activity in this field, possibly because monoclonal antibodies would be of uncertain value against virus hidden in different cells.

Combinations of any of these methods may be more effective than any single one. Most AIDS patients need general supportive care (item 5), as they are usually run down and weakened by the disease and may have anemia.

The status of these treatments that are presently important will be discussed in turn, and the nature and properties of the different drugs and vaccines that have been developed will be presented as well.

U.S. Decision to Relax Rules on Experimental Drugs

The Food and Drug Administration (FDA) has always had very strict rules and specified stringent procedures for clearing a new drug for testing on humans. Tests are to be carried out first on human cells in tissue cultures, and then with animals, followed by short- and long-term tests on human volunteers. It can take 5 years or more before enough data are obtained on the effectiveness and toxicity of any new drug to propose its unlimited use in humans.

It is clear that in the case of AIDS this procedure is much too long. With thousands dying each year and many more thousands of victims clamoring for any kind of hope in the form of a cure, the pressure for faster testing became overwhelming, and in early 1987 the FDA took action on proposals made by the Reagan administration and accepted new rules.

Dr. Frank E. Young, commissioner of the FDA, says the proposed new rules will essentially formalize procedures already used to make the drug AZT available to many AIDS patients even before it had passed all clinical tests and regulatory hurdles designed to prove that it is safe and effective.

If an experimental drug for a life-threatening condition begins to look promising in clinical trials, he states, the new rules will allow it to be made available for the treatment of patients who are not participating in the clinical trials but who could benefit from its use.

In addition, the new rules make two concessions to the drug industry. First, they allow drug companies to charge patients for promising drugs. Before, experimental drugs were provided free. Second, if it is believed that a promising drug should be restricted, the burden of proof is shifted to the government rather than requiring the drug company to prove the drug should have unlimited use. The latter is a very important concession. Dr. Young estimates that drugs might become available 2 or 3 years earlier with these new regulations. He also warns that patients who use less than fully tested drugs face a greater risk than is normally the case. Dr. Young also says that the government will propose a streamlining of the entire drug research and approval process.

Passage of an AIDS Drug Testing Law in California

By 1991 California expects to have 50,000 patients with active AIDS, costing the state $2.5 billion in medical care. Consequently, it is seeking means to speed up the process of finding, testing, and marketing new drugs. California already has the authority to approve new drug applications and to permit their investigational use. Manufacturers may seek approval for testing and sale under state law without complying with federal requirements as long as the drug is manufactured and distributed only within the state. California is the only state at present with the authority to develop new drugs for AIDS and other diseases.

AIDS Victims' Search for a Cure

Prior to 1987 physicians had only palliatives (drugs that give relief from pain but have no chance of providing a cure) to offer AIDS patients. Now azidothymidine has been approved for certain AIDS victims, and all AIDS patients can obtain it if their doctor prescribes it. Dozens of new drugs and treatments are in the pipeline. AZT, while able to arrest the progress of the disease and improve the status of many patients, has by no means proved to be a cure. It has, in addition, serious side effects. Complete information about AZT is provided below.

People with AIDS are often not content to put all their eggs in a basket of AZT pills. They are frantically searching out and trying other means to improve their health status. Doing nothing doesn't work, the victims rightly claim.

Michael Callen, an AIDS patient, has written a 145 page manual for newly diagnosed AIDS victims called "Surviving and Thriving with AIDS." He advises, "Ask around, network with other people with AIDS." He lists his own experiences, including taking isoprinosine, naltrexone, DNCB, gamma globulin, Bactrum, dapsone, and acyclovir (intravenous and oral), undergoing plasmaphoresis (a blood-cleansing process), receiving transfusions of packed red cells, and whipping up daily a "poor man's AL-721" (lecithin, oil, and juice). Callen belongs to the "try anything" school. Some health care experts worry that AIDS sufferers are uselessly depleting their resources and wasting their time and efforts taking ineffectual drugs. They are also easy marks for unscrupulous salespeople who prey on them with promises of help.

But many of these people facing certain death have a much different point of view. They point out that some drugs ease their suffering, that others may add months to their lives, and that the rest, even if worthless, bolster their spirits. When there was nothing to try, they say, there was no hope. Now at least there is hope and a feeling that they have some control over whether they will live or die.

Chemical Antiviral Agents or Drugs

Finding a drug to fight AIDS virus is a particularly difficult problem for two reasons. First, the virus, like other retroviruses, gets inside the cell and becomes an integral part of it. When integrated into the DNA it may remain hidden there for years and while it is in this form we do not know of any way a drug can select the infected cell. If the virus is stimulated to become active, grow, and make proteins and other copies of itself, then it is possible to find drugs that may interfere with these processes. Unfortunately, the drugs that interfere, also interfere with normal cell growth and this may cause serious side effects.

Second, as the virus infects brain cells, many antiviral drugs cannot reach these cells in adequate concentrations because of the natural blood-brain barrier that normally protects brain cells by keeping out all kinds of extraneous material. What is needed is a drug that is not too toxic to normal cells, can get by the blood-brain barrier, and is not too rapidly excreted or broken down in the body. AZT meets some of these requirements well, but it is still quite toxic. In the following discussion of drugs, those with an asterisk following the name are being clinically tested.

Azidothymidine* (trade name Zidovudine)

This drug is a close relative of thymidine, a compound required by the body for making DNA. Thymidine is known as a nucleotide and is one of the four different nucleotides that go into making the double-helical structure of the DNA molecule. It is what is called the rate-limiting nucleotide, meaning that in a resting, non-dividing cell, three of the nucleotides and the enzymes to make them are present in adequate quantities, but thymidine is not. When a cell is stimulated to make DNA and divide, one of the first things it does is to make the enzymes needed to synthesize thymidine. Once thymidine is present, DNA synthesis can proceed.

If DNA synthesis takes place in the presence of AZT, the latter drug competes with thymidine and may be incorporated into the DNA. Whenever this happens, synthesis of the DNA chain is blocked because the azido group breaks chain formation (Figure 7-1).

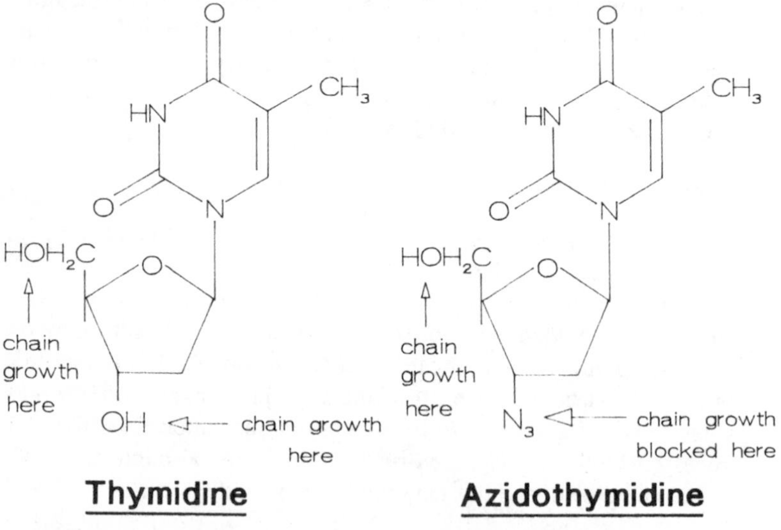

Figure 7-1 **Structures of thymidine and azidothymidine.**

The result is that short chains of DNA are made which are of no use for making copies of viral RNA. Virus production is therefore stopped. The structures of AZT and thymidine are shown in Figure 7-1 for comparison, and the sites where chain growth is stopped are indicated.

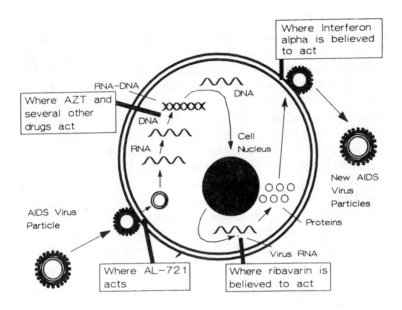

Figure 7-2 Drugs used in AIDS treatment and how they may work.

Figure 7-2 shows the sequence of viral replication in a cell and where AZT and some other drugs probably interfere.

AZT was synthesized over 20 years ago and shown in 1974 to be a general inhibitor of retrovirus replication. It is very effective in stopping AIDS virus replication *in vitro* and is effective against widely different strains of HIV. It should also be useful against other immunodeficiency retroviruses such as those that affect monkeys, cats, and cattle, as well as against lentiviruses that infect sheep and other animals. It will probably be useful in treating HIV-2 infections, but it is too early to tell since the latter variant of HIV was discovered only a short time ago.

AZT, in addition to terminating chains of DNA, affects other aspects of nucleotide metabolism in cells. For example, it reduces the cellular level of thymidine triphosphate, its natural counterpart, and this ability undoubtedly increases its effectiveness. AZT also reduces the level of deoxycytidine triphosphate in cells. The latter nucleotide is another of the four direct precursor nucleotides of DNA, and this lowering also augments the effectiveness of AZT.

The U.S. Health Service and Burroughs-Wellcome have recently reported on 282 patients in phase II tests of AZT, which are extensive examinations of the effects of the drug in large numbers of patients. AIDS victims receiving AZT had a significantly lower death rate than those receiving placebos (pills similar in appearance to the drug being tested but containing no medication). There were 16 deaths in the placebo group and only 1 in the group receiving AZT. The AZT group also had a lower incidence of lymphomas (cancer of the lymph gland), Kaposi's sarcoma, and opportunistic infections. They gained weight and showed some improvement of immune function. The results were so good, in fact, that the Data Safety Monitoring Board decided it would be unethical to continue using placebos and began to give all patients AZT. These tests spanned a period of only 6 months, so little is known about long-term toxicity, the possibility of relapse, the development of allergies, and the long-term prognosis of those taking the drug.

One drawback of AZT is that it fails to enter white cells called macrophages. These cells can be infected with AIDS virus, and since they roam the entire body they can carry the disease to the brain and to other cells.

Side effects of AZT

Since AZT can interfere with DNA replication, it can unfortunately interfere with the growth and division of normal cells. Most important among these are bone marrow cells, which eventually supply all the white and red cells of the body as well as the platelets needed for blood clotting. Although AZT suppresses AIDS virus replication, there is also bone marrow suppression with resulting neutropenia (too few white cells), anemia (too few red cells), and lowered ability to fight disease. If bone marrow suppression by AZT becomes serious, treatment may have to be stopped or the dose lowered.

Dr. Hiroaki Mitsuya and Dr. Samuel Broder began administering AZT to AIDS patients in July 1985. The drug has many good features. It can be taken orally, and it is rapidly absorbed. Best of all, it shows excellent penetration of the blood-brain barrier which excludes most drugs. The drug has a short life in the body, so it has to be administered every 4 hours around the clock.

During short courses of administration these investigators found that partial restoration of the immune system took place and that patients showed good overall clinical improvement. In patients with dementia, AZT brought about dramatic neurological improvement, but how long this will last is not known.

AZT is being tested in detail in many hospitals around the United States and at present is probably being used in over 16,000 patients worldwide. Many doctors prescribe it for their patients on demand even before these patients show disease symptoms.

AZT as a preventative for the development of active AIDS infection

Many physicians involved in testing drugs against AIDS virus believe that one of the most important studies is a phase II (large scale) clinical trial set up to determine whether AZT can repress development of the disease in patients who are infected with the virus but show no symptoms.

Unfortunately, these trials are not going well. Although begun in September 1986, more than a year later only half of the 1562 patients needed had been enrolled at 19 medical centers in the United States. It is now likely that another year will be needed to find the requisite participants, and it will be another 3 years before the results are compiled and evaluated.

The difficulties have been many. At first not enough drug was available, there were problems at the federal level in financing, there were administrative mistakes, and above all there was a serious reluctance of many AIDS virus carriers to enter the trial. It is a controlled study with about half the patients receiving placebos. AIDS victims and even AIDS carriers shun placebo experiments, and with good reason. They are afraid they might not get a drug that could cure them, at least in part, or even prevent the disease. In New York and San Francisco, only a handful of patients have been enrolled.

Despite the problems the trial will go on, and if it shows that a significantly fewer number of the AIDS virus carriers who receive AZT develop disease symptoms than placebo patients, this could be a very important finding. It will not necessarily slow the epidemic unless at the same time the transmissibility of the disease is reduced. The trial is not set up to determine this. For carriers, however, knowing they could stave off the disease symptoms into the far future, at least, would be a boon.

Cost of AZT

AZT is a very expensive drug. It is estimated that over a period of a year, when the normal dose is given, it will cost about $10,000. Treatment with the drug may have to continue for an indefinite time, perhaps several years. Fortunately, no patients are at present being denied the drug because they cannot afford it. Most health insurance organizations, Blue Cross, Medicare, and others, have authorized payment for the drug for insured patients. Furthermore, New York City officials have appropriated an emergency sum of money, about $6.4 million, to provide *all* patients who might benefit from the drug with an adequate supply. Congress is being asked for a quick appropriation of $30 million to augment the funds being provided by states and cities. It is not likely that anyone will be denied the drug. Of course, as the number of cases gets into the hundred thousands, the demand for money for this and other, probably as expensive, medicines will soar. I am confident this demand will be met in our society. However — and this is a big "however" — victims in the Third World may have a serious problem. It is obviously necessary for the more industrialized nations to furnish funds and medicines for all who need them throughout the world.

Ribavirin*

Ribavirin has been known for many years. Its manufacturer, ICN Pharmaceuticals, claims it is useful for treating AIDS virus infections, but these claims have been refuted and the FDA has not approved it for this use.

The structure of the drug is shown in Figure 7-3.

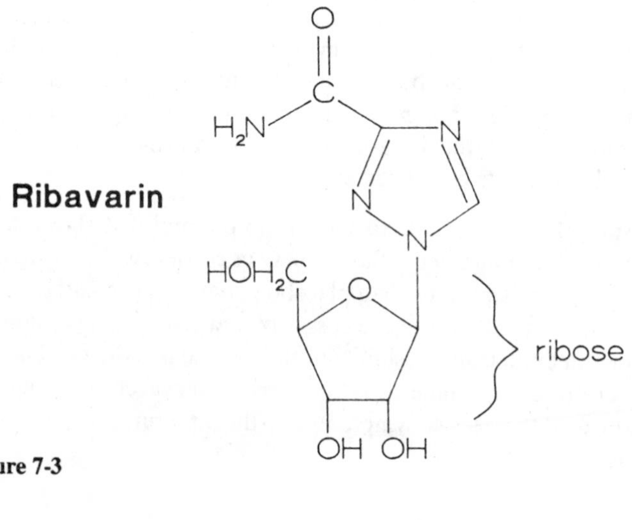

Ribavarin

ribose

Figure 7-3

Since the ribose has its normal complement of OH groups, this drug does not act as a chain terminator for either DNA or RNA. Thus it differs from AZT. The base ring above the ribose has an extra nitrogen, is smaller (five atoms instead of six), and has an unusual group attached to it. It probably works by being incorporated into RNA which, by virtue of the drug's presence, is abnormal and cannot function as normal retrovirus RNA would.

A clinical study was done with 163 patients in the early stages of AIDS. They had had depressed levels of T4 lymphocytes and swollen lymph glands for at least 3 months, but no other symptoms. Of 56 patients who took a placebo, 10 developed full-blown AIDS. Of the 55 patients who took a daily dose of 600 milligrams of ribavirin, 6 progressed to AIDS. However, of the 52 patients who took 800 milligrams of ribavirin daily, none developed the fatal disease.

These results have been highly criticized on several grounds. First, they are only for 6 months. After a year, the picture may be quite different. Second, the placebo group had a much higher percentage progressing to AIDS than would be expected. It has been suggested that this group included most of those who were among the sickest participants. This would tend to make the groups receiving the drug look better. Finally, the difference in drug dosage between the 600- and 800-milligram groups, 200 milligrams, would hardly be expected to give rise to such a great difference in the number of those getting AIDS, namely, 6 and none, respectively.

These results, which look promising but may not be, have been seized upon by those infected with AIDS, but still either without symptoms or in the earliest stages of the disease, as offering hope of protection. Unfortunately, they are too preliminary, and possibly suspect, to warrant taking the drug, but obviously, to those without hope, these results are hope.

Consequently ribavirin is at a premium for AIDS patients and is avidly sought by them in 12 other countries, including Mexico, that sell the drug. In the United States the drug is approved only for treatment of a sometimes fatal respiratory infection in children caused by a virus. ICN Chemical Company has been developing ribavirin (trade name Virazole) for 16 years as therapy for hepatitis A, herpes, influenza A and B, measles, chicken pox, dengue fever (which is being seen more frequently in this country), and lassa fever (a highly fatal disease found in Africa).

At the International AIDS Conference held in Washington in 1987, the results of a follow-up test on ribavirin were reported. The test was carried out at 6 different medical centers in the United States and utilized 212 patients suffering from AIDS-related complex. After 28 weeks, ribavirin had no significant effect in preventing death or blocking the progression to AIDS. In fact, 6 of the patients who received the drug died compared to only 2 who received the placebo.

Fourteen patients taking the placebo progressed to AIDS, as did 12 who were given 800 milligrams of ribavirin daily, and 7 given 600 milligrams of drug also progressed to AIDS. The conclusion was that ribavirin had no significant effect in this experiment.

Dr. Peter Mansell, of the Institute for Immunological Disorders in Houston, presented results for a healthier group of patients in another experiment. This group consisted of 163 homosexual men suffering from lymphadenopathy syndrome, mainly swollen lymph glands, which is the first sign of AIDS. In this test ribavirin delayed the progression to AIDS, and only mild side effects of the drug were observed. These results were, however, sharply challenged by Dr. Frank Young, commissioner of the FDA who claimed that, again, the placebo group contained some of the sickest patients. Only careful examination of each patient's history would prove this, and this has not been done.

Despite Commissioner Young's violent opposition to ribavirin, he later relented and cleared the way for limited clinical trials of the drug. It will be used in a group of 32 patients with AIDS-related complex to determine whether it can prevent progression of the disease.

Combining AZT and ribavirin: Ribavirin antagonizes the effect of azidothymidine

Separately, both drugs inhibit HIV replication, but by different mechanisms. AZT interferes with DNA chain synthesis, and ribavirin interferes with the processing of RNA after it is synthesized. Use of the drugs together may be beneficial by addition of the inhibitory effects of the two drugs. When they were tested together, however, using cells in tissue culture, ribavirin was found to interfere with the action of AZT. This interference occurred when a variety of different conditions were tried. Dr. Markus W. Vogt and his colleagues at Massachusetts General Hospital, Infectious Disease Unit, Harvard Medical School, who reported the work, pointed out that a similar interference may occur during clinical trials of the two drugs in combination and that carefully controlled conditions would have to be used. Apparently ribavirin interferes with the conversion of AZT to the triphosphate, which is necessary if AZT is to be placed in the DNA chain and terminate it.

Acyclovir*

Acyclovir is another nucleotide drug, one based on guanine. It has been licensed by the FDA for treating herpes, as a salve applied directly to the herpes blisters and also internally. It does not cure herpes, but when taken internally appears to lessen the severity of the outbreaks and to make them occur less frequently.

Dr. Mitsuya and Dr. Broder, at the National Cancer Institute, who, as already mentioned, have been studying the effects of AZT, found that acyclovir and AZT acted synergistically against AIDS virus growing in cells in tissue culture. "Synergistic" means that when the two drugs are used together, they are far more effective than the sum of their two activities. For example, if each drug separately inhibits the growth of the virus 10%, when used together they might inhibit growth by 50% instead of the 20% expected. The experiments were done with tissue cultures, and there is no guarantee that the same synergism will be observed in the body, but there is at least a good chance that it will. The combination of AZT and acyclovir is being clinically tested at present. The structure of acyclovir is shown in Figure 7- 4.

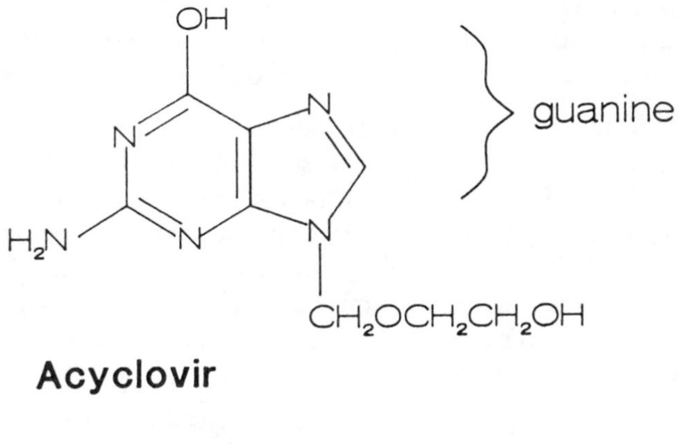

Acyclovir

Figure 7-4 The structure of acyclovir.

Other Drugs Being Tested for AIDS

AL-721* (Praxis Pharmaceuticals and Ethogen Corporation)

This compound is a lipid mixture containing neutral glycerides, phosphatidylcholine, and phosphatidylethanolamine in a 7:2:1 ratio, respectively. It interferes with HIV infectivity, possibly by disrupting the virus' membrane. No adverse effects were observed in a 6-week clinical trial. Oral administration leads to partial degradation in the intestinal tract, which does not appear to interfere with the mixture's therapeutic potential.

A recent homemade recipe is the following:

6 1/2 tablespoons of butter

5 tablespoons of PC-55 (a commercially available lecithin concentrate)

3/4 cup of water

Mix the PC-55 and water in a blender. Melt the butter and slowly add it to the mixture. Mix 3 to 5 minutes until even in color. Pour into an ice cube tray and freeze. One thing to be said for this medicine is that it is not likely to harm anyone at the rate of several frozen cubes a day.

In early clinical trials AL-721 reduced HIV reverse transcriptase activity and improved immune function and clinical signs.

Ampligen* (Dupont, HEM Research)
Ampligen is produced by HEM Research, Inc., a private Rockville, Maryland company now in partnership with DuPont. This drug has been tested with only 10 patients and is now in the process of being investigated in larger trials employing randomized tests using placebos.

Ampligen was given to patients with AIDS, ARC, or only swollen glands — a symptom of the beginning stages of AIDS. Six of 7 patients with AIDS or ARC showed a reduction in virus in their blood. All 10 patients had an improved immune response as determined by skin tests, while 7 of 8 showed stable or increased levels of helper T cells. A variety of clinical symptoms were reduced, including swollen glands, yeast infections, fatigue, and weight loss. Side effects included nausea and flu-like symptoms.

Dr. William Mitchell, a professor of pathology at Vanderbilt University who is cooperating in the trials, explained that the drug works like a biological response modifier, triggering the production of interferons and tumor necrosis factor (hence the side effects which both of the two latter substances initiate).

It is not yet known whether the drug crosses the critical blood-brain barrier to reach AIDS virus in infected brain cells or whether it can enter macrophages which probably help spread the infection throughout the body.

Ampligen is a mismatched double-stranded RNA. Such products are known to be potent stimulators of interferon production by cells.

Ansamycin, Rifabutin* (Adria Laboratories)
This antibiotic is a potent inhibitor of reverse transcriptase and other similar enzymes. It is used principally to treat AIDS patients suffering from the opportunistic infection *Mycobacterium avium-intracellulaire*. The drug is able to cross the brain-blood barrier and is being tested in AIDS patients with neurological symptoms.

Azimexon
This compound is a chemically modified immune stimulant. Early trials showed improvement in immune function and symptoms in ARC patients but not in AIDS patients. A slight toxic effect is mild hemolysis (disintegration) of red blood cells.

Carrisyn*, polymannoacetate (Carrington Laboratories)
This polysaccharide (or complex sugar) is made from the common sugar mannose which is widely distributed in nature. It is believed to prevent lipid coated viruses from penetrating host cell membranes by binding thymidine on the virus particles. Eight AIDS patients given the drug orally showed clinical improvement and no toxic effects. Clinical trials will be continued.

Cyanothymidine, CNT
This compound is a drug like AZT that can act as a chain terminator. It appears to be as active as AZT in tissue culture, but studies on the drug in humans have just begun. See Figure 7-5.

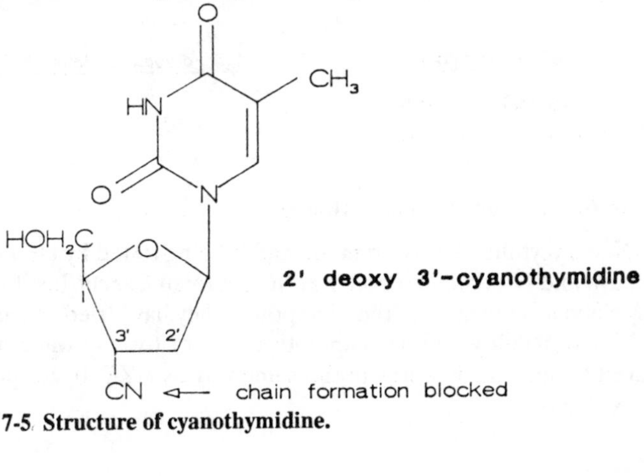

2' deoxy 3'-cyanothymidine

CN ◁— chain formation blocked

Figure 7-5. Structure of cyanothymidine.

Cyclosporin a

In October 1985 three French doctors announced that cyclosporin a, a well-known drug used to suppress the immune system after kidney, heart, and other transplants, had produced for the first time "spectacular biological improvement" in two AIDS patients. This statement was immediately vehemently criticized as completely irresponsible because it was based on only two patients treated for 8 days. The criticism turned out to be well founded, because the patients died soon after and the drug proved to be useless. One might have predicted this for a drug that suppresses the immune system in patients whose immune system has already been nearly destroyed by AIDS virus.

Dideoxycytidine*, DDC

This compound belongs to a class of nucleotides that lack a group on both the 2' and 3' carbons of ribose and differ from the normal nucleotides used to make DNA, which have a hydroxyl group on the 3' carbon. Figure 7-6 shows the relationship.

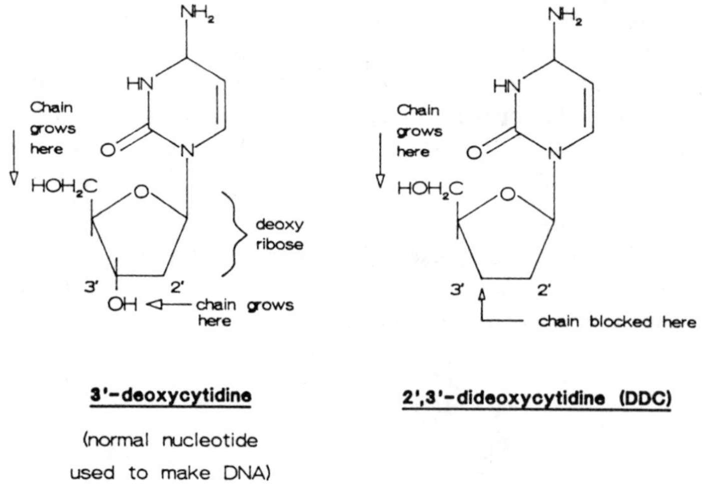

3'-deoxycytidine

(normal nucleotide
used to make DNA)

2',3'-dideoxycytidine (DDC)

Figure 7-6 Structure of dideoxycytidine

Dideoxycytidine has been made and is being tested by Dr. Hiroaki Mitsuya and Dr. Samuel Broder at the National Cancer Institute and they claim it is the most potent compound they have tried. It has good oral bioavailability and a comparative lack of toxicity when administered to animals. It works in the same way as AZT, by terminating DNA chains.

It is interesting to note that dideoxynucleotides can suppress AIDS virus replication and protect sensitive helper T4 cells *in vitro* for long periods without interfering with the function and survival of these T cells. One explanation for the selective effect of dideoxynucleotides on AIDS reverse transcriptase is that the viral enzyme is more easily fooled into accepting a dideoxynucleotide than is the mammalian enzyme (DNA polymerase).

Extensive testing of dideoxycytidine is underway. Unfortunately, early clinical trials with it had to be stopped because the patients began to develop peripheral neuropathy—pain and loss of sensation in the hands and feet. This condition was reversible in some patients, and it is hoped that with lower doses it will not occur. Also, it has been suggested that alternate weekly use of AZT and DDC might be beneficial and avert these nerve effects as well.

Doxorubicin hydrochloride, adriamycin* (Adria Laboratories)
This highly toxic agent is useful in treating several types of cancer. It inhibits DNA synthesis and HIV replication and infectivity in tissue culture. It is being used in a phase II trial involving AIDS patients with Kaposi's sarcoma.

Eflornithine* alpha-difluoromethyl ornithine, DFMO (Merrell Dow)
This antiprotozoan agent is being used successfully to treat *Pneumocystis carinii* pneumonia in AIDS patients who cannot tolerate the standard therapy for this disease — pentamidine or trimethoprim sulfamethoxazole.

Foscarnet*, Trisodium phosphonoformate
This Swedish drug has been used to treat cytomegalovirus infections, one type of opportunistic infection occurring in AIDS patients, and also to treat herpes.

It inhibits the reverse transcriptase activity of HIV. Problems in formulation (making the drug up for injection) and serious side effects have been encountered. No results in AIDS victims have been reported.

Fusidic acid
This antibiotic has been known since 1962. According to a group of investigators in Harrow, England, and another in Copenhagen, Denmark, the drug is effective *in vitro* and also has produced striking clinical improvement in a 58 year-old Danish man with AIDS.

The drug is relatively free of side effects and can be given orally. Its cost is less than 1/10 that of AZT. Interestingly, it was first tested in patients (being an approved antibiotic) before it was tested against cells in tissue culture. In the AIDS patient mentioned, it was being used to treat a tuberculosis infection of the lungs. The patient's fever cleared up, he gained weight, and remains well.

An important property of the drug is its ability to penetrate many types of cells and tissues including granulocytes, macrophages, bone and fatty tissue (bone marrow).

It has been mentioned that, now that AZT is available, AIDS patients will not participate in a drug test that involves the use of a placebo. This makes it more difficult, of course, to test any drug. The answer is to test two similar groups of patients, one receiving AZT and the other fusidic acid, and all new drugs now are being compared to AZT rather than to placebos.

Ganciclovir* (Burroughs-Wellcome)
This drug is a close relative of acyclovir and is being used to treat cytomegalovirus infections, particularly of the eye, in AIDS patients (AIDS retinitis). Combination with AZT appears to be too toxic to blood-forming elements of the immune system. (It is described in more detail in Chapter 6).

Heparin
This compound is a common blood anticlotting agent in the body. It is reported to protect cells in tissue culture against AIDS virus.

HPA 23, ammonium 21-tungsto-9-antimoniate
This compound is a complex chemical containing tungsten and antimony, two toxic elements. It was used to treat Rock Hudson. It has been shown to inhibit reverse transcriptase of several retroviruses *in vitro* and to have some tendency to check the growth of HIV, but no therapeutic benefit has been documented in AIDS patients.

Immunthiol, diethyldithiocarbamate* (Merieux Institute)
Several French investigators claim that this substance, which is a well-known chelating agent (one that removes metals, including toxic heavy metals like lead, from solution or from the body), is useful for treating AIDS-related complex. Eight of 12 patients showed clinical improvement, including reduced fever, a gain in weight, and increased numbers of T4 cells. The patients have been taking the drug for from 3 months to 2 years, and significant side effects have been absent. It is now being clinically tested in the United States.

Imreg-1* (Imreg Incorporated)
This biological response modifier is obtained from white blood cells. It has been reported to be able to increase production of interleukin-2 and gamma-interferon, two biological response modifiers that are important for the growth and maintenance of white cells and for priming other body cells to resist viral attack. A recent claim by the company that makes it that the drug when administered to patients with ARC reduced the risk of progression to AIDS was supported by two panels of scientists. The drug has essentially no side effects.

Inosine pranobex, isoprinosine, inosiplex
This compound is a chemically synthesized complex salt containing para aminobenzoic acid and a derivative of inosine, a nucleotide related to the four in DNA. It has antiviral properties and is also an immune modulator. It was originally developed to enhance memory in the elderly, and has been found to improve the immune functioning of ARC patients in one study.

Alpha-interferon*,
Beta-interferon*, and
Gamma-interferon*
There are three major varieties of interferon: alpha- and beta-interferon are produced by most cells of the body in response to virus infection, and gamma-interferon is produced by cells of the immune system. *In vitro*, they check the growth of HIV and may cause regression, in some cases, of Kaposi's sarcoma accompanying AIDS virus infection. (See also Biological Response Modifiers.)

Interleukin-2*
This protein is made by lymphocytes and is a growth factor for them. Although useful for treatment of some cancers, it has not yet proved to be of benefit to AIDS patients. Trials are continuing, however, using interleukin-2 in combination with other drugs. (See also Biological Response Modifiers.)

D-Penicillamine* (Degussa Corporation, Carter-Wallace, Merck)
This compound is a portion of the penicillin molecule that has physiological actions of its own. It is often helpful in treating rheumatoid arthritis and Wilson's disease (a rare defect in copper storage) and it also inhibits HIV reproduction in humans. In tests carried out at George Washington University Medical Center, it suppressed the virus but also depressed T-cell levels in a number of AIDS patients with continually swollen glands. A high dose completely inhibited HIV

replication in pre-AIDS patients, and this effect persisted for 24 weeks after therapy ceased.

Nonoxynol-9
This compound is a widely used spermicide employed in most contraceptive creams, gels, and sponges. Even at a low concentration it kills HIV in about 30 seconds. Its use in a concentration of no less than 5%, in combination with a condom, should be mandatory for any male who might risk transmitting AIDS virus to a sex partner.

Peptide T* (Peninsula Laboratories)
It is claimed that this peptide blocks HIV infection by blocking the T4 sites where the virus attaches to cells. The effects claimed for it in AIDS patients are highly controversial and are described in detail later in this chapter.

Suramin
This drug is an antiparasitic agent. It is a strong inhibitor of HIV reverse transcriptase, but it also inhibits biological functioning of the immune system in AIDS patients. There is little clinical evidence that it can help these patients. In addition, it has severe side effects and cannot cross the brain-blood barrier. It is no longer being studied as a useful agent for treating AIDS.

Trimetrexate* (Warner Lambert)
This antimetabolite has a potent effect against the vitamin folic acid needed for nucleotide synthesis. It is also an anticancer drug and is being used to treat AIDS patients with *P. carinii* pneumonia who cannot tolerate standard therapy or in whom standard therapy has failed. A lethal dose is given, followed immediately by a rescuing dose of the vitamin folic acid. Human cells are rescued but not protozoan cells.

New Drugs Not Yet Being Clinically Tested

AME, amphotericin beta-methyl ester (Waksman Institute of Microbiology, Rutgers University)
This water soluble, antifungal antibiotic binds to cholesterol irreversibly. For this reason it is hoped it will bind to the HIV virus membrane which, since it is derived from human cell membranes, is rich in cholesterol. It may interfere with virus infectivity and also the ability of cells to bind the virus.

AS-101, Ammonium trichloro(dioxyoethylene-O,O') tellurate
This drug has immune-stimulating properties and minimal toxicity. It induces interleukin-2 production and proliferation of human lympho-

cytes *in vivo* and directly enhances the ratio of T4 to T8 cells in cultured cells from AIDS patients.

Castanospermine and 1-deoxynojirimycin (Fred Hutchinson Cancer Research Center)

Castanospermine is extracted from the seeds of an Australian chestnut tree. Workers at the University of Amsterdam and the Netherlands Cancer Institute in Amsterdam report that these two related drugs hamper the processing of sugar molecules important for the recognition and fusion of cells and viruses. Both these compounds greatly reduced the ability of infected cells to fuse with uninfected cells. In addition, the ability of HIV to spread infection after budding from infected cells was greatly reduced. Apparently, sugar molecules on cells that would normally attach to the gp120 protein are altered so they no longer can. Tests have been done in tissue culture and are now being performed in animal models. The results have been confirmed by others.

CS-87, 3′-azido 2′, 3′-dideoxyuridine

This compound is a very close relative of AZT but lacks the methyl (CH 3) group shown in Figure 7-1. Although it is 50-fold less potent than AZT, it is also only 1/23 as toxic to bone marrow cells.

DDA 2′, 3′dideoxyadenosine (Bristol-Myers)

This drug is very similar to DDC but has adenosine instead of cytidine as the parent nucleotide. It is less potent than DDC but also less toxic. Clinical testing is expected to begin early in 1988.

Treatment of *Pneumocystis carinii*

This is the most common opportunistic infection occurring in AIDS victims, and many are killed by it. Others may survive several bouts of the disease, only to be finally killed by the third or fourth attack. Treatment of the pneumonia cannot cure AIDS, but curing the pneumonia prolongs and makes life easier for those with AIDS.

Two drugs have been used to fight the pneumonia — which is caused by a parasite. One is an antibiotic, trimethoprim-sulfamethoxazole which kills the organism but causes allergic reactions in as many as 60 to 70% of the patients. A second drug is pentamidine, which also kills the parasite and is effective in many patients but can damage the kidneys and bone marrow to the extent of precluding its use. In patients already severely weakened in general, and with depressed bone marrow, the use of this drug is risky. Patients with a second bout of *Pneumocystis* are less likely to tolerate either drug a second time.

A possible third alternative is the drug trimetrexate which is highly toxic alone but is given with the antidote Leucovorin (folic acid). This combination has been used successfully in treating cancer patients. About 70% of 49 AIDS patients receiving this treatment have tolerated the drugs and survived the pneumonia. Leucovorin is the trade name for an essential vitamin, folic acid, small amounts of which are necessary in humans for the manufacture of nucleic acids. Trimetrexate is a potent anti-folic acid agent which is highly toxic to bone marrow cells.

Two other drugs being tested are Dapsone, originally developed to treat leprosy, and Fansidar, an antimalarial drug. Dapsone can damage the bone marrow, and Fansidar can cause severe allergic reactions, but they can help some patients who cannot tolerate other drugs.

To circumvent some toxicity problems, drugs can be placed in solution and given to patients in the form of an inhalant, as a mist or spray. In this way the drug mainly reaches the lungs where it is needed, and its toxic effects on other organs are diminished. Some of the drug that is sprayed might reach the liver and kidneys, but hopefully in lower concentrations than if it were given by mouth or injection.

If this reduced toxicity can be tolerated, it might be possible to give the drugs continually to patients at risk to pneumonia and thus prevent the disease from ever occurring. Efforts to accomplish this are under way. Dr. Donald Armstrong at Memorial Sloan Kettering Cancer Center in New York City has treated 220 AIDS patients with an aerosol containing pentamidine. He reports positive results but needs further time to evaluate them. Dr. Michael Lange of St. Luke's Roosevelt Hospital Center is more optimistic and believes that the use of Dapsone or pentamidine as a spray is very effective in preventing pneumonia in patients who already have had one occurrence of the disease or whose immune system is so damaged that they are likely to develop it.

Some General Thoughts on Drug Therapy

If a drug is developed that limits, but does not eliminate, the expression of AIDS virus, lifelong therapy may be necessary to protect infected persons. If this is so, the toxicity of the drug must be relatively low and the cost must be modest. AZT does not appear to meet these requirements.

Since AIDS virus can hide so well in the body, no drug may be able to root it out completely and provide a permanent cure. The best one might be able to hope for in drug therapy is keeping the virus in check and preventing the development of AIDS or ARC. A person might be able to continue leading a normal life under these circumstances but there would still be a possibility of transmitting the disease during sexual activity.

Biological (Immune) Response Modifiers

Granulocyte macrophage colony stimulating factor (GM-CSF)
This factor is one of the body's natural proteins, and belongs to the class of biological (immune) response modifiers. These substances act as growth stimulants for one or more cells in the immune system. Dr. Jerome Groopman at New England Deaconess Hospital in Boston has treated 16 patients with the protein. He reports that all patients' white blood cell counts resumed normal levels. In addition, patients with anemia had increases toward normalcy in their red cell counts. Side effects were minor including, mild aches, chills, and fever. Phlebitis, an inflammation of the veins, occurred in four patients.

GM-CSF is now being extensively tested in the treatment of AIDS, as well as in the treatment of cancer. Many types of cancer give rise to abnormalities in the immune system, including anemia and neutropenia (a low white cell count). Both conditions weaken patients and make them more susceptible to bacterial and other infections. Dr. Groopman also believes that GM-CSF may block the replication of HIV based on the finding that five out of nine patients experienced a lowering of viral proteins in their blood after treatment. The drug may be especially useful in patients who have both AIDS and some cancer such as Kaposi's sarcoma, lymphoma (cancer of the lymph glands), breast cancer, or lung cancer.

Suppressor T cells
The class of lymphocytes attacked by AIDS virus include the helper T cells, so called T4 or CD4 cells. In addition to this class, there are several other classes of T cells that have different receptors and different functions. One important group includes the T 8 or CD8 cells, suppressor cells functioning to damp down the immune system and prevent it from running out of control at the height of an infection.

Dr. Jay A. Levy and a group of colleagues at the University of California Medical School in San Francisco believe that these suppressor lymphocytes act to control the AIDS infection. They theorize that this may explain why some people infected with AIDS virus have not become ill. It is possible, they believe, that patients who have become ill can be treated by enhancing the body's supply of suppressor T cells.

The San Francisco group studied blood samples from three healthy men who had antibodies to AIDS virus in their blood indicating prior infection, but no detectable virus. When suppressor T cells were removed from the blood samples, the virus began to grow. When the suppressor T cells were added back to the samples, the growth of the virus was again inhibited. Further research suggested that the patients' own cells were more effective at inhibiting HIV than were suppressor cells from another person and that the suppressor T cells from the AIDS patients produced an unidentified substance that attacked the virus.

As a method of treatment, suppressor T cells would be removed from the patient's blood and treated with a growth factor such as interleukin-2 to stimulate them to grow and divide. Then the greatly increased numbers of cells would be reinjected into the AIDS victim.

Other scientists have remained skeptical about this interpretation of Dr. Levy's results and are not convinced that what appears to work in the test tube and petri dish will also work in human AIDS patients. However, further clinical testing of the theory would undoubtedly be worthwhile, and the new technique may be valuable, particularly, in combination with various drugs like AZT that suppress virus growth.

Interferons and other immune modulators
Interferons are proteins produced by cells infected by viruses or subjected to a large variety of other infections and stimulants. Interferons released by infected cells are taken up by uninfected cells and prime the uninfected cells to resist the viral infection and destroy the virus if it enters the primed cell.

This system is obviously of great importance to the body in its defense against disease. About 20 different interferons are produced in the body, all with slightly different properties and actions. Many interferons are manufactured commercially by new biotechnology developments using recombinant DNA techniques. The human genes for interferons are isolated and placed in bacteria or other suitable microorganisms which then use them to make large quantities of the respective interferons. These compounds can then be isolated in bulk quantities and highly purified for clinical use.

Is AIDS linked to gamma-interferon deficiency?
A research team at Cornell University Medical College headed by Dr. Henry W. Murray has linked AIDS to an inability of T cells to produce

gamma-interferon. Gamma-interferon is produced principally by cells of the immune system (other interferons are produced by almost all cells of the body) and so is very important in protecting immune cells from viruses like AIDS.

The Cornell researchers found that when T cells from 14 AIDS patients were exposed to specific infectious agents, cells from 13 of the patients completely failed to produce gamma-interferon. This could explain, in part at least, the breakdown of the immune system of patients which causes them to die of opportunistic infections. Treatment of macrophages with gamma-interferon enabled the macrophages to kill invading microorganisms and inhibit others. Several programs are presently underway for testing this treatment method alone and in conjunction with other AIDS remedies.

Tumor necrosis factor and gamma-interferon
Genentech, Inc., which makes tumor necrosis factor, has begun testing it against AIDS in combination with gamma-interferon. TNF is a natural cancer-fighting factor produced by the body when a cancer is growing. Dr. David V. Goeddel reports that the two substances reduced the amount of virus produced by cultured human cells in the test tube, as well as selectively killing cells that were already infected with HIV. The company is going forward with clinical trials of the combination. TNF is a very toxic material causing a wasting syndrome called cachexia. In addition, interferons produce side effects like the flu, including fever, aches, tiredness, loss of appetite, and sometimes mental symptoms.

Vaccines as a Cure for AIDS

In theory, a vaccine can be made for any infectious disease, whether it is viral, bacterial, or protozoan.

What is a Vaccine?

A vaccine is a preparation made from an infecting agent that can be injected into a person and will elicit an immune reaction. The preparation will not give the person injected the disease (possibly a slight fever and some soreness may occur) but will confer protection from a later invasion by the live infectious agent. Sometimes booster shots are needed after the initial injection. (For example, booster shots are recommended for tetanus every 5 years.)

Vaccines can be made from viruses, bacteria, and protozoa by

1. Heating the microorganism to kill it

2. Inactivating the microorganism with chemicals, for example, formaldehyde

3. Inactivating the microorganism with X-rays

4. Coupling a virus, or part of a virus, to another virus which is harmless or to which one is already immune; for example, vaccinia virus which has been used in smallpox vaccines in the past

5. Using one or more protein products from a virus or other microorganism for injection

6. Using parts of one or more protein products (peptides) from a virus and then injecting them.

In each case the killed or inactivated organism or the proteins or peptides from it must be injected into the person being immunized. The immune response is maximum after 1 to 2 weeks and then dies away, but the person is immune to the disease by virtue of memory cells which will recognize the live invader and respond to it so quickly that no effects will be felt. Immunity may last for years to decades to a lifetime.

Polio, a virus disease, has been conquered by the Salk vaccine. Vaccines are routinely prepared for new influenza viruses that appear from time to time. Smallpox, a virus disease, has been eliminated from the globe by means of a vaccine. A vaccine for *Salmonella*, a bacterium that causes food poisoning, is ready for testing. Also, a new vaccine for chicken pox has been made. Hundreds more vaccines are available for a large variety of diseases.

Why not a vaccine for AIDS?
AIDS is a complicated disease, and the answer to this question is a complicated one that must be divided into several parts. The different factors that make if difficult to prepare a vaccine against AIDS or test it are considered in turn.

1. *There are at least two major forms of AIDS virus:*
The virus that has already spread throughout the world is HIV. However, another form which is considerably different from HIV, namely, HIV-2, has appeared in Africa and will undoubtedly spread from this focus. Separate vaccines would be needed for HIV and for HIV-2. The two could probably be combined so that a single injection (or a series of injections) for immunization could be given. Complicating the situation is the fact that HTLV-I, the virus that causes a fatal leukemia

after about a 20 to 30-year lag period, is being passed, along with HIV, by about 5% of those infected with HIV. A third vaccine would be necessary to prevent its spread.

2. *All AIDS viruses are undergoing continuous variation (mutation)*: This variation may be considerable. It is found to occur principally in virus proteins that are not essential for reproduction or growth control. Thus the glycoprotein the virus uses for attachment to cells and the coat proteins that cover the virus vary most, while the reverse transcriptase (*pol*) and control proteins *tat* and *trs* vary little. A number of variant forms of the virus may be isolated from a single patient. If a vaccine is made for a particular type of HIV, in a year or two enough variation may have taken place to render it ineffective. The HIV is varying in all AIDS patients and there may now be dozens to hundreds of virus types. This continual drifting makes it difficult to pin the virus down with a single vaccine or even a multiple vaccine which would be much more difficult to prepare.

One way to get around making new vaccines continually, however, is to prime lymphocyte white cells against AIDS virus, as has been achieved by using a vaccinia-AIDS combined virus as a vaccine. The primed lymphocytes are less fastidious than antibodies in attacking minor variants of the AIDS virus proteins which may arise in the course of an infection. The primed lymphocytes provide cell-mediated immunity; that is, they attack human cells to which AIDS proteins or parts of proteins (peptides) are attached.

The situation with influenza virus is not quite the same. Variations rarely take place in a fairly big jump. A new, distinct type of virus appears and does not change significantly for a year or many years. The virus may rapidly infect large populations, but if a vaccine has been made for the new variety, it will be effective in the entire infected population.

3. *The AIDS virus may be hidden in cells in a form that is unresponsive to the immune system*: In Chapter 2 it was explained that when AIDS virus gets into cells its RNA is copied into DNA and that the DNA of the virus may then be inserted into the cell DNA and become part of the hereditary material of the cell. When it is in this form, the immune system does not recognize the virus DNA as foreign, and the virus DNA may stay inert in the cell for many years until some stimulus, perhaps another infection, triggers it to become active. Multiple copies of AIDS virus may then be rapidly made and spread through the blood, infecting various

white cells, brain cells, and others and bringing on the manifestations of the disease. The virus may also spread from cell to cell without entering the blood and in this way pretty much escape the immune system, particularly antibodies that have been made on initial contact with the virus or after injection of a vaccine.

The above are three major problems involved in the making of a vaccine against AIDS virus. There are others, but vaccines have already been made and new ones are in the testing stage. Assuming that one has been made, there will still be a large number of other problems and dilemmas concerning who should get the vaccine, for how long, how the results should be monitored and followed, and so on. For example,

Once a vaccine is available who should get it?
Assuming a safe vaccine has been made, who should get it? Persons who have antibodies to AIDS virus in their blood have already been infected with the virus and have mounted an immune defense against it. Nevertheless, their antibodies appear to be ineffective or weakly effective at most and do not destroy the virus. ARC or AIDS may develop after a number of years anyway. Why bother to give already infected persons the vaccine?

One could hope that the vaccine-induced antibodies and killer cells might be stronger or better able to destroy the virus and virus infected cells than the antibodies and cells already present. Certainly a new vaccine should be tried in already infected persons, at least on a voluntary basis.

It should be voluntary because there is a possibility that some vaccines will make the disease worse. This happened when sheep suffering from visna virus infection (an immunodeficiency disease) were given a vaccine prepared against visna virus and their disease became worse.

Who among uninfected persons should get the vaccine?
Obviously, any homosexuals who do not have a positive test for anti-bodies to AIDS virus would constitute a good group for testing the vaccine's efficacy, along with intravenous drug users and prostitutes not already infected with AIDS virus. Perhaps teen-agers would be another good group on which to try the vaccine.

Eventually, if the vaccine proves to be safe and effective beyond a reasonable doubt, then perhaps it should be given to everyone.

Determination of the effectiveness of any vaccine is bound to be troublesome and certainly a lengthy procedure covering many years. What kind of a control group would one use for comparison? If a person does not get AIDS, does it mean the person was not exposed to the disease or was exposed and warded off the infection because the vaccine established immunity?

The only positive result would be an unfortunate one where a person developed AIDS even after having been given the vaccine. This would suggest that the vaccine was either ineffective or that perhaps some other disease (herpes, influenza) compromised the immune system so that AIDS virus was able to get a foothold even though the vaccine may have initially produced immunity.

There are many questions and as yet no answers. That is why experts are conservative in predicting when an effective vaccine will be available. The consensus is that it will be about 5 years, but this may be wishful thinking. Nevertheless, active research is being conducted to produce many different kinds of vaccines, and some of them are being tested in animals and even humans in Zaire and in the United States.

Some African countries with heavy concentrations of AIDS infection in urban areas are especially good places to test vaccines, as many additional people are likely to be exposed. The nature of some of the vaccines being prepared and how they are being tested are described below.

Preparation and testing of different kinds of vaccines

Dr. Daniel Zagury, from the University of Pierre and Marie Curie in Paris, and his colleagues in France and Zaire have used the coat protein of AIDS virus inside vaccinia virus, a harmless virus formerly used in smallpox vaccinations. Dr. Zagury injected the combination virus into himself and into several Zairian volunteers to determine its effect.

French AIDS researcher in daring experiment

Among scientists there are always a few who in their anxiety to make progress are willing to overstep the boundaries of careful, painstaking experimentation to reach their goal. No one can argue that the goal, a cure for AIDS, is not an important one, but Dr. Zagury has been the object of severe criticism for using himself as an experimental animal to test an AIDS virus vaccine. Joining him in the experiment were 10 African AIDS patients who were injected to see if their immune systems could be bolstered and the ravages of the disease stopped. Also, 10 uninfected Africans and a French colleague were injected to measure their body's response to the vaccine.

Some scientists feel that Dr. Zagury's experiment was scientifically meaningless. Others admire his boldness. The preliminary results of his experiments, which were presented at the Third International Congress on AIDS in Washington D.C., were impressive. He reported that he had succeeded in obtaining a large amount of antibodies and helper T cells that killed the virus in a test tube and may perhaps be able to kill an invading HIV particle or an infected cell in the body. The only way this could be determined would be for Dr. Zagury to infect himself, however no one expects him to be bold enough to do that. Nevertheless, an important point has been proved, namely, that the recombinant vaccinia-HIV virus Dr. Zagury used can provoke antibodies against AIDS virus and helper T lymphocytes that can kill AIDS virus-infected cells in humans.

In an article in *Nature* Dr. Zagury and his colleagues report that the vaccine stimulated the production of antibodies against the coat protein and also primed white cells (killer lymphocytes) which can attack infected cells. It still has to be established whether these immune responses could successfully fend off invasion by AIDS virus. The cell response (cell-mediated immunity) is especially important, as the cells might be able to attack different variants of the virus, while the neutralizing antibodies might be restricted to the type of coat protein in the vaccine. Further studies on this vaccine are being watched with interest.

Two groups in this country are using this technique as well. One group, headed by Dr. Shin-Lok Hu of Oncogen Company in Seattle, placed the envelope gene, which makes the glycoprotein of HIV, into vaccinia virus. They used macaque monkeys for subjects, and the monkeys made antibodies to the AIDS glycoprotein. Furthermore, monkey white cells were triggered to produce an immune response against AIDS virus. The second group, consisting of Dr. Bernard Moss and his co-workers at the National Institute of Arthritis and Infectious Diseases and the National Cancer Institute, treated monkeys with a similar recombinant vaccinia virus, removed the monkeys' white cells, and exposed these cells to live AIDS virus infected cells in a test tube. The monkey white cells did not become infected with AIDS virus. A word of caution is in order: vaccinia virus is harmless to people who are healthy, but it can cause serious infection in anyone with a weakened immune system. To prevent this from happening, Dr. Charles Flexner, at the Laboratory of Viral Diseases, National Institute of

Allergy and Infectious Diseases, and co-workers found that when a gene for interleukin-2 was placed in the combined *vaccinia*-HIV-protein construct in a way that allowed interleukin-2 to be made and expressed in the cell, as well as outside the cell, hairless mice (which have an almost complete lack of T cells) were protected from an otherwise fatal infection from the *vaccinia*. This technique would be expected to work in humans, since the immune systems of humans and mice are similar, but extensive testing would have to be done to make sure.

Less promising results with recombinant vaccinia virus were obtained when it was tested using nine chimpanzees. Four were given the vaccine-HIV recombinant, and five were given a control vaccinia vaccine with no HIV. After the animals were immunized they were given a high or low dose of AIDS virus. Although the chimpanzees given the recombinant HIV-vaccinia vaccine had antibodies to HIV and T cells that responded to HIV, all four had HIV virus in their lymphocytes, indicating that the vaccine did not protect them from subsequent infection. One of the animals given the plain vaccinia vaccine and then a high dose of AIDS virus developed substantial and persistent lymphadenopathy (swollen lymph glands, sore throat, fever), but the four animals immunized with the recombinant vaccine and then given a high dose of HIV showed no symptoms of disease.

This experiment suggests that vaccinia-HIV glycoprotein is not promising as a candidate vaccine. It does not prevent subsequent infection with AIDS virus, although it is possible that it might slow down or prevent the appearance of disease symptoms. One animal is hardly enough to support this possibility, and tests with humans will have to be run on a large scale to obtain a firm conclusion.

AIDS Vaccine Workshop

A scientific workshop on AIDS vaccines was held at the National Institutes of Health in March 1987. Gerald Quinnan of the FDA predicted that clinical trials for an AIDS vaccine would be conducted in the United States soon.

Vaccine trials in the United States

Plans for the first test of a vaccine have been announced by Micro-GeneSys of West Haven, Connecticut, and the federal government. This is the first test to be authorized in the United States and will be conducted on 81 volunteers at the National Institutes of Health by the end of 1987. The study will investigate only the safety of the vaccine and the degree to which it stimulates the formation of protective antibodies. It will not try to determine if a person can truly be protected against AIDS which would require a much longer and more complicated large-scale test involving hundreds to thousands of patients.

MicroGeneSys vaccine was the first to be thoroughly tested in animals including mice, guinea pigs, rabbits, Rhesus monkeys, and two chimpanzees. The vaccine is cultured from an insect cell. If the initial 6-month study is successful, a longer, 100 to 200-patient study lasting a year will be necessary, and if this is successful, the full-scale test mentioned above will be carried out. Still not clear is how it will be determined whether the recipients have been exposed to AIDS virus and if the vaccine is effective.

A second AIDS vaccine, a recombinant made from vaccinia virus and AIDS virus coat proteins, was approved for testing late in 1987 by Oncogen, a subsidiary of Bristol-Myers. Thirty to 60 healthy volunteers, homosexuals not infected with AIDS virus, will be given the vaccine and compared to a like group given plain vaccinia vaccine. The initial tests will be to determine the vaccine's safety and the particular type of antibodies it will force the immune system to produce. This vaccine suffers from the already mentioned defect of possibly not working against variants of HIV.

Three major questions were addressed at the vaccine workshop.

1. What is an acceptable result for a vaccine trial? Protection against infection, protection against viral transmission to another person, or protection against the onset of active disease in an already infected person, or any combination of these?

Obviously protection against all three would be ideal, but some researchers believe protection against infection may never be achieved.

2. How well do the results of preclinical tests (in tissue culture and in animals) predict a vaccine's usefulness in treating humans?

There appears to be a general consensus that the results obtained in a test tube or in animals do not predict very well what will happen in the human. Chimpanzees illustrate this. They can be infected with AIDS virus and not develop the disease. None of the virus vaccines made so far protect chimpanzees from infection. However, this does not mean that the same results will be obtained in humans as in chimpanzees. After all, the latter do not get the disease, while humans do, and this is a big difference. Dr. Jonas Salk has cautioned against using chimpanzees for vaccine screening.

Dr. Patricia Fultz of the Federal Centers for Disease Control reports that Rhesus macaque monkeys can be infected by HIV-2 the new virus spreading in the African population. This finding is deemed to be important in providing a better model for the testing of vaccines.

3. Which human populations should receive test vaccines?

With regard to this question, there has been a shift in thinking to include groups already infected with AIDS, particularly children born to AIDS-infected mothers.

Despite the misgivings of other scientists, Dr. Jonas Salk, chief discoverer of the live anti-polio vaccine, has been developing a vaccine based on whole AIDS virus. He hopes to have it ready for testing by early 1988. Dr. Neil Flynn, chief of the AIDS unit at the University of California Medical Center in Sacramento, says, "We don't offer any false hopes or promises, in fact the subject could get worse." He is referring to the fact that the vaccine will be tested in people already exposed to the virus. It is intended to keep those already infected from developing the disease and possibly reduce their infectiousness.

Use of Viral Protein Pieces to Make an AIDS Vaccine

A group of scientists led by Dr. Scott D. Putney of Repligen Company of Cambridge, Massachusetts, has prepared a genetically engineered piece of the outer coat glycoprotein (gp 120) of HIV. This piece can be made in quantity and when injected into animals causes them to form antibodies that can neutralize HIV in a test tube. Goats produce antibodies to the fragment to the same extent that they do to the whole protein. Thus the whole protein may not be necessary to make an effective vaccine against AIDS. It is not yet known, however, whether these antibodies when made by humans can protect them against the virus. Also, because many strains of HIV exist, antibodies to a fragment may protect against only some strains. The recombinant protein fragment is unable to prevent HIV infected cells from binding to uninfected cells or to the T4 receptor of lymphocytes. This may be a drawback to this type of vaccine, but research and testing are continuing.

Vaccine work at Genentech is producing a slightly larger version of the glycoprotein of HIV by culturing mammalian cells. This gp 130, when inoculated into rabbits or guinea pigs, also causes them to produce antibodies to gp 120 which neutralize HIV *in vitro*.

Anti-Idiotype Vaccines

Dr. Hilary Koprowski, head of the Wistar Research Institute in Philadelphia, is working with this novel approach. Antibodies are made to HIV by infecting an animal (sheep, guinea pig, and so on) with the virus. The antibodies (called idiotype antibodies) are isolated and purified and then injected into a different animal (mouse or pig). Antibodies against the antibodies are then produced. The primary antibodies against HIV can be considered to be related to HIV as a glove turned inside out is related to a glove turned right side out. The secondary antibodies turn the virus right side out again and therefore bear the image of the original HIV in their structure (anti-idiotype antibodies).

Since anti-idiotype antibodies carry the image of HIV, it is possible that injection of these antibodies into the body will produce antibodies against them that will also be effective in neutralizing HIV virus itself. Anti-idiotype antibodies may therefore serve as a vaccine similar to HIV but without any risk of producing the disease. Some success has already been obtained with anti-idiotype vaccines against cancer in animals. However, it is a long shot that such a vaccine will be effective in preventing AIDS, and much work remains to be done to effectively produce anti-idiotype antibodies in quantity and to test their effectiveness in humans.

Anti-Thymosin Antibodies

Thymosin alpha-1 is a hormone secreted by the thymus gland. It acts primarily on helper T cells (T4 lymphocytes), enhancing the expression of T-cell markers produced during maturation of cells, and also stimulates the production of interleukin-2 and gamma-interferon. Thymosin alpha-1 has also been found to restore helper T-cell function and prolong survival in clinical trials with patients with lung cancer who have been treated with radiation.

In patients with AIDS or ARC, thymosin alpha-1 levels were found to be reduced below normal. Also found in the blood of these patients was a protein like thymosin alpha-1 but without its biological activity. The origin of this protein was a puzzle resolved by the finding that the *gag* coat protein of HIV has in some portions of its structure, regions very similar to thymosin alpha-1. The body produced antibodies to these portions which mimicked thymosin alpha-1 and these antibodies reacted positively in tests for the hormone.

A group of investigators led by Dr. P. S. Sarin at the National Cancer Institute prepared antibodies to thymosin alpha-1 in rabbits and found that these antibodies effectively blocked AIDS virus replication in cells in tissue culture. These workers suggested that anti-thymosin antibodies might prove useful as a basis for developing a novel vaccine for AIDS virus. However, one problem with this is that antibodies against an important hormone like thymosin alpha-1 will probably reduce the levels of this hormone, which appears so necessary to the well-being of the immune system, to a point that will do more harm than good. Injections of thymosin alpha-1 itself might be of benefit to AIDS patients in view of its biological actions as described above.

Protection of Volunteers Who Test AIDS Virus Vaccines

Any person who volunteers to test an AIDS vaccine will thereafter become positive in the ELISA test for antibodies to AIDS virus. Such a person, however, will not have the virus in his or her blood or cells and will not be able to transmit the disease to another person.

To protect such individuals from the usual stigmas affecting those who test positive for AIDS virus antibodies, or from discrimination in insurance, housing, and the job market, each volunteer will receive a notarized document saying that he or she has developed AIDS virus antibodies as the result of a vaccine trial. The Bureau of Engraving and Printing is working to produce counterfeit-proof identification cards which will be needed if any large-scale use of a vaccine becomes feasible.

It will be possible to obtain proof of whether a person has had a vaccine or a natural infection of AIDS virus by running a Western blot test. An individual injected with vaccine will develop antibodies only to the protein or possibly two proteins present in the vaccine. A person with a natural infection will develop antibodies to at least several HIV proteins, including *env*, gp120, gp41, *gag*, p55, p24 p17, and *pol*. The Western blot test does not distinguish between injection of a vaccine made from the whole virus and a natural infection, however, and in this case an identification card would have to be the proof.

Use of Substances That Block the Entry of AIDS into Cells

Peptide T
This substance was developed by Dr. Candace B. Pert of the National Institute of Mental Health and has been approved for testing in AIDS

patients. The efficacy of peptide T, which works to block the T4 receptor on helper lymphocytes, is highly controversial. Dr. Pert and scientists of the Oncogen unit of Bristol-Myers strongly support peptide T's utility, but Dr. William Haseltine, of the Dana Farber Cancer Institute in Boston, as well as other academic and industrial labs, are skeptical of its usefulness.

Dr. Pert treated only four patients in a small pilot study; and the results were promising, but the number treated was too small to be convincing, and a larger study of 50 patients is now underway.

If free peptide T, which is part of the envelope glycoprotein of AIDS virus, is injected into a patient, it will attach to the peptide T receptor on the cell membrane, thus preventing the virus from attaching to the cell. Attachment is necessary if the virus is to be drawn into the cell and infect it.

It is interesting that peptide T was isolated from brain cells, which have receptors probably identical with the receptors on T4 lymphocytes. High concentrations of these receptors were found on surface cells of the cerebral cortex and the hippocampus, which are regions of the brain known to be involved in higher mental functions. These functions are often impaired in AIDS patients because the virus can attach to the receptors and infect these particular brain cells.

Peptide T has eight amino acids in a string — alanine, serine, threonine, threonine, threonine, asparagine, tyrosine, and threonine. This many threonines so close together is unusual, and scientists have named the compound, T peptide for this reason. (Note that the peptide is part of the virus HIV glycoprotein and not the T cell receptor protein, but it is the part of the glycoprotein that gives the good fit with the receptor.)

Peptide T is also similar to vasoactive intestinal peptide, a nerve peptide long known to exist in the human intestine as well as in regions of the brain. This nerve peptide is believed to be important in regulating emotion, perception of pain, and related functions. Its receptors also fit the key attachment of the AIDS virus. Thus the virus could also invade intestinal cells.

The planned trials of peptide T will use synthetic copies and variants of peptide T in an effort to block the receptors and halt progression of the disease. A long-range possibility is to string together many repeat tandem sequences of peptide T, and possibly variants of it, in a protein which can be used directly as a vaccine or to provoke formation of a vaccine in animals. This vaccine could then be used in humans.

Use of CD4 receptor to prevent AIDS infection

CD4 is the protein receptor on helper T4 cells, as well as other cells (e.g. in the brain), that attracts HIV. The receptor binds firmly to the virus, and the receptor with bound virus is then taken into the cell, allowing the virus eventually to multiply and spread the infection.

For several years Dr. Richard Axel and his colleagues at Columbia University in New York City have been studying this binding process, showing that CD4 protein plays a crucial role in the cellular spread of the virus. These and other investigators asked, Why not inject large quantities of CD4 protein into humans and fool the virus into thinking it was attaching to cells? If enough of the decoy protein is picked up by the virus, the virus may be unable to enter cells it normally attacks.

CD4 protein could benefit AIDS patients in several ways. First it may directly prevent the spread of virus to healthy cells. Also, it could prevent infected cells from clumping together with healthy cells, which they do through CD4 protein. Finally, cells infected with AIDS virus constantly shed a viral protein that sticks to the CD4 of healthy helper T4 cells, targeting them for destruction by the patient's own immune system. Pure CD4 protein could conceivably sop up this protein and protect healthy T4 cells.

Many different research groups are working on this approach. Scientists from Genentech and Dr. Jerome Groopman's laboratory at New England Deaconess Hospital in Boston report that they can insert the gene for CD4 into animal cells which then make the protein. The protein can then be isolated and purified. In tissue culture CD4 protein has prevented over 99% of cells from being infected with AIDS virus. How effective CD4 would be in the body is not yet known. Also, it is possible that the protein could produce undesirable side effects. It is, in addition, not expected that CD4 could eliminate all the AIDS virus in an infected person, but it might be combined with AZT or other drugs or immune factors to stop the multiplication of HIV and keep a person healthy. Dr. Samuel Broder of the National Cancer Institute says, "It all sounds good," but it is estimated that it will be several years before adequate clinical testing can be completed.

It was shown by Dr. Carolyn Dolye and Dr. Jack L. Strominger, the latter who is Higgins Professor of biochemistry at Harvard University, that the CD4 surface protein cell marker or receptor binds specifically to other cells that bear class II histocompatibility proteins. This means of course that the AIDS virus glycoprotein, gp120, which firmly binds this CD4 protein, must have a sequence in common or very similar to that of a class II histocompatibility protein.

Prospects for Treatment of AIDS — Chemicals and Immune Stimulants

According to experts, AZT is at present the best hope of many AIDS patients. The use of dideoxycytidine together with AZT may be more effective. It is very likely that the use of some combination of biological response modifiers—such as gamma-interferon and tumor necrosis factor or interleukin-2 and GM-CSF will be helpful in stimulating the immune system and the development of killer cells capable of destroying AIDS virus-infected cells. We already know of some treatments that do this. It may be possible to take these killer cells outside the body and, on treatment with the proper growth factors, greatly augment their number. Reinjection into the patient could result in wholesale killing of infected cells with resulting clinical improvement. Finally, an agent such as AL-721 or nonoxynol-9, when used intravenously or orally, may further kill or prevent growth of the virus. A combination of all three therapies may be expected to give long-term remission of AIDS in sick patients and long-term prevention of the expression of AIDS in well patients who have been infected with HIV. This triple combination could be in place within a year. Better drugs and vaccines, however, are a few years down the road. Hopefully, a vaccine based on an invariant protein of HIV will protect infected and uninfected alike but this hope remains for the near future, perhaps the next 5 years.

I remain confident that AIDS will be essentially conquered in highly industrialized countries by the year 2000. Taking care of the Third World will require a massive effort, like that waged against smallpox, and will take longer.

Vaccines

Preliminary tests on vaccines are already being carried out on human volunteers. The development of successful vaccines for widespread use still appears, however, to be at least 5 years away. Even if they were ready for widespread use, many dilemmas concerning whom to test, how to test, what observations to make, and many other questions have not been answered. It is not possible to predict whether a vaccine can be prepared that will prevent one from getting AIDS or that will prevent the development of AIDS in a person already infected.

Widespread government financial and technical help will be necessary to make large quantities of any potentially useful vaccine.

Pharmaceutical companies will have to be spared the possible serious liabilities that might result from any harmful side effects of a vaccine. Otherwise they will not be able to participate in its manufacture and dissemination.

At this moment there is serious doubt about whether AIDS can be combatted solely by a vaccine.

Dextran sulfate has been suggested to be a useful drug in treating AIDS. Dextran is a polymer made by bacteria in which the common sugar of the blood, glucose, has been linked together in a specific way in mostly linear chains but with some cross links between chains. Sulfuric acid groupings are then added to the glucose units in the laboratory to give dextran sulfate.

The drug has blocked the AIDS virus from destroying cells in laboratory tests. It is presently being tested in the United States. Dextran sulfate is not available for medical use in the United States but has been obtained by an estimated 2,500 Americans, chiefly from Japan. New laws allow Americans to import by mail up to a 30 day supply of an experimental drug even if it has not been approved for use in the United States.

Since the molecular weight and degree of branching of dextrans from different bacterial sources can vary greatly, as can the number of sulfuric acid groupings placed on the dextran, it is not at all clear what is the optimum drug to use. Different dextran sulfates may have markedly different medical efficacy against the AIDS virus. Testing all the possibilities is going to take considerable time.

Core antigen, antibody levels vary as disease progresses

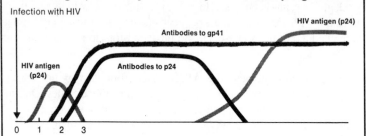

Infection with HIV

HIV antigen (p24)

Antibodies to gp41

HIV antigen (p24)

Antibodies to p24

0   1   2   3

Months after infection

A hypothetical patient's profile shows the inverse relationship between two key HIV markers—the core antigen p24 and antibodies raised against it. p24, which appears in blood soon after infection, is neutralized by a rising tide of anti-p24 antibodies. As long as the level of these antibodies remains high, the patient's condition is stable. But months or years later, when the virus starts replicating again, its stepped-up production of p24 overwhelms the immune defenses by complexing all the available anti-p24 antibodies. By contrast, the level of antibody to the transmembrane glycoprotein gp41 remains fairly constant

Source: Abbott Laboratories

CHAPTER 8
HOW TO GET HELP FOR AIDS

Introduction; God's Love We Deliver; The government's policy on AIDS research; AIDS research at the National Institute of Arthritis and Infectious Diseases (NIAID); What to do if you test positive for AIDS; The President's panel on AIDS; How the 1988 presidential candidates look at AIDS.

"You can't tell if someone has been infected by the AIDS virus by looking at him or her. But you aren't in danger of getting the disease unless you engage in risky behavior with someone who is infected."

— Anthony S. Fauci, M.D.
Director, National Institute of Allergy and Infectious Diseases and Coordinator of the National Institutes of Health AIDS Research

8

HOW TO GET HELP FOR AIDS

Introduction

The office of the Surgeon General of the United States and the medical news departments of the *Journal of the American Medical Association* and the journal, *Occupational Health and Safety* have all compiled lists of resource centers in the United States that provide information about AIDS. Most of these centers supply free printed information of various kinds to anyone who wants to learn more about the disease. State and city sources of information also have printed information, as do many local sources — schools, churches, health departments, community groups of all kinds, and private physicians. There is a tremendous wealth of information available, and if one cannot obtain answers to all of one's questions, there are numerous hot lines that may be able to help.

Some of these groups are listed in appendix 1. Although those included are mostly formal organizations, there are many informal groups, particularly among gays, that are well provided with information and can be very helpful. While they are largely information sources rather than welfare groups, most of them have information on how to actually find support, financial aid, housing, medical care, medicines, counseling, psychiatric care, and the like.

God's Love We Deliver

An organization with such a noble name sounds like a missionary group or perhaps a florist that specializes in flowers for religious purposes. Nothing of the sort. It is a small group that provides gourmet meals for about 30 AIDS victims and it is located in a kitchen in West Park

Presbyterian Church in New York City. It was founded by Ganga Stone who worked as a volunteer at Cabrini Hospice. One day she was asked to take food to the home of a man with AIDS. She was distressed at how bad he looked and how terrified and lonely he seemed to be. So she began to deliver take-out meals to three or four people, teaming up with her roommate Jane Ellen Best. They used their own money, bringing whatever was requested in the way of food. The organization grew and was funded in part by the state health department and money from donation cans left around the city. Volunteers always appeared when needed. Other donations for a cooler and a delivery van appeared unsolicited.

The meals are large and are delivered between 11 a.m. and 2:30 p.m. so they can be eaten for both lunch and dinner. A recent meal consisted of duck pate, swordfish kabobs, basmati rice, red cabbage salad, and baked stuffed apple. Rich, nutritive hot soups are commonly served. Patients that are too sick to eat complex rich meals get simpler purees.

Stone hopes the organization can expand soon by setting up drop-off points where volunteers can pick up and deliver food. Part of the job of those who deliver is to talk to and cheer up the patients. In return, the stories, thoughts, and feelings of some of the people the volunteers have met are being recorded, perhaps to benefit others with AIDS, perhaps to benefit us all. (Excerpted from an article by Trish Hall in *The New York Times*, October 14, 1987, with the kind permission of the editors.)

The Government's Policy on AIDS Research

After a late and slow start, the U.S. government is revving up to provide AIDS research and treatment at a faster rate. Federal AIDS funding from 1984 through 1988 is indicated in Table 8-1. Millions more are being spent by private companies for AIDS research.

Critics of the administration say that the money appropriated is not nearly enough, and this is undoubtedly true to some extent. One area that is seriously underfunded is treatment and rehabilitation of intravenous drug users, the most critical source of AIDS virus transmission. Millions more are needed for this.

The government has received good mileage for its research money. Never in history has so much been learned about a virus so fast. We now know more about the AIDS virus than any other. Paradoxically, because of its complexity, we need to know much more, particularly about treatment with chemicals and vaccines. This kind of knowledge comes slowly and with difficulty and is somewhat dependent on the

Table 8-1 Federal AIDS funding in millions of dollars[a]

	1984	1985	1986	1987	1988[b]	1989[b]
Public Health Service	61	109	234	494	791 (950)[c]	1145
Federal Medicaid share	0	0	130	210	375	
Veteran's Administration	6	12	24	30	44	
Department of Defense	0	0	79	74	52	
TOTAL	66	121	467	808	1421	

[a]Source: Office of Management and Budget.
[b]Estimated.
[c]Actually appropriated by Congress.

number of patients available. Unfortunately for the country, this number is still increasing rapidly, but the point of leveling off may only be a few years away. Education is another area that is starved for funds. The government should be giving assistance to the states, in addition to running its own programs. Although some funds for this purpose are being spent by the Public Health Service, they are far from adequate.

How much funding is enough? Throwing money at a problem will not always solve it. There has to be an expanding base of specialists of all categories — epidemiologists, molecular biologists, virologists, medical research practitioners, physicians, psychologists, paramedical personnel, and others — who are familiar with the disease. Also, educational experts and, particularly scientists with a knowledge of AIDS and who can communicate with the public are greatly needed. With expanding numbers of such groups, more money could be used effectively and efficiently.

For the present (1988) the Institute of Medicine of the National Academy of Sciences says $1 billion for research and a billion dollars for education should be enough. The amount appropriated, $1.421 billion, does not compare favorably with this estimate at all, especially if one considers that much of the $1.421 billion will go for the treatment and care of indigent patients. The Institute of Medicine hasn't even given a figure for this expense, but it is clear that for 1988 at least $2 billion dollars will be necessary. Twenty thousand patients at $100,000 per year will require $2 billion.

AIDS Research at the National Institute of Arthritis and Infectious Diseases (NIAID)

Headed by Dr. Anthony S. Fauci, the National Institute of Arthritis and Infectious Diseases (NIAID) has a budget that has doubled from a few years ago and is now at $600 million. Is this enough to oversee research on drug and vaccine development for *all* infectious diseases, including AIDS? Of course other institutes, particularly the National Cancer Institute, and other agencies contribute much to the AIDS program. One should not overlook the Federal Centers for Disease Control which have done so much to let us know where we stand with respect to AIDS' spread and transmission.

NIAID's research program has six major divisions:

The natural history and epidemiology of the disease

The nature of the virus itself

The pathogenesis of AIDS

Drug therapy

Vaccine development

Rebuilding of the immune system

This is obviously a very big program, and to ensure effective progress NIAID probably requires a major investment in new laboratories, equipment, and personnel. None of this has as yet been done.

If NIAID is to take the lead in these areas, it must stay abreast of all activity in industry, government, and academia and also integrate the efforts, provide direction, see that there is no waste or duplication of effort, and exercise leadership.

Many of the following facilities have already been set up

AIDS treatment evaluation units

National cooperative drug discovery groups

AIDS clinical studies groups

NIAID vaccine evaluation units

Special AIDS hospitals.

These organizations are listed in Appendix 2.

The Public Health Service has set up a task force on AIDS, and the major areas, those persons in charge, and the chain of command are shown in Figure 8-1.

One of the big problems mentioned by many leaders in the field is dissemination of information. Industry is pictured as being particularly lax in this respect. Everyone now knows that any useful finding of a new

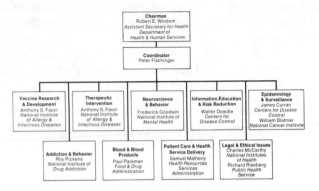

Figure 8-1 The Public Health Service task force on AIDS.

drug, a vaccine, or some new fact about the virus might be capitalized in the hundreds of millions of dollars range. One scientist says, "The sharing of data and ideas is significantly less than in other fields I have been in. I had never before seen such a lack of candor in discussing new ideas and the sharing of approaches. What we have is a series of close mouthed relationships." This of course is unfortunate because science thrives best when there is openness and give and take concerning ideas and data.

Scientists at NIH can accept consulting fees from industry. This does not sound like a good idea because industry does not want its new developments discussed until they are ready for marketing or patenting. This lack of communication could lead to many problems, duplication of effort, production of a faulty product, greater time and cost to develop a product, and other difficulties. Under many circumstances these problems could be condoned, but, in the case of AIDS, where lives hang on the need for maximum speed and efficiency in the development of new ideas, there is no excuse for such lack of communication.

Under NIAID, 19 AIDS treatment evaluation units have been set up around the country, and additional centers are being established. Cooperative drug discovery groups and clinical studies groups have also been set up (Appendix 2). However there is some criticism of NIAID's direction. They have been accused of taking their own favorite drugs and forcing their network to look at them instead of allowing the network to do their own drug development work. A similar network for drug development set up by the National Cancer Institute has been allowed considerable latitude to develop its own ideas.

There are also many complaints from drug companies about the difficulty of new drug development. The FDA is pictured as giving no clear policy guidance and of trying to predict the probability of success of a new drug rather than allowing investigators to go quickly to phase I tests that are designed to determine its safety and efficacy.

Small companies have complained that NIAID favors the larger companies and that good, innovative ideas are not being heard. Criticism that the government is still moving too slowly is frequent. Michael Callen of the People with AIDS Coalition says, "We don't have time for the research systems already in place to move at the glacial pace for which bureaucracies are famous."

Despite the complaints, bruised egos, duplication of effort, and wrong leads followed, everyone working on the AIDS problem, and the number is now in the tens of thousands, is moving in the same direction—to cure the disease and prevent its transmission. Like an army trying to find its way through a dark, impenetrable forest, eventually these researchers will get through to light and safety.

What To Do If You Test Positive for AIDS

It's entirely possible that I have AIDS. In 1984 I had an attack of acute appendicitis and had to have immediate surgery. Unfortunately, I had just started to take an anticoagulant a week before; my blood was unclottable, and the surgeons could not operate until it was. They gave me at least 6 pints of serum intravenously to flush the anticoagulant out of my blood. Serum is blood from which the cells, red and white, have been removed. It contains all the viruses and any other harmful material that donors may have contributed.

I have strongly emphasized that anyone who might have AIDS should have a test done. It's important to know where and how to have this done. The best idea is to ask your physician or, if this is not convenient, call the local public health service, Red Cross, or blood bank for directions to the nearest laboratory where they are being performed. Most often the testing is free or will be paid for by your health insurance. Large cities have a number of free AIDS testing stations set up. Try to stay away from local concerns that might be advertising quick tests for $29.95 with results in 5 hours. The results may be of dubious validity and involve only a single test which is not enough.

Be aware also of the meaning and interpretation of the tests (Chapter 5). The first test done will be an ELISA. If positive, it should be repeated. If positive the second time, you should have a Western blot test done, and only if this test is positive should you believe that you are infected with AIDS virus.

If your tests are negative don't buy the champagne quite yet. If you have had a sexual contact or intravenous injection of a drug within the past 6 months, remember it may take that long for antibodies to the virus to build up in your blood to the point where they will give a positive test. Have another test in 6 months.

A single ELISA is just not enough. Anywhere from 1 to 5% of the tests may give a false positive. That's why it is necessary to repeat the ELISA and then run a Western blot test.

Let's assume you really are positive. Do you panic? Certainly not — start thinking of the positive aspects. First of all, data indicate that it takes an average of at least 5 years for AIDS to develop, and it may take a lot longer for some. There are people who have been carrying AIDS virus for 8 to 9 years with no sign of the illness. Then, even if you get the disease, the onset is slow and a large number of people with AIDS disease have survived 5 years or more. In 10 years it is quite likely there will be drugs or vaccines that will prolong life indefinitely or even provide a cure. You may easily live to three score and ten.

One of the things you must do is to read and agree to practice the responsible behavior listed at the end of Chapter 9. You must be a responsible and moral person and remember virtue is its own reward.

Another thing you must do is take good care of yourself. The longer you stay healthy, the longer the virus may remain dormant. Eat properly, exercise regularly, avoid stress, get enough sleep, and above all have an optimistic attitude. You have to believe you can win against AIDS. I feel confident that there are people with AIDS alive today who are going to win. You could be one of them. It would probably be a good idea for you to confide the results to your doctor, and if you feel very upset and depressed, get counseling to help you face up to your problem.

By the way — my test for AIDS was negative, and I am not usually that lucky.

The President's Panel on AIDS

W. Eugene Mayberry, an administrator at the Mayo Clinic in Rochester, Minnesota, was named head of the President's Commission on AIDS. He has been an administrator at the Mayo Clinic since 1971 and chaired its board of governors since 1976. He is a scientist who has done significant work with thyroid hormones and is described as a good leader and organizer. The panel was charged with issuing a preliminary report after 90 days and a final report after 1 year and then go out of business. Its purpose is to advise the President and relevant secretaries about the public health dangers of AIDS and related conditions, including their medical, legal, ethical, social, and economic impact. The panel will also make recommendations to federal, state, and local officials about steps they can take to protect the public from AIDS, assist in finding a cure, and care for patients.

Other members are

Colleen Conway Welch, professor and Dean of Nursing at Vanderbilt University in Nashville who represents the views of the nursing profession.

John J. Creedon, chief executive officer of the Metropolitan Life Insurance Company in New York City, who has been involved in examining the implications of the AIDS epidemic for the insurance industry; his company is conducting a major AIDS education plan.

Theresa L. Crenshaw, San Diego director of the Crenshaw Clinic which specializes in treating sexual problems; she argues that changes in sexual behavior are needed to stem the threat of AIDS.

Richard M. DeVos, cofounder and president of the Amway Company.

Burton J. Lee, practicing physician and former president of the medical staff at the Memorial Sloan-Kettering Cancer Center in New York City—a major AIDS treatment center; his specialty is treatment of lymphomas or cancers of the lymph glands.

John Cardinal O'Connor, Archbishop of New York whose archdiocese has been active in helping AIDS patients.

Penny Pullen, Republican leader of the Illinois State House of Representatives, who has sponsored bills requiring AIDS antibody testing of marriage license applicants and requiring health officials to trace the sexual contacts of infected people.

Cary SerVaas, Indianapolis physician and journalist, who as editor and publisher of the *Saturday Evening Post* has turned the journal into a medically oriented magazine for the common citizen; she was chosen for her educational know-how.

Woodrow A. Myers, Jr., health commissioner of Indiana, a state known for starting one of the best and earliest AIDS education programs.

Frank Lilly, Chairman of the genetics department at Albert Einstein Medical Center in New York; he is familiar with retroviral diseases similar to AIDS. He is the only homosexual on the committee.

William B. Walsh, founder, president, and medical director of HOPE, a project which brings health care and health education to areas of the developing world.

Admiral James D. Watkins, Chief of Naval Operations from 1982 to 1986.

The President's AIDS panel was beleaguered with criticism soon after it was formed. Among other things it was accused of being stocked with right-wing ideologists, antihomosexuals, and scientific illiterates. Its chairman, Eugene Mayberry, resigned along with the co-chairman, Woodrow Myers, Jr., early in October 1987, probably because of internal bickering and dissent within the ranks. Admiral James Watkins was then appointed the new chairman, and left behind was a highly conservative group.

The commission had met only twice before this happened, once to listen to public criticism and once to get advice from Congress. Basically it had no staff to help it. The executive director of the commission, who was hired to assemble and organize the staff was fired in September 1987, not long after the commission was formed. She had not been replaced even 4 months later. Frank Lilly pointed out that people with real expertise with AIDS were needed for the commission. One member, Theresa Crenshaw, has at various times suggested that AIDS can be passed through casual contact and that some individuals should be quarantined. Penny Pullen has called for mandatory testing of hospital patients, marriage license applicants, prisoners, and those convicted of sex-or drug-related crimes. SerVaas, who edits the *Saturday Evening Post* and serves as president or research director for several medical societies she has founded, drives around in a 34-foot-long mobile home called an "AIDS mobile" and stops in shopping malls and church parking lots to test individuals for HIV. The AIDS mobile crew is not interested in testing homosexuals whom SerVaas considers "deviants."

It was doubtful if the commission would be able to fulfill its broad mandate, which is to advise the President about virtually all aspects of the AIDS epidemic, including moral and ethical issues, scientific needs, and more. Fortunately the new chairman, Admiral James Watkins, former Chief of Naval Operations, was able to do something constructive.

To fill the panel seats vacated by the two resigning chairmen, Kristine M. Gebbie, chief health officer in Oregon, and Beny J. Primm, president of the Urban Resource Institute, a nonprofit organization that operates clinics for intravenous drug users in Harlem and Brooklyn, were appointed. Both appointments were praised by public health workers and AIDS activists.

Gebbie is a nurse who has headed the Oregon Health Department for the past 9 years and presently chairs an AIDS task force for the Association of State and Territorial Health Officials. Primm is a doctor and is credited with being a physician with technical competence and political courage.

The commission released a preliminary report in December 1987, and final recommendations to the President are to be ready by June 1988. It has met in Washington to hear from agency chiefs and department heads and is scheduled to meet in New York, San Francisco, and Nashville, Tennessee.

In their preliminary report to President Reagan the committee said it would concentrate on four issues that, it seemed to imply, the federal government and other groups have not adequately addressed. These issues are

1. The lack of drugs for treating AIDS patients

2. The lack of valid data on how the disease is spreading

3. The need for home care and other out-of-hospital care for AIDS patients

4. The lack of programs for treating intravenous drug abusers at a high risk of infection.

The Chairman of the President's Panel on AIDS presented the commission's major report in March 1988. The chief recommendations were for a $2 billion a year program above present spending to expand treatment programs on drug abuse and to improve health care services.

The recommendations were broad going beyond the AIDS epidemic to address major problems in the health care system and they were detailed, for example commenting on the need to have computer programs and link-ups among all the researchers reporting the results of drug experiments to treat AIDS.

There were 180 recommendations in all most of them given with very little analysis to explain the basis for the recommendations. Staff members said the analysis would be given in the final report due on June 24, 1988.

Briefly some of the recommendations are:

- "Treatment on demand" for all drug users with a sustained effort on drug abuse prevention costing about $1.7 billion a year including research, treatment and education.

- A significant expansion of health care and related services for those infected with AIDS virus including the training of more doctors and nurses to treat AIDS patients to serve in impoverished areas where many AIDS victims are found. Also recommended was the training and hiring of 32,000 drug treatment specialists and setting up 3,300 drug centers for drug abusers.

- The commission pointed out the need for increased access by a broader spectrum of the infected population to a greater variety of experimental treatments.

- Improving the limited access of certain individuals to drug trials including women, children, HIV positive asymptomatic individuals, certain minority populations, and others.

The critical comments on the report were almost universally favorable in the media and by special groups such as gays and ethnic minorities who have a high percentage of AIDS cases. The complete report is available from the Superintendent of Documents and larger libraries.

How the 1988 Presidential Candidates Look at AIDS

Republicans
Vice-President Bush, in talks given in New York City, has called for more federal money for research and education. He says education

would be a number-one priority of his administration. (He is referring here to all educational costs, not just those for AIDS.)

Democrats
Governor Michael Dukakis heads the National Governors' Task Force on AIDS. He has expanded testing and counseling sites for the disease, ordered state agencies to develop public service announcements and explicit teaching guides, and channeled government money directly into medical research. He holds himself ready to consider different AIDS testing plans but has doubts on the reliability of such tests.

AIDS is likely to be a big issue in the 1988 campaign and the lines are already fairly well drawn. In general, the Republicans favor fairly extensive mandatory testing, informing others with the "right to know" about the presence of infection and educational efforts that stress abstinence or sex only within marriage. Condoms, while approved as partly preventing the transmission of AIDS virus, are not stressed. They favor increased spending for research and care of AIDS victims.

The Democrats by and large are less certain of the value of widespread mandatory testing, and their educational program is for frank discussion with school students starting at about the seventh grade. They also favor greatly increased spending for research and treatment.

Prospects of Babies Infected with HIV by Contaminated Blood Transfusions

Many young children received blood transfusions before 1985 when testing of blood donors was instituted. A considerable number of these children became infected with HIV. A new study with 20 children has shown that one third of the children have died or are ill with AIDS, one third have had more than the usual number of childhood diseases but are relatively normal, while the final third have no evidence of any damage to their immune system and are healthy and developing normally.

These results give hope that many of the children who now become infected from AIDS-infected mothers at birth may be able to resist the disease for longer periods of time than the average of two years, that was suggested, passed before the babies exhibited clinical AIDS symptoms and die. Furthermore, early studies on treating young children with AIDS with AZT have been quite promising and it may be possible with this drug to benefit their health and prolong their lives considerably.

CHAPTER 9
PSYCHOLOGICAL, ETHICAL, AND LEGAL PROBLEMS OF AIDS

Introduction; Sentencing of an AIDS carrier to prison; Should doctors refuse to treat AIDS patients?; American Medical Association ruling on treatment of AIDS patients; Decision of New York State medical colleges on treating AIDS; Problem of notification and privacy; Private patient and doctor confidentiality; American Civil Liberties Union stand on AIDS; Children with AIDS going to school; Should sex partners of AIDS victims be informed?; Supplying condoms to federal prisoners; Legal aspects of AIDS: divorce; Rights bill on AIDS; Should free needles be given to drug addicts to help curb AIDS?; AIDS and the right to die; Other types of legal issues involving AIDS; Anonymity of blood donors; The Catholic Church's stand on AIDS; Corporate policies toward AIDS; Should physicians (or dentists) with AIDS be allowed to practice?; Responsible behavior for AIDS victims.

9

PSYCHOLOGICAL, ETHICAL, AND LEGAL PROBLEMS OF AIDS

Introduction

Making a judgment concerning what is right to do about an AIDS problem is not easy. A logical way to begin is to adopt the premises:

1. One wants to maximize the safety of society by preventing the spread of the disease.

2. One wants to give an individual the maximum freedom compatible with premise 1.

Some reactionaries would argue that the only way to accomplish premise 1 would be to test all individuals for AIDS and lock up those who test positive. This is obviously a draconian and unworkable suggestion on moral, ethical, legal, and practical grounds. Considering only the latter, where would one lock up the 1 to 2 million people in this country who are believed to be infected?

A majority of those who have AIDS virus can be depended upon to either refrain from sex or to take measures minimizing the possibility of transmitting the disease to another person by using a condom, sterilizing creams or jellies, and so on. Even so, the skeptics would cry, What about those who don't care if they spread the disease? Only a few people like this are needed to spread AIDS to many others who are uninfected. These few who might be amoral or vengeful or desirous of "getting back" at society because of their treatment by it are a problem that is only beginning to be approached. Some of these approaches are discussed in this chapter.

Sentencing of an AIDS Carrier to Prison

An Army medical instructor has been sentenced to 2 months in the stockade and given a dishonorable discharge for having sexual relations with three female soldiers without telling them he carried AIDS virus. He also had sexual relations with four others but was not charged with those contacts. The young man, who was 28, has also been demoted from the rank of sergeant to private and stripped of military benefits. Does the punishment fit the crime? I think not. It is possible that all seven women will get AIDS, and if they do they will likely die.

It is difficult to know what the right punishment would be. Should society make it impossible for him to have sex again? This could be accomplished by a moderately simple operation. But then he could transmit the disease through infected needles.

In 5 months he will be discharged from the Army and free to go into civilian life with no restraints on his activities. Will he infect others again? Very possibly. I don't know how the Army caught him, but since the Army has tested all its personnel for AIDS it's easy to know who has it and who does not. In civilian life he will be anonymous, and anyone infected by him will probably be unaware of it for some time and possibly unable to make the connection to him. There is therefore a significant dilemma concerning what is the best course to follow in such cases. Perhaps if it is known who the sex partners are, they could be informed and tested at 6-month intervals to see if AIDS antibodies develop. There are presently no civilian laws that would restrict this army man from sexual activity.

Of course Army law is not civilian law. However, a whole body of civilian law with regard to AIDS is springing up, and soon there will be textbooks on AIDS-related law and Supreme Court decisions on AIDS laws. Eventually these laws will accomplish, in the best possible way, what is desired in the two premises stated above.

Should Doctors Refuse to Treat AIDS Patients?

A news story not long ago reported that one quarter of 258 doctors in training at New York hospitals believe it is not unethical to refuse to treat people suffering from AIDS. A heart surgeon from Milwaukee quoted in an editorial says, "I've got to be selfish; I've got to think about myself; I've got to think about my family. That responsibility is greater than to the patient." Another heart surgeon writing to the same paper believes that the public has not been fully informed about the degree of risk involved. He continues, "As a heart surgeon my hands are constantly immersed in a sea of blood from the patient and from countless numbers of donated units of blood and blood products." "During the performance of nearly every operation on the heart, inevitable breaks in the rubber gloves and in the skin of the surgeon occur because of contacts with sharp objects. . . If a surgeon elects to operate upon an AIDS patient, he makes a personal voluntary decision that at the same time commits dozens of operating room assistants and other nurses involved in postoperative management of such patients to a high degree of risk." The same doctor also points out that there is very little chance that a patient with active AIDS disease will recover from such an operation because of his weakened immune system and high susceptibility to infectious disease.

For the same reasons, many dentists refuse to treat AIDS patients or even known homosexuals. Dental surgeons and dentists who do extractions are particularly exposed to blood and blood aerosols, as are all dental assistants and hygienists who work on such patients.

The viewpoints expressed by these and many other physicians and dentists who do not want to risk the dangers of treating AIDS patients have raised a hurricane of protest. Contrary views are just as vehemently presented.

Kenneth M. Prager, writing on the Op-Ed page of the *New York Times* on October 23, 1987, says, "I too have a wife and children to support and I hope to spend decades more with them. But if every doctor who loved his family and life followed the Milwaukee doctor's logic, who would be left to treat AIDS patients?"

Dr. Prager believes that the risks threatened by open heart and other procedures have been exaggerated. He points out that when one considers the hundreds of thousands of contacts between AIDS patients and medical personnel, only a few infections have been reported and these usually entailed serious mistakes in omitting elementary precautions or carelessness in handling blood, syringes, scalpels, and needles.

The fact that some doctors refuse to treat AIDS victims will of course only increase the irrational and often hysterical fear that uninformed people have of catching the disease. While it is certainly true that some risk exists for anyone who treats AIDS patients and a higher risk exists for surgeons, all of these physicians took the Hippocratic oath to serve those who are sick without question or preference. Failure to uphold the oath demeans not only the individual but the whole profession.

American Medical Association Ruling on Treatment of AIDS Patients

The American Medical Association is one of the largest and most powerful professional societies in the world. It has great political and economic clout.

It has stated that "A physician may not ethically refuse to treat a patient whose condition is within the physician's current realm of competence" only because the patient has been infected with AIDS virus, noting that this is a long-standing position of medical ethics. "When an epidemic prevails, a physician must continue his labors without regard to the risk to his own health."

About 250,000 doctors, or slightly less than half of all U.S. physicians, are members of the AMA. The statements above were prepared by a nine-member panel including a medical student and eight doctors, one of whom was a resident in training.

The statement by the AMA describes the doctor's duty in this way: "A person who is afflicted with AIDS needs competent, compassionate treatment. Neither those who have the disease nor those who have been infected by the virus should be subjected to discrimination based on fear and prejudice, least of all by members of the health care community."

A spokesman for the Federal Centers for Disease Control says the government knows of 12 cases in which health care workers have been infected by AIDS virus. Eight were in the United States and four in other countries. Some of these workers were pricked with contaminated needles, and others were briefly exposed to large amounts of blood from infected patients and had cuts or abrasions through which the virus may have passed.

The American Medical Association does not enforce its rulings but says that most physicians will comply. In theory, if a physician refuses to do so, complaints may be filed by patients, and a physician, after a hearing, can be expelled from the state and/or national group. Unfortunately such expulsion is not likely to have much effect on his or her practice.

Decision of New York State Medical Colleges on Treating AIDS

New York State's 13 medical colleges state that any faculty member, hospital resident, or medical student who refuses to treat an AIDS patient will be dismissed.

This is the first regulation by any medical organization that establishes strong penalties for refusal to treat AIDS victims and goes far beyond any earlier ruling. A statement by this association, whose members include private schools, calls for "due process" consisting of appropriate review and consultation concerning the facts.

Problem of Notification and Privacy

A very serious conflict exists between the needs of an individual to have knowledge of his or her AIDS infection kept in the strictest confidence and the need of society to know who has AIDS. This problem has many ramifications.

Should doctors notify state health departments when they diagnose an AIDS case? In most states at present it is mandatory for a physician who diagnoses a case of AIDS to report it to the state department of health. The reason is obvious. The state needs to know where the cases are and to get all possible information about the victim it can: age, sex, sexual preference, intravenous drug use, and so on. With this information the state can keep tabs on the disease, learn about movements of infected people, prepare educational programs where needed, and estimate hospital care needs.

A TV program:
A Case of AIDS
("Frontline," PBS)

Reviewed by Martha Bayles in the *Wall Street Journal*

It's hard to mourn for Fabian Bridges, a 30-year-old AIDS victim buried in a pauper's grave ... in Houston. Not only was he ill with a fatal disease, he also consciously infected others – as many as six men a night, who paid, sometimes, for the privilege of having sex with this gloomy, remote, acne- scarred stranger who admitted to a TV interviewer that "I'm at the point now where I just don't give a damn."

There is nothing sensational about the documentary which was shown on a special edition of PBS's "Frontline". Film makers from

"Frontline" and WCCO-TV (a CBS affiliate in Minneapolis) followed Mr. Bridges from city to city during the last year of his life, talking with his family, his doctor, and the various officials who could not control his behavior without violating his rights. Mr. Bridges comes across as pathetic rather than threatening – a scruffy little plague ship adrift in the lower depths.

Neither does the film flatter the institutions Mr. Bridges drifts through. In Indianapolis, a judge drops minor theft charges in order to get Mr. Bridges out of a city jail and buys him a one-way bus ticket to Cleveland, where the city council learns about him and half-heartedly debates the issues, but can find no better way to deal with him than to send him on to Houston.

It's striking that only once in the film does anyone attempt to rebuke Mr. Bridges. Unfortunately the rebuker is a doctor in Houston whose bluff, offhand manner is unpersuasive, even to the viewer. Watching Mr. Bridges interact with other authority figures, from police to his own mother, we sense that nobody is getting through to him; he loathes the rest of the world even more than he loathes himself.

Thus, the documentary has two contradictory effects. First, it raises questions about individual rights vs. public health. As one Cleveland councilman observes, there are laws on the books establishing quarantine for a list of dangerous diseases, but the list does not yet include AIDS. Other means of preventing a citizen from pursuing this or that sexual activity are few and far between. The most authorities in Houston can hope for is an arrest for solicitation, which will take Mr. Bridges off the streets for only a couple of hours.

The second effect is probably unintended: By showing us so much about poor Fabian Bridges, the film distances us from the problem of AIDS. Mr. Bridges's life is so marginal, so degraded, that we can't help but identify with the Houston vice officer who throws up his hands at the suggestion that Mr. Bridges could be put away if he were caught initiating a sex act with a policeman. "Not me," he says, laughing along with his fellow officers. Watching the penniless, drug-taking, dying Mr. Bridges, most viewers will think the same thing: Not us.

Yet think again. Mr. Bridges is a marginal person, but in his carelessness and self-absorption, he embodies certain tendencies that are definitely "us." Describing a one-night stand with a stranger, he says, "I liked him because he was affectionate," and then adds that he expressed this liking by performing anal intercourse – thereby exposing the kindly stranger to a high risk of death.

In his narcissistic inability either to deny his impulses or to face up to their consequences, the late Fabian Bridges is not so different from a great many other people, both heterosexual and homosexual, who look to strangers not just for sex, but for a simulacrum of love and intimacy. The brutish promiscuity of certain gay bars and bathhouses is alien to most of us. But the use of casual sex for comfort, entertainment, or distraction is not. And because we are easy and tolerant about sexual relations in general, we are in for a terrible shock: Epidemiologically speaking *AIDS is already out of the closet.* (Italics added.)

Some gay organizations have acted responsibly, such as the group in Houston that took Fabian Bridges off the streets when no one else could. Yet true responsibility must go further, into acceptance of the danger in its true proportions. We must all rise above resentment and sound the alarm, because it's too late now to point anything but a microscope.

Many doctors are under great family pressure not to report a case of AIDS as such, and because of the havoc such a report can wreak if it becomes known, some acquiesce and may instead report pneumonia, Reiter's syndrome, lymphadenopathy, or something else—but not AIDS. There is consequently a significant underreporting of the disease. In many earlier instances, AIDS in intravenous drug users was reported as some other disease. This occurred to such an extent in New York City that when death certificates were combed to find the misreported cases, cases among intravenous drug users actually were numerically greater than those involving homosexuals.

Of course many physicians can make an honest mistake, but this is becoming more difficult to do all the time as the disease becomes better recognized in all its various manifestations.

In theory, once the health department receives notification, the fact that a person has AIDS should be held in strictest confidence. Or should it? What if the person is promiscuous and doesn't care whom he infects? What if the mate of the person doesn't know he or she is infected? What if a doctor is going to carry out surgery on the person, or a dentist is going to work on his or her teeth. Shouldn't all the people involved be notified of their risk?

The American Medical Association has addressed this problem in its discussion of the obligations of a physician with respect to AIDS. It states that "Doctors have an ethical obligation to recognize the rights to privacy and to confidentiality of the AIDS victim. These rights are absolute until they infringe in a material way on the safety of another person.

"If," it goes on to say, "the doctor learns that a person infected with the AIDS virus is endangering others, the doctor should try to persuade the person from activities that might result in further transmission of the disease. If rational persuasion fails, the doctor should notify the local authorities so they can take the steps needed to protect other people such as the sex partner of the infected individual."

I wonder how many doctors carry through on this and would be surprised if many do. First of all, an infected person would probably be very reticent to talk about his sex partners. Second, he or she would probably readily agree to be careful, but not necessarily carry this out. If the doctor feels that this might be the case, and if all else fails, the AMA advises that the doctor may be obliged to notify the endangered third party if local authorities do not do so.

Private Patient and Doctor Confidentiality

A man who was told by his doctor that he had AIDS asked the doctor to keep the information confidential. He said he was going to file for divorce from his wife and that the information, if known, would complicate matters.

The physician tried to get the patient to tell his wife so she could be tested, but the man refused. The doctor finally informed the woman, but in doing so he risked substantial damages under Massachusetts' strict confidentiality law which requires written consent from a patient to relate AIDS test results.

Other cases like this have occurred, and they are greatly straining the sanctity of the doctor-patient relationship. But the argument is strongly made that this sanctity must be breached whenever another person could be harmed. The right to privacy is absolute except when it infringes on another person's right to safety from harm, and it is in fact the doctor's duty to prevent this harm from occurring.

It is probably true that confidentiality is being breached more and more. Even in California, which has the strictest confidentiality laws in the country, the authorities have steadfastly refused to prosecute health care officials and physicians who violate this confidentiality.

One result of this is that some individuals may be reluctant to undergo tests for AIDS in any setting in which they believe privacy is not possible. This might include refusal to be tested at all for AIDS virus antibodies.

On the federal level, an aide to Senator Edward M. Kennedy says that the Massachusetts Democrat's comprehensive bill on AIDS would, among other things, free doctors from criminal and civil liability if they informed members of the family or known sex partners of a patient infected by AIDS virus. This is but another example of the right of society to protect itself taking precedence over the legal rights of the patient.

American Civil Liberties Union Stand on AIDS

The American Civil Liberties Union is against any compulsory testing for AIDS virus and against all government efforts to trace and identify sexual contacts of those suspected of harboring AIDS virus.

This is not in conflict, they assert, with sound health policies. The ACLU points out that many public health officials strongly oppose mandatory testing and contact tracing. Also, they state, these officials oppose it because they believe such programs would make it harder, not easier, to limit the spread of AIDS virus. These programs would drive people away from health authorities. Voluntary testing is the answer, the ACLU believes, with safeguards so that infected people will not be publicly identified and thereby subjected to loss of a job, insurance, or housing and to social ostracism.

The ACLU is worried that unfounded fear will lead us to abandon our concern for individual rights and to embrace policies that falsely promise deliverance. Mandatory testing and contact tracing will not deliver us from the threat of AIDS. To argue otherwise is counter-productive in terms of both public health and civil liberties, it believes.

There are, of course, contrary views to those of the ACLU and some of these have already been presented in chapter 5.

Children with AIDS Going to School

There is nothing parents are more fiercely protective of than their children. When parents learn that children with AIDS virus are attending the same school as their children, there is often a dramatic, even hysterical, outbreak of fear. Meetings are organized, petitions are circulated, and if all else fails, children are kept home from school. All this is a pity, because an educational program for parents and children attending a school expecting an AIDS-infected child could probably avert trouble before the child arrives. Good communication and education efforts by the school, with physicians and other experts on AIDS at hand to talk and answer questions at PTO and other meetings could result in children with AIDS being admitted without even a raised eyebrow.

Children who are well informed about a disease are remarkably unafraid and are usually very solicitous of peers who might have it. This has been demonstrated time and again with respect to AIDS in more enlightened schools. It is clear therefore that if a child tests positive for AIDS virus but is otherwise healthy, he or she should be allowed to attend school. It isn't necessary to advertise that this child or that child has AIDS, but the principal of the school, the school nurse and other medical staff, and the child's teachers should be informed. Then if anything happens to the child, such as a fall or a cut, they would be prepared to take the proper precautions.

Of course, the risk to other children is not zero. A child with AIDS virus might be involved in a fight and be hit in the nose, getting blood on the fist of his attacker. Since it is always possible that the attacker may have a cut on his hand, there would be a very small chance that some virus could gain entry into the uninfected child.

The argument to be made is that all children are at some risk going to school. The greatest risk is probably from the school bus. School buses are often involved in accidents; they are even hit by trains at railroad crossings, and children are injured or killed. Parents seldom stage uprisings over these dangers. Naturally one wants to be as careful as possible in operating a school bus and to see that all possible precautions are taken, such as warning signals at any railroad crossings. The same is true, of course, about AIDS. Perhaps all school children should be warned about getting into fights in which blood might be spilled.

I think it can be said with considerable confidence that the risk of a school child getting AIDS from another child with the disease is probably less than that of being injured in a school bus accident. There have been thousands of families with an AIDS victim *living* with the family, but I know of no case in which another family member caught the disease.

Suppose a child is developing the symptoms of AIDS. Early symptoms like swollen glands will not be very important and will not make the child feel sick or be more contagious to others. In general, a child with progressive AIDS should be allowed to attend school as long as he or she feels well enough. This is a judgment perhaps best made by a physician. If the child feels sick or is very weak or develops any mental symptoms, then of course he or she should be kept at home. By taking AZT the child may recover enough to go back to school.

At its 135th annual convention in 1987 the American Medical Association said, "There is no reason to exclude these (AIDS) children from public schools because they cannot (are highly unlikely to) infect other children." (my parentheses). The 3000 physicians in attendance also voted to create a national network to provide information about the virus to schools and communities.

Lawsuits against schools that ban students with AIDS
The Fairfax County school system in Virginia is one of the largest (130,000 students) and most highly rated in the nation. School authorities told the parents of a 5 year old girl that she could no longer attend classes because her medical record indicated she suffered from a serious contagious disease and she was banned by state law. The parents filed suit, contending that the exclusion violated a federal law that bars discrimination against the handicapped. Students in Florida, California, and Indiana with AIDS have won similar court cases based on this law. The Fairfax suit requested confidentiality for the child and her parents, and this has been maintained. It seems likely the little girl will win her suit.

Should Sex Partners of AIDS Victims Be Informed?

If one is talking about married couples, the answer is certainly yes. It is hoped that everyone who is married and has tested positive for AIDS virus antibodies will tell his or her spouse. While this might be disconcerting (to make an understatement) to an uninfected spouse, it will at least encourage the latter to take an AIDS test and, if it is negative, use condoms and other protection during future sexual encounters. Of course many of these AIDS victims could have been infected by a blood transfusion or contaminated needle. If they are hemophiliacs, or were required to use other blood products, they might also have picked up AIDS virus.

What if a supposedly faithful spouse comes home one day and confesses to having AIDS without having one of the above risk factors? Then it would appear that that spouse has been unfaithful. Can the uninfected spouse sue for a divorce and get one? This is a legal problem, but adultery has always been grounds for divorce, and there have been cases already in which a divorce was granted under these conditions.

The large majority of sex partners of AIDS virus-infected persons are not spouses. Should these partners be informed? In this case it is probable that the infected person, fearing rejection or retaliation of some sort, would not inform the partner, thus exposing him or her to a high risk of catching the disease. This failure to inform is immorality of the highest order. It involves condemning a person to a highly lethal disease with little chance that he or she can avoid the infection. At present there is no body of law addressing this question, either to punish the transgressor or to protect the victim. There certainly should be. There are even a few efforts being made to locate these partners and inform them of their risk.

One effort is being made by the New York City Department of Public Health headed by Dr. Stephen P. Joseph. He estimates that 400,000 people in New York City are infected with AIDS virus and that so far there have been over 13,000 cases of the active disease. With this large pool of infected persons there is a very real chance of the disease running out of control. Consequently a new program is being initiated in which the AIDS patients of almost 4000 doctors in New York City will be urged to identify their sex partners so they can be warned of their risk of infection.

This will be a voluntary program, and if any AIDS patients do not wish to inform their partners themselves, city health workers will do it. The names of all persons involved, both AIDS patients and their partners, will be held in strictest confidence. A similar program has been initiated at the health department's clinics for venereal diseases and AIDS testing centers. There has not been a great response to the notification program at the clinics or testing stations, and that is why it is being expanded to include the offices of thousands of doctors. I do not predict a great response to the expanded program. Even though the sex partners will not be told who the person is that listed them, most partners know with whom they have had sexual relations. There is bound to be, therefore, considerable reluctance to list these persons.

Dr. Joseph has recently said that the growing epidemic might force the city to consider mandatory testing for anyone at substantial risk of infection, such as prostitutes and sex and drug offenders, as well as a crackdown on all forms of prostitution.

While it might be justified to carry out mandatory testing of these groups, the problem of what to do with persons who test positive has not been answered at all. I don't think anyone has ever been jailed for having a disease. Certain disease carriers (e.g., "Typhoid Mary") have been prohibited from having any contact with food, but a whole new body of law is required for those who spread AIDS indiscriminately.

Somewhat along the lines of what we have been discussing is a decision by the State Supreme Court of New York that prison officials can deny conjugal visits to inmates with AIDS. The court was sharply divided four to three. An inmate and his wife had sued prison officials, arguing that their constitutional rights had been violated, that the decision was arbitrary and capricious, and that the inmate had been discriminated against on the basis of a handicap, affliction with AIDS.

One judge, Fritz W. Alexander, II, voting with the minority, wrote, "The basis for the prison official's determination—to shield practitioner-wife from infection should the two decide to engage in sexual relations—invades an area of personal decision making between a married couple embraced by their marital privacy right."

Some ethicists have a view contrary to this opinion. They believe the mores of our society have progressed to the point where an individual is always protected from harm despite willingness to undergo it. Thus the court compels parents to permit children to have operations or to receive blood transfusions that are lifesaving, even if they are against the religious beliefs of the parents. People who attempt suicide are always prevented from doing so if they are caught in time. Most states have laws against reckless endangerment and having sex with an AIDS virus carrier could certainly be considered reckless endangerment with the AIDS carrier as the violator. Perhaps these laws should be used more often to jail AIDS virus infected offenders. Such offenders, once they are known and have a prison record, might be more reluctant to offend again with the prospect of a harsher sentence if they are caught a second time.

Supplying Condoms to Federal Prisoners

In Vermont, prison inmates can get condoms on request, and a similar pilot program has been tried in New York City jails. The Reagan administration has, however, ruled out giving condoms to federal prisoners. Robert Brutsche, medical director of the Federal Bureau of Prisons, says that since homosexual sex is against prison regulations, it would be inconsistent for the authorities to pass out condoms.

Here again is the dilemma: Is it better to be consistent or to perhaps prevent new cases of AIDS? I will let the reader answer this one.

Dr. Brutsche says the administration plans to conduct tests every 6 months on all new inmates not found to be carrying AIDS virus. By tracking this group as long as they are imprisoned, officials hope to learn about the risk of AIDS exposure among new prisoners.

Legal Aspects of AIDS: Divorce

If a husband or wife has not received a blood transfusion and becomes infected with AIDS virus, the spouse must assume it is the result of either intravenous drug use or extramarital sex. If drug use is eliminated, it can be attributed to a sexual encounter.

Not surprisingly, most of the legal cases have arisen in New York and California, which between them share about half of the nation's AIDS cases. Only a handful of cases linking the disease and divorce have been reported thus far, and almost all have been disputes over child custody or visitation rights. But in more and more cases the question of AIDS comes up. Often the wife will say, "I think my husband has been unfaithful. He should be tested for AIDS." No-fault divorce laws and laws allowing equal distribution of property often make it easy to get a divorce, provided both of the spouses are willing. Adultery is no longer much of a factor, and only when there is disagreement over custody of the children is it necessary for lawyers to step in and wrangle over the details.

Some of the problems arising that have not yet been worked out by lawsuits are the following:

●Should an AIDS victim be granted visitation rights for children?

●What should wives of men who contract the disease do? There are a number of possibilities. She might wish to continue the marriage. Sex is possible with the husband with the use of condoms and antiseptic creams but will not be 100% safe. The woman might sue for divorce or, as some lawyers have suggested rather ghoulishly, simply wait until the husband gets the disease and dies, thereby gaining all the property. However, it is possible for the husband to will his share to someone else. A husband whose wife acquires AIDS has the same options.

●What if a partner in a sexual encounter gets AIDS or some other sexually transmitted disease? Is the infected partner liable to a damage suit? A few years ago a case involving the transmission of genital herpes set a precedent. A court in Minneapolis ruled that a woman who had contracted herpes from a boyfriend could collect damages under his homeowner's insurance policy since the transmission took place in the boyfriend's home. The insurance company settled out of court for $25,000. As a result of this suit, insurance companies have changed their policies to exclude coverage for sexually transmitted disease at home. There are other possible ways to collect. For example, a New York court ruled that a wife who caught genital herpes from her husband could sue for divorce and collect damages based on her husband's gross negligence and fraud in failing to disclose that he had herpes. The decision in this case has not yet been reached.

Rights Bill on AIDS

Representative Henry A. Waxman, a Democrat from California, has introduced a bill in Congress with the following provisions:

1. It establishes a civil penalty of up to $2000 for the unauthorized disclosure of names and other information obtained through AIDS counseling and testing.

2. It provides that no one may discriminate against an otherwise qualified individual in employment, housing, public accommodations, or government services solely by reason of the fact that he or she is infected by AIDS virus or is regarded as being infected (homosexual, drug abuser).

3. A civil penalty of up to $2000 must be paid by anyone who illegally discriminates against anyone with AIDS virus.

The Reagan government has come out against the bill, stating that most states protect the confidentiality of medical information and that these provisions would create an expensive and burdensome new federal administrative enforcement bureaucracy. Dr. Otis R. Bowen, a former Secretary of Health and Human Services, says states should be free to adopt or reject civil rights laws protecting AIDS victims according to local conditions. He admits that those infected by HIV have suffered discrimination.

It is clear that this discrimination has occurred, and it seems to be continuing at an accelerated pace as the number of AIDS victims rises. It therefore appears to be high time to pass Representative Waxman's law or a similar one. The Privacy Act of 1974, which limits the disclosure of medical records and other personal data held by the federal government, contains numerous exceptions under which disclosure can occur without the patient's knowledge.

Should Free Needles Be Given to Drug Addicts to Help Curb AIDS?

I think one's immediate gut response to this is to say yes. AIDS virus has spread more rapidly among intravenous drug users than among any other group. It is estimated that New York City has over 200,000 intravenous drug users and that 50 to 60% of them are infected with HIV. Still, if one could prevent infection in about 100,000 persons, this would seem to be worthwhile.

The health commissioner of New York City, Dr. Stephen C. Joseph, has suggested selecting a small group of addicts to be used in a trial to see if further spread of AIDS virus can be prevented. If successful, wider distribution of free needles would be carried out.

Unfortunately, time is against such a small-scale test. It could take 6 months to a year to obtain even a possibly invalid test of the value of distributing free needles. In that length of time many of the remaining uninfected addicts could become infected. It may be too late to help present intravenous drug users in New York City. One might ask if there is any potential harm in giving sterile needles and syringes to drug addicts? The only possible harm that comes to mind is that some potential customers for intravenous drugs might have refrained from using them because they know about the custom of sharing needles and that they will probably get AIDS and die. If they are assured of clean needles and syringes, this might overcome their reluctance to use intravenous drugs.

Sterling Johnson, Jr., New York City's special prosecutor for narcotic cases, says, "Free needles just would not work. The users would get them and sell them. The next logical step would be the creation of city-supervised shooting galleries to insure that sanitary needles were being used. Surely such an idea would be unthinkable. Aren't you implicitly saying that New York is the place to come if you want to do drugs? This is the wrong message to give."

Johnson also points out that addicts will not use clean needles. In the heat of the moment they will not take out a new hypodermic syringe and unwrap it. They will take a needle, any needle, and pass it around. He says that raids have been carried out and boxes of clean needles stolen from pharmaceutical houses were found all over the place, but with dozens of addicts lying about, they have found only one bloody needle among them. Despite the views of Johnson, a private antidrug abuse agency, Association for Drug Abuse Prevention and Treatment

(*Adapt*), plans to offer free sterile needles and syringes to the public in New York City. The president of *Adapt*, Yolanda Serrano, says that her agency is prepared to face prosecution, loss of financing, and loss of tax-exempt status to protect the public and save lives. The use of needles without a prescription is unlawful in New York State.

Adapt was formed in 1980. It has 10 full-time staff members and hundreds of volunteers who work in all the boroughs of New York City counseling drug addicts to stop using drugs and enter treatment.

The other approach is, of course, successful enforcement of the antidrug trafficking and use laws, but no reasonable person expects this to happen soon.

AIDS and the Right to Die

A patient with ARC prepared a will saying that he wished no medical treatment if it would not result in "a meaningful quality of life." Presently he is in a coma with a serious brain infection, and his legal guardian has sued the hospital to discontinue treatment.

The hospital, however, has refused, contending it is possible that the patient could recover at least partial health by AZT treatment and that he would have to be consulted again about his wishes. A judge of the State Supreme Court of Manhattan (New York) says that the law cannot be concerned with the patient's long-term prognosis but only his current health. Because the guardian cannot prove that the case is hopeless, the doctors do not agree that it is hopeless, and the state has not defined the legal powers of a "living will," the judge has upheld the hospital's right to continue treatment.

This case raises many questions:

Treatment for AIDS changes every 6 months or so. Even though a case may look hopeless today, in a few months new advances may change the picture. Is it not best to support the person with AIDS as long as possible?

How does one define "a meaningful quality of life"? Everyone has a different concept of what this means.

The symptoms of AIDS are so varied that no possible living will can cover all the eventualities.

If the patient should recover enough to be conscious and lucid, he could say, "I want no further treatment," and his wishes would then have to be obeyed.

Other Types of Legal Issues Involving AIDS

Only a legal treatise could address all the possible legal actions arising from the AIDS epidemic. Several types of cases have already been mentioned and discussed, and the following also pose interesting questions:

- Challenging of wills: A 28 year old man who committed suicide after learning he was infected with HIV left half his assets to a church run by his homosexual lover. The family has moved to set aside the will, claiming the man was exposed to the AIDS virus by his lover.
- Issue of negligence. A Chicago woman filed suit seeking $12 million in damages after she was bitten by a ticket agent in a scuffle. The ticket agent tested positive for AIDS virus. She is seeking compensation for infliction of emotional damages, charging the airline with negligence in hiring.
- A charge of attempted murder: A 28 year old man was charged with attempted murder for knowingly selling his AIDS-infected blood. District Attorney Ira Reiner of Los Angeles said the man had sold his blood at least once to a Los Angeles blood company, Plasma Production Associates, and was in the process of making a second attempt when he was caught. At the time he was arrested, there was in fact no law covering what he did. Although the state senate passed a bill prohibiting anyone who tests positive for AIDS virus antibodies from donating blood, any law which might be finally enacted cannot be applied retroactively. More than likely, it will be impossible to prosecute him and, in fact the case against him was dismissed.

Anonymity of Blood Donors

There have been a number of cases in which suit was brought against a hospital or an individual involving donated blood which was contaminated. The blood was given to a patient who needed blood, and the patient subsequently contracted AIDS and died. These cases involved transfusions given before the blood supply was considered safe — before 1985 when testing of all donors for AIDS antibodies was initiated.

In all cases the anonymity of the blood donor has been upheld, and no damages have been awarded to the patient or the surviving family of the AIDS victim. Although there are a large number of individuals who received transfused blood or blood products before 1985, and who might be infected with the AIDS virus because of this, these individuals are not likely to be able to successfully bring a court case for damages.

The Catholic Church's Stand on AIDS

The religious implications of AIDS are profound. But no religion has faced the moral dilemma of the Catholic Church, because it alone has consistently held that artificial contraception of any kind is immoral and, in the eyes of the church, sinful. And we have learned that one way for reducing the risk of transmitting AIDS sexually is to use condoms.

It was rather surprising, therefore, to find that in a policy paper, "The Many Faces of AIDS: A Gospel Response," the administrative board of the United States Catholic Conference, which has the authority to speak for the nation's bishops, takes a very compassionate view. The paper warns repeatedly against stereotyping homosexuals as carriers of the disease. The approach the conference suggests, is, briefly

- To support legislation and education programs that seek to provide accurate information about AIDS
- Increase public support for drug treatment programs, including elimination of the cause of drug addiction, poverty.

And the statement, in its entirety, that provoked considerable surprise:

"In such situations (acknowledging that not everyone will act according to Catholic precepts) educational efforts if grounded in the broader moral vision outlined above, could include accurate information about prophylactic devices or other practices proposed by some medical experts as potential means of preventing AIDS. We are not promoting the use of prophylactics but merely providing information that is part of the factual picture. Such a factual presentation should indicate that abstinence outside of marriage and fidelity within marriage as well as the avoidance of intravenous drug abuse are the only morally correct and medically sure ways to prevent the spread of AIDS. So-called safe sex practices are at best only partially effective.

They do not take into account the real values that are at stake or the fundamental good of the human person."

The document has been widely interpreted as giving Catholic education programs the license to mention condoms provided they indicate that using them is wrong. A footnote to the paper quotes Thomas Aquinas: "Those who govern rightly tolerate certain evils lest certain goods be impeded or also lest some greater evil obtain."

The document provoked a lively debate among American bishops: John Cardinal O'Connor, the Archbishop of New York, Bernard Cardinal Law of Boston, and Archbishop Edmund Szoka came out strongly against any softening of the prohibition against condoms. However, a large group has supported the controversial passage. Each Catholic, I suppose, will have to do what he or she thinks is morally right, since there is a division of opinion. Undoubtedly the matter will be considered again, certainly at a meeting of 300 bishops in 1988 and perhaps even by the Pope.

Only a few days after the document was released, Archbishop John L. May of St. Louis, president of the U.S. Catholic Conference, wrote to John Cardinal O'Connor and told him that the questions raised by the paper would be reintroduced at the meeting of the full body of bishops to be held in the spring of 1988. So the question of whether Catholics can teach about condoms or use them to prevent AIDS is still far from settled. Archbishop May emphasized that the report had not been changed or withdrawn, but would remain in effect until the meeting of all the bishops.

Kathleen Kaveny, a candidate for a Ph.D. in religious ethics and a law degree from Yale University, points out that discussion would be more fruitful if a distinction between the contraceptive and prophylactic functions of condoms were made. It would then be possible to describe a situation in which their use would be entirely acceptable according to traditional Catholic analysis according to the time-honored "rule of double effect."

As an example she describes, a newly married Catholic couple who want to start a family but discover that the hemophiliac husband has contracted AIDS through a blood transfusion. To foster the unitive good of marital intercourse, they could use condoms without violating the teachings of the Humanae Vitae. If asked why they were using condoms, their answer would be "to prevent the transmission of AIDS." Thus the end, aim, or primary effect is entirely acceptable.

Corporate Policies Toward AIDS

Many companies have had no experience with AIDS and have the attitude that "It can't happen to us." As the number of cases mounts, however, no company will be untouched and some coherent policy will be needed. There have been accounts in the newspapers of workers who were fired because it became known that they had AIDS. Often the firing was prompted by a hysterical reaction from co-workers. In some cases, where the victim sued, the company was forced to rehire the individual with AIDS.

A few companies, particularly in AIDS-ridden San Francisco, have adopted specific personnel policies for handling AIDS problems in the workplace. Others have decided to treat AIDS as they would any fatal sickness. This means that stricken employees can continue to work as long as they are able to perform their jobs and are in no danger to themselves or other co-workers. They will continue to receive all company benefits, which in many cases include comprehensive health care.

Quite a few companies in San Francisco have developed a system called case management. This ensures care and support for AIDS patients who are moved, after hospital care, to special homes or hospices for AIDS victims. Case management has drastically cut medical care costs to about $30,000 to $40,000 for each AIDS sufferer, from diagnosis to death, compared to $100,000 to $150,000 in other parts of the country. It is in the companies' interest to treat AIDS patients effectively and efficiently. It could cost companies, who pay 80% of their workers health care benefits, up to $50 billion a year by 1991 for workers with AIDS. Case management could undoubtedly save billions for these companies.

Surgeon General C. Everett Koop has put forth a suggested AIDS policy for corporations:

- Treat AIDS within existing policy for life-threatening illnesses.
- Allow employees with AIDS to work as long as they can.
- Require that AIDS patients perform their jobs satisfactorily or offer them jobs with less responsibility.
- Encourage sensitivity on the part of co-workers toward an employee with AIDS.

- Do not grant a transfer request of an employee who is afraid to work with a co-worker who has AIDS if such a transfer is inconsistent with other transfer policies.
- Maintain the confidentiality of health records of persons who test AIDS virus-positive but who are not ill.
- Implement an educational policy on AIDS.
- Consider case management for an AIDS victim for humanitarian and economic reasons.

There are two federal laws that frightened AIDS-free employees may resort to when they want protection from co-workers who are carriers of AIDS virus: (1) The Occupational Safety and Health Act requires work sites to be free of known hazards. Fortunately, today, nearly all experts will agree that there is no hazard from casual contact with an AIDS carrier. (2) The National Labor Relations Act states that employees cannot be penalized for refusing to work out of a genuine fear for their safety. This appears to be a question of education. No one who is well informed about AIDS should fear for his or her safety if there is an AIDS virus carrier working in the office.

In June 1986, the U.S. Justice Department issued a memorandum stating that firing an employee based on an irrational fear of contagion is not prohibited by federal law and is therefore not discriminatory. This, needless to say, was followed by a wave of firings. AIDS patients quickly fought back with lawsuits claiming a violation of their civil rights. Most of them won, and at present 21 states and many cities have laws or court rulings that make AIDS a "protected handicap" so that employers cannot fire employees just because they have the disease.

It is claimed that very few companies require testing of prospective employees for AIDS antibodies. Such testing is specifically prohibited in California, Florida, Massachusetts, and Wisconsin. As the number of AIDS victims increases, however, there may be an increased demand for these tests. Some lawyers point out that there really is no way in which testing as a condition for employment could be considered lawful.

Should Physicians (or Dentists) with AIDS Be Allowed to Practice?

There is no law at present that prevents medical personnel with AIDS from practicing. This applies both to symptom-free carriers of AIDS virus and to those who might have mild beginning symptoms.

One question arises immediately:

Is it immoral for the medical practitioner to conceal from his or her patients the fact that he or she has AIDS? Should patients have the right to make a choice as to whether they want to continue with a doctor who has AIDS?

I think the physician or dentist should carefully examine this question and make the most moral judgment possible. If there is any reasonable doubt about keeping his illness secret or about being optimally alert mentally, it appears that the physician would have no option but to conclude practicing.

I think that once a decision is made to tell patients that a physician or dentist has AIDS, the practice will disintegrate to essentially nothing. There is ample evidence for this. Dr. Robert J. Huse, a pediatrician, brought a lawsuit against a former roommate who was spreading rumors that the doctor had AIDS. He thought the lawsuit would be kept private, but the local newspaper published the story of the suit with a banner headline across the entire front page. Within a week of the disclosure, his practice had dropped from 15 to 20 per day to 4 or 5. Although many parents called to tell him of their support, his practice was no longer profitable and he closed it. One of his few options, he noted, was to go into the practice of treating AIDS patients.

In England, the British Health Department says that doctors with AIDS can continue practicing and that patients do not have the right to be told that their physician is infected with the virus except where there is a risk of blood-to-blood contact, such as for some surgeons. It seems to me that British doctors still have to make the moral judgments outlined above.

Responsible Behavior for AIDS Victims

In the preface it was stated that if the AIDS epidemic is to be contained in the United States, the population would have to obey strict behavioral precepts. The need for highly altruistic and moral behavior has been emphasized repeatedly herein and also by a wide variety of scientific, medical, religious, political, and educational leaders. What then is the behavior needed? Fortunately it is not difficult to define this in a way that would be endorsed by most individuals. At a minimum the following is required:

1. Anyone who has had the *slightest chance* of contracting AIDS *by any means* should voluntarily subject himself or herself to an AIDS

test. If risky activity is continued, the tests should be continued at 6-month intervals.

2. Any person who tests positive for AIDS virus antibodies should:

a. Refrain from sexual activity with another person who is not known to be infected with AIDS virus, or

b. Tell a sexual partner that he or she is infected and if the other partner is willing to have sex, use a condom and, preferentially a disinfectant like nonoxynol-9.

c. Refrain from sharing needles.

3. Every pregnant woman should have a test for AIDS virus antibodies in the first trimester. If the test is positive the woman should consider an abortion.*

a. If a woman with AIDS has had a child, the child should not be nursed.

Of course, if a cure is found for AIDS, these precepts may have to be changed or modified.

If everyone obeyed these suggestions we would see a gradual decline in AIDS to a level of perhaps a few sporadic cases, which, by the time this level is reached, should be readily amenable to treatment if not cure.

I am enough of a realist to know that not everyone in the world will obey these suggestions let alone hear of them. All the same, I believe that enough people will agree with these precepts and will do what is necessary to finally conquer AIDS.

---

*Although there is about a 50% chance that a child born to an AIDS virus-infected mother may not contract the disease, many would argue that the woman does not have a moral right to take that chance.

APPENDIX 1

Sources of Information About AIDS

National Sources

Federal Centers for Disease Control
Atlanta Georgia
General information 800-342-AIDS
In Atlanta 404-329-3524

In addition to many pamphlets on every aspect of the AIDS virus and disease, the FCDC have compiled guidelines for health care professionals, research workers, and others who might be exposed to the virus to protect personnel from infection.

National Institute of Allergy and Infectious Diseases
Office of Research Reporting and Public Response, Bethesda, Maryland.
301-496-5717

AIDS Action Council, Federation of AIDS-Related Organizations
729 Eighth St. S.E.
Washington, D.C. 20003
202-547-3101

American Association of Physicians for Human Rights
P.O. Box 14366
San Francisco, CA 94119
415-558-9353
In the Bay area, 415-673-3189

American Red Cross AIDS Education Office
431 18th St. N.W.
Washington, D.C. 20006
202-737-8300

Gay Men's Health Crisis
P.O. Box 274, 132 West 24th St.
New York, NY 10011
212-807-6655

Hispanic AIDS Forum
c/o APRED
835 Broadway, Suite 2007
New York, NY 10003
212-870-1902 or 870-1864

Lambda Legal Defense and Education Fund
666 Broadway, 12th Floor
New York, NY 10012
212-995-8585

National AIDS Network
1012 14th St. N.W., Suite 601
Washington, D.C. 20005
202-347-0390

National Coalition of Gay STD Services
P.O. Box 239
Milwaukee, WI 53201

National Gay and Lesbian Task Force
1517 U Street, N.W.
Washington, D.C. 20009
202-332-6483

National Hemophilia Foundation
Soho Building, 110 Greene St., Room 406
New York, NY 10012
212-219-8180

National Lawyers Guild AIDS Network
211 Gough St., Suite 311
San Francisco, CA 94102
415-861-8884

National Lesbian and Gay Health Foundation
P.O. Box 65472
Washington, D.C. 20035
202-797-3708

National Sexually Transmitted Diseases Hotline
American Social Health Association
800-227-8922

United States Public Health Service
Hubert Humphrey Building, Room 721 H
200 Independence Ave. S.W.
Washington, D.C. 20201
202-245-6867

Local Organizations

Arizona
  Phoenix
  Arizona Stop AIDS Project
  736 East Flynn Lane
  Phoenix, AZ 85014

  Tucson
  Tucson Alternative Lifestyle Health Association
  101 W. Irvington Rd., Room B2
  Tucson, AZ 85714

  Tucson AIDS Project
  80 West Cashing St.
  Tucson, AZ 85701
  602- 792-3772

California
  Berkeley
  Gay Men's Health Collective
  2339 Durant Ave.
  Berkeley, CA 94704-1670
  415-644-0425

  Pacific Center for Human Growth
  2712 Telegraph Ave.
  Berkeley, CA 94705
  415-841-6224

  Garden Grove
  AIDS Response Program
  Gay and Lesbian Community Services Center of Orange County
  12832 Garden Grove Blvd., Suite E
  Garden Grove, CA 92643
  714-534-0862
  Hotline 714-859-6482

Long Beach
Long Beach Project Ahead
2017 E. 4th St.
Long Beach, CA 90804
213-439-3948

Long Beach Dept. of Health
2655 Pine Ave.
Long Beach, CA 90806
213-427-7421

Los Angeles
Aid for AIDS
8235 Santa Monica Blvd., Suite 311
West Hollywood, CA 90046
213-656-1107

AIDS Project LA
7632 Santa Monica Blvd.
West Hollywood, CA 90046
213-876-8951
Hotlines 213-876-AIDS and
800-992-AIDS (southern California only)

People with AIDS-LA
QDc/o Trainor
1752 N. Fuller
Los Angeles, CA 90046

Southern California Mobilization against AIDS
1428 N. McCadden Place
Los Angeles, CA 90028
213-463-3928

Sacramento
California Dept. of Health Services
AIDS Activities
1812 14th St., Room 200
Sacramento, CA 95814
916-445-0553

Sacramento AIDS/KS Foundation
1900 K Street, Suite 201
Sacramento, CA 95814
916-488-AIDS

San Diego
San Diego AIDS Project
P.O. Box 89049
QDSan Diego, CA 92138
619-543-0300

Owen Clinic
University of California Medical Center
225 Dickinson St.
San Diego, CA 92103
619-543-3995

Beach Area Community Clinic
3705 Mission Blvd.
San Diego, CA 92109
619-488-0644

San Francisco
AIDS Interfaith Network
2261 Market St. #502
San Francisco, CA 94114
415-928-4673

AIDS Worried Well Group, Operation Concern
1853 Market St.
San Francisco, CA 94103

Lesbian and Gay Health Services Coordinating Committee
Department of Public Health
101 Grove
San Francisco, CA 94102
415-558-2541

People with AIDS/SF
415-861-7309

San Francisco AIDS Foundation
333 Valencia St., 4th Floor
San Francisco, CA 94103
415-864-4376 or 863-2437
Hotline 800-367-2437

Shanti Project
525 Howard St.
San Francisco, CA 94105
415-777-2273

San Jose
AIDS Hotline 800-342-3437

Colorado
Denver
Colorado AIDS Project
P.O. Box 18539
Denver, CO 80218
303-837-0166

Connecticut
Hartford
AIDS Coordinator
State Dept. of Health Services
150 Washington St.
Hartford, CT 06106
203-566-1157

New Haven
AIDS Project/New Haven
P.O. Box 636
New Haven, CT 06503
203-624-2437

District of Columbia
Whitman-Walker Clinic
1407 South St.
Washington, D.C. 20009
202-332-2437

St. Francis Center
5417 Sherier Place, N.W.
Washington, D.C. 20016
202-363-8500

Florida
Key West
AIDS Action Committee
901 B Durval St.
Key West, FL 33040
305-294-8302

Ft. Lauderdale
Health Crisis Network
305-674-7530

Miami
Health Crisis Network
P.O. Box 52-1546
Miami, FL 33152
305-634-4636

Tampa
Tampa Bay AIDS
P.O. Box 350217
Tampa Bay, FL 33695- 0217

Georgia
Atlanta
AIDS Atlanta
404-876-9944

Hawaii
Honolulu
Life Foundation
320 Ward Ave., Suite 104
Honolulu, HI 96814
808-527-2211

Illinois
Chicago
AIDS Action Product
Howard Brown Memorial Clinic
2676 N. Halsted
Chicago, IL 60614
312-871-5777

People with AIDS-Chicago
c/o Hall
3414 N. Halsted St.
Chicago, IL 60657

Sable Sherer Clinic
Fantus Health Center of Cook County
Chicago, IL 60612
312-633-7810

Kentucky
  Lexington
  Lexington Gay Services Organization
  P.O. Box 11471
  Lexington, KY 40511
  606-231-0335

Maryland
  Baltimore
  Gay Community Center of Baltimore Health Clinic
  241 Chase St., 3rd Floor
  Baltimore, MD 21201
  301-837-2050

Massachusetts
  Boston
  Fenway Community Health Center
  AIDS Action Committee
  16 Haviland St.
  Boston, MA 02215
  617-267-7573

  Mayor's Task Force on AIDS
  City Hall, Room 608
  Boston, MA 02201

  Haitian Committee on AIDS in Massachusetts
  117 Harvard St.
  Dorchester, MA 02124

Michigan
  Detroit
  Venereal Disease Action Coalition
  United Community Services
  51 W. Warren Ave.
  Detroit, MI 48201
  313-833-0622

  Royal Oak
  Wellness Networks, Inc.
  P.O. Box 1046
  Royal Oak, MI 48068
  800-521-7946, ext. 3582
  In Michigan 800-482-2404, ext. 3582

Minnesota
  Minneapolis
  Minnesota AIDS Project
  1436 W. Lake St.
  Minneapolis, MN 55408
  612-824-1772

Missouri
  St. Louis
  AIDS Task Force
  c/o Dept. of Anthropology
  Washington University
  St. Louis, MO 63130

Nevada
  Las Vegas
  Southern Nevada Social Services
  P.O. Box 71014
  Las Vegas, NV 89109
  702-733-9990

New Jersey
  New Brunswick
  New Jersey Lesbian and Gay Coalition
  P.O. Box 1431
  New Brunswick, NJ 08903

  Trenton
  AIDS Office
  New Jersey Department of Health
  Health and Agriculture Bldg.
  Trenton, NJ 08625
  609-633-2751

New Mexico
  Albuquerque
  Common Bond
  P.O. Box 1191
  Albuquerque, NM 87131
  505-266-8041

  Espanola
  New Mexico Physicians for Human Rights
  P.O. Box 1361
  Espanola, NM 87532

Santa Fe
AIDS Task Force
P.O. Box 968
Santa Fe, NM 87504

New York
Buffalo
Buffalo AIDS Task Force
P.O. Box 38, Bidwell Station
Buffalo, NY 14222

New York City
AIDS Resource Center
24 W. 30th Street, 10th Floor
New York, NY 10001
212-481-1270

Gay Men's Health Crisis
Box 274, 132 W. 24th Street
New York, NY 10011
212-807-6655

New York State AIDS Institute
212-340-3388

Community Health Project
208 W. 13th Street
New York, NY 10011
212-675-3559

People With AIDS Coalition
Box 125, 263 W. 19th Street
New York, NY 10011
212-627-1810

Rochester
AIDS Rochester
1063 East Main Street
Rochester, NY 14608

Stony Brook
Long Island AIDS Task Force
SUNY
Stony Brook, NY 11794
516-385-2437

White Plains
Mid-Hudson AIDS Task Force
Gay Men's Alliance
255 Grove Street
White Plains, NY 10601

North Carolina
 Durham
 AIDS Project
 Lesbian and Gay Health Project
 P.O. Box 11013
 Durham, NC 27703
 919-683-2182

 Wilmington
 GROW, A Community Service Corporation
 P.O. Box 4535
 Wilmington, NC 28406
 919-675-9222

Ohio
 Cincinnati
 Ambrose Clement Health Clinic
 3101 Burnet Ave.
 Cincinnati, OH 45229

 Columbus
 Open Door Clinic
 237 E. 17th St.
 Columbus, OH 43201
 614-294-6337

Oregon
 Portland
 Cascade AIDS Project
 408 SW 2nd Ave.
 Portland, OR 97204
 503-223-8299

Texas
 Dallas
 AIDS Task Force, Dallas Gay Alliance
 P.O. Box 190712
 Dallas, TX 75219
 214-528-4233

Houston
KS/AIDS Foundation
3317 Montrose, Box 1155
Houston, TX 77006
713-524-AIDS

Utah
Hotline 303-831-6268

Virginia
  Richmond
  Richmond AIDS Information Network
  Fan Free Clinic
  1721 Hanover Ave.
  Richmond, VA 23220
  804-358-6343

  Headwaters
  The Elisabeth Kubler-Ross Center
  South Route 616
  Headwaters, VA 24442
  703-396-3441

Washington
  Seattle
  Northwest AIDS Foundation
  P.O. Box 3449
  Seattle, WA 98114
  206-587-0306

  Seattle AIDS Support
  206-322-AIDS

  AIDS Information Line
  Seattle-King County Department of Public Health
  206-587-4999

Wisconsin
  Milwaukee
  Brady East STD Clinic
  Milwaukee AIDS Project
  1240 E. Brady St.
  Milwaukee, WI 53202
  414-272-2144

Canada
AIDS Committee Toronto (ACT)
P.O. Box 55, Station F
Toronto, M4Y 2L4 Ontario, Canada
416-926-1626

Where to Obtain Free Pamphlets that Provide Information on AIDS

The U.S. Public Health Service and the American Red Cross have compiled literature providing *basic* AIDS information. This literature is available at no cost and, although brief, provides accurate general information focusing on the means of transmission of AIDS virus.

Leaflets
The following publications (up to 50 copies) may be obtained by writing to AIDS, Suite 700, 1555 Wilson Boulevard, Rosslyn, VA 22209:

AIDS, Sex and You

Facts About AIDS and Drug Abuse

AIDS and Your Job — Are There Risks?

Gay and Bisexual Men and AIDS

AIDS and Children — Information for Parents of School Age Children

AIDS and Children — Information for Teachers and School Officials

Caring for the AIDS Patient at Home

If Your Test for Antibody to the AIDS Virus Is Positive . . . "

Other Materials Available Free of Charge
Surgeon General's Report on AIDS (October 1986). Write to AIDS, P.O. Box 14252, Washington, DC 20044 (up to 50 free copies).

Facts About AIDS. Write to AIDS, Suite 700, 1555 Wilson Boulevard, Rosslyn, VA 22209 (up to 50 free copies).

Write to Office of Public Inquiries, Centers for Disease Control, Building 1, Room B-63, 1600 Clifton Road, Atlanta GA 30333 for the following pamphlets(up to 50 free):

What Everyone Should Know About AIDS (also available in Spanish)

Why You Should Be Informed About AIDS (for health care workers)

What Gay and Bisexual Men Should Know About AIDS

AIDS and Shooting Drugs

APPENDIX 2

NIH funds network of AIDS centers across U.S.

AIDS treatment evaluation units

Memorial Hospital for Cancer & Allied Diseases, New York City
Johns Hopkins Hospital, Baltimore
U of Washington, Seattle
U of Miami, Miami
Massachusetts General Hospital, Boston
Tulane U Medical Center, New Orleans
Institute for Immunological Disorders, Houston
San Francisco General Hospital, San Francisco
Albert Einstein College of Medicine, New York City
New York U Medical Center, New York City
U of Minnesota Health Science Center, Minneapolis
Duke U Medical Center, Durham, N.C.
U of Rochester, Rochester
UCLA School of Medicine, Los Angeles
U of Pittsburgh, Pittsburgh
USC Medical Center, Los Angeles
Stanford U School of Medicine, Stanford
Mount Sinai Medical School, New York City
U of California, San Diego

National cooperative drug discovery groups

Memorial Sloan-Kettering Cancer Center, New York City
Duke U Medical Center, Durham, N.C.
Purdue U, West Lafayette, Ind.
U.S. Army Medical Research & Development Command, Fort Detrick, Md.
U of Texas Medical Branch, Galveston, Tex.
Stanford U School of Medicine, Stanford
Biogen, Cambridge, Mass.
Dana Farber Cancer Institute, Boston
U of Miami School of Medicine, Miami
George Washington U School of Medicine, Washington, D.C.
Emory U School of Medicine, Atlanta
State U of New York School of Medicine, Buffalo

State U of New York School of Medicine, Stony Brook
U of Alabama School of Medicine, Birmingham
City of Hope National Medical Center, Duarte, Calif.
Worcester Foundation for Experimental Biology, Worcester, Mass.

AIDS clinical studies groups

U of Texas Health Science Center, San Antonio
U of Massachusetts Medical School, Worcester
New Jersey Medical School, U of Medicine & Dentistry of New Jersey, Newark
Milton S. Hershey Medical Center, Hershey, Pa.
Ohio State U Medical Center, Columbus, Ohio
U of Cincinnati College of Medicine, Cincinnati.
Robert Wood Johnson Medical School, U of Medicine & Dentistry of New Jersey, Piscataway
St. Luke's/Roosevelt Institute for Health Sciences, New York City
Indiana U School of Medicine, Indianapolis
Case Western Reserve School of Medicine, Cleveland
U of North Carolina School of Medicine, Chapel Hill
Children's Hospital, Boston
Cornell U Medical College, New York City
Northwestern U Medical School, Chicago
Washington U School of Medicine, St. Louis, Mo.
George Washington U, Washington, D.C.
State U of New York, School of Medicine, Stony Brook

NIAID vaccine evaluation units

U of Rochester, Rochester
U of Maryland, Baltimore
Johns Hopkins U, Baltimore
Marshall U, Huntington, W.Va.
Vanderbilt U, Nashville
Baylor College of Medicine, Houston

If Your Test for Antibody to the AIDS Virus Is Positive...

American Red Cross

U.S. Public Health Service

T he virus* that causes AIDS (acquired immune deficiency syndrome) may have infected as many as 1 to 1½ million Americans.

Many people who are infected with the virus have not developed any symptoms, while others have had relatively minor illnesses. The most serious form of illness caused by the virus is AIDS, which involves loss of the body's natural immune defenses against disease.

The AIDS virus is primarily spread by sexual contact and by sharing of contaminated needles and syringes among users of intravenous drugs. The virus can also be transmitted from infected mothers to their babies during pregnancy, at birth, or shortly after birth (probably through breast milk). In a small number of cases, the virus has been spread through blood transfusions and through blood products used to treat patients with hemophilia and other blood clotting disorders.

The AIDS Antibody Test

Antibodies are substances produced in the blood to fight disease organisms. When antibodies to a specific organism are found in a person's blood, they indicate that the person has been infected by that particular organism.

Since spring 1985, a test for antibody to the AIDS virus has been used by blood collection centers to keep donated blood and plasma that might carry the virus from becoming part of the nation's blood supply. The antibody test is also available—through private physicians and at clinics in most states—to people who may want to know their antibody status. Those considered to be at risk of infection include men who have had sex with another man since 1977; people who inject illegal drugs, or who have done so in the past; people with symptoms that suggest AIDS virus infection; people from Haiti and Central African

---

**The virus that causes AIDS and related disorders has several different names: HTLV-III, LAV, ARV, and most recently HIV. In this brochure it is called "the AIDS virus."*

countries, where heterosexual transmission seems to be more common than in this country; male or female prostitutes and their sex partners; sex partners of persons who are infected or are at increased risk of infection; people with hemophilia who have been treated with clotting factor products; and infants of high-risk or infected mothers.

What Does a Positive Antibody Test Mean?

If your test for AIDS antibody is positive, it usually means that you have been infected by the virus. Occasionally, however, a person may have a positive test result even though he or she has never been exposed to the AIDS virus. This is called a "false positive" reaction. To be sure that the test result is truly positive, the test is repeated, and in some cases a different type of laboratory test may also be performed.

A positive test result *does not* mean that you will get AIDS—many people with a positive test either remain free of symptoms or develop less serious illnesses. The antibody test cannot tell you whether you will eventually develop signs of illness related to AIDS virus infection—or, if you do, how serious that illness might be.

A positive test result *does* indicate that you have been infected by the AIDS virus and most probably can transmit it to others, *even if you show no symptoms.* It's likely that you will carry the virus in your body throughout your life.

How Can I Protect My Health?

After getting the results of your test, you should see a doctor for a checkup and follow-up care. Your doctor will want to discuss your situation with you thoroughly, answer your questions, make sure that you receive the counseling you need, and check you at regular intervals to help you maintain your health.

How Can I Protect Others?

To protect others from getting the virus from you, there are some important steps you should take:

- Be sure to tell your sex partners about your positive test result. Avoiding sex would eliminate any risk of spreading the virus by sexual means; however, if you and your partner decide to go ahead, be careful to protect him or her from contact with your body fluids, which may carry the AIDS virus. ("Body fluids" includes blood, semen, urine, feces, saliva, and vaginal secretions.) *Use a condom,* which will help reduce the chances of spreading the virus, and avoid practices, such as anal intercourse, that may injure body tissues and make it easier for the virus to enter the bloodstream. Oral-genital contact should also be avoided, as should open-mouthed, intimate kissing.
- People who have been your sex partners may have been exposed to the AIDS virus. If you have used intravenous drugs, anyone you have shared needles and syringes with may have been exposed too. You should tell these persons about your positive test result and urge them to seek counseling and antibody testing from a doctor or health clinic.
- Don't share toothbrushes, razors, tweezers, or other items that could become contaminated with blood.
- If you use drugs, consider enrolling in a drug treatment program to help protect your health. Remember that needles and other drug equipment must *never* be shared.
- Don't donate blood or plasma, body organs, other body tissue, or sperm.
- Clean spills of blood or other body fluids on household or other surfaces with freshly diluted household bleach—one part bleach to 10 parts water. (Don't use bleach on wounds.)
- When you seek medical help, tell the doctor, dentist, eye doctor, or other health worker who gives you care about your positive AIDS antibody test, so that steps can be taken to protect you and others.

• If you are a woman with a positive test result, consider avoiding pregnancy until more is known about the risks of transmitting the AIDS virus to your baby. If you do become pregnant, it's important to see a doctor for regular care during your pregnancy. Because the AIDS virus has been found in breast milk, you should not breastfeed your baby.

What About the Ordinary Activities of My Daily Life?

You should be careful to follow the normal practices everyone needs to maintain good health: Eat a well-balanced diet, exercise, rest, and try to manage your life in a way that avoids undue stress. But there's no reason to change your activities in ways beyond those that have already been discussed.

Your positive test status should not affect your contacts with people at work or in social situations. Special precautions are not necessary: The AIDS virus is not spread by ordinary nonsexual contact such as shaking hands, sharing an office, coughing or sneezing, preparing or serving food, or sharing toilet facilities.

Your relationships with family members and friends should continue to be close and supportive. Hugging, kissing on the cheek, and other forms of affectionate behavior that don't involve exchange of body fluids do not spread the AIDS virus.

It should be stressed that scientists have not found a single instance in which the AIDS virus has been transmitted through ordinary nonsexual contact in a family, work, or social setting.

A Final Word...

The news that you have had a positive result on your AIDS antibody test is not easy to receive. For your follow-up care, it's best to establish a close relationship with a doctor you trust, so that you can speak openly about your feelings, problems, and any fears you may have. Above all, ask questions—and seek assurance from any health professional who takes care of you that all information related to your health will be kept in the strictest confidence.

The U.S. Public Health Service has made AIDS and other AIDS virus-related illnesses its number one priority. Scientists all over the country are working to find ways to eliminate the AIDS virus as a threat to health. A great deal of research progress has been made—and made quickly—and there is every reason to expect these advances to continue at an even faster pace.

More information about AIDS and AIDS-related illnesses can be obtained from—
- Your doctor.
- Your state or local health department.
- The Public Health Service's toll-free hotline: 1-800-342-AIDS.
- Your local chapter of the American Red Cross.

If you would like information about drug treatment programs, call the toll-free hotline of the National Institute on Drug Abuse: 1-800-662-HELP.

APPENDIX 4

AIDS

WHAT IT IS
AND
HOW TO AVOID IT

THE
UNIVERSITY OF
CONNECTICUT

Student Health Services
Division of Student Affairs and Services

AIDS

WHAT IS AIDS?

AIDS stands for Acquired Immune Deficiency Syndrome. This is the name given to a complex of health problems first reported in the United States in 1981.

AIDS is caused by the human immunodeficiency virus (HIV), and is the final stage of a disease process which may begin years earlier. HIV attacks a very important white blood cell in the body, the T4 helper cell. This affected cell normally functions as the "orchestrator" of the immune system.

As HIV continues to reproduce itself, it usually causes progressive deterioration of the immune system, leaving a person increasingly vulnerable to diseases that persons with intact immune systems easily resist. Most people with AIDS die. They are unable to fight "opportunistic infections" such as Pneumocystis carinii pneumonia (PCP) and Kaposi's sarcoma (KP — a rare cancer), which would usually not pose a threat to their lives.

Numerous people infected with HIV have many of the symptoms of AIDS but have not yet developed the life-threatening diseases characteristic of full-blown AIDS. These people are frequently referred to as having AIDS Related Complex or ARC.

WHO GETS AIDS?

Anyone can get AIDS. AIDS is an equal opportunity killer. It does not care about race, gender, age, or sexual orientation. The educational focus is no longer on what were previously considered the *high-risk groups*, but instead is on *high-risk behaviors*. This change has occurred because *the people at highest risk in reality are those who consider themselves at such a low risk that they practice unsafe behaviors.* Groups previously identified as higher risk in this country such as gay and bisexual men*, have become increasingly knowledgeable about AIDS and most have put their energies into practicing safer behaviors, in other words, into *prevention*.

The currently "safer" status of gays and bisexuals is not yet reflected adequately in AIDS statistics because new cases of AIDS are the clinical outcome of viral infections which occurred as long as five or more years ago. Most were not at that time informed about the disease and preventative behaviors.

Although the risk group categories remain constant, several new trends are evident in Connecticut. Over 50% of the new cases of AIDS in this state are now IV drug users, their sexual partners and their children. There is an increase in women and children with AIDS. A disproportionately high number of Blacks and Hispanics now have AIDS. There is a decrease in the proportion of gays and bisexuals with AIDS.

Regardless of the trends which have been observed, those groups considered at highest risk remain:

- Gay and Bisexual Men
- IV Drug Users
- Recipients of Contaminated Blood Products
- Sexual Partners of Above Groups (or partners of persons previously infected by above groups)
- Infants Born to Mothers Infected with AIDS Virus

The AIDS statistics of the next decade are being shaped by behaviors of people today. Unfortunately, the people who will have AIDS in the future are the people we know and spend time with now. Whether you are one of these people tomorrow depends on your actions today. You can *choose* not to get AIDS.
It should be noted that AIDS cases in some countries are primarily heterosexual.

HOW COMMON IS AIDS?

By mid-1987, more than 34,000 cases of AIDS were reported in the United States. In Connecticut, there were over 400 reported cases, with the number of cases doubling approximately every 12 months. Experts think that for every person who has AIDS, there are five to ten who have ARC and 50-100 who are infected with HIV, but have no symptoms. It is estimated that about 340,000 people have ARC and 1.5 to 4 million people are currently infected with the AIDS virus. *These millions have no symptoms and look like everyone else, but they are able to transmit the virus.* Most of them have no idea that they are infected and capable of passing the virus to others.

If those estimates are not shocking enough, it has been projected that by 1991, at least 270,000 people will have full-blown AIDS, about 2.5 million will have ARC, and as many as 20 million Americans will be carrying the AIDS virus.

Connecticut currently ranks as number 14 among states in total AIDS cases. Considering its proximity to New York (ranked #1) and New Jersey (ranked #5), it is a wonder its rank is not higher in the nation. College students, in a very high risk age group, flock to Florida (ranked #3) for vacations and semester breaks which no doubt increases their risk of becoming infected. It is noteworthy that seven cities in Connecticut are ranked in the top 50 nationally for risk of AIDS.

AIDS

IS THERE A TEST FOR AIDS?

No, there is currently no test for the AIDS virus in clinical use. The only tests available are for HIV antibodies, which the body develops in response to exposure to the virus. Testing for antibodies is like looking for footprints in the sand. If footprints are found, it is thought that feet had at one time been there. Likewise, if a person tests positive for antibodies, it is presumed that this person had been infected by the virus at some time in the past.

HIV antibody tests are available in numerous locations in Connecticut. Anonymous sites for counseling and testing are preferable for those who need to be tested. This list is available through the State AIDS Program, **566-1157**, for those at higher risk.

HOW IS AIDS TRANSMITTED?

The AIDS virus has been found in blood, semen, vaginal secretions, saliva, tears, urine, and breastmilk. AIDS has only been transmitted through the exchange of blood, semen or vaginal secretions. Blood exchange is the most effective means of transmission.

It is helpful to think of AIDS as a blood-borne sexually transmitted disease, comparable to hepatitis B. AIDS is a very fragile virus. It dies in less than a second outside of the body. You need to try pretty hard to get AIDS or to give AIDS to someone.

AIDS is transmitted in one of four ways. A **conscious choice** is involved in each of these four activities:

1. Sexual Contact (with the exchange of blood, semen or vaginal secretions)
2. IV Drug Use (including skin popping)
3. Blood Transfusions
4. Mother to Baby (before or during birth)

AIDS has never been transmitted by casual, social contact. Even families living with people with AIDS, participating in normal household activities, have failed to get AIDS.

AIDS is not transmitted between people sitting in a classroom, sharing a room, eating together or even swimming or using a whirlpool together. Nor is AIDS transmitted by sneezing or coughing. It is safe to spend time with, touch and hug people who have AIDS.

DO PEOPLE WITH AIDS LOOK SICK?

No, most do not look sick, although people with full-blown AIDS have episodes of severe illness. The large majority of people carrying the AIDS virus look and feel fine. Therefore, the people with whom you should avoid sexual or blood contact are the people you might least expect to be carrying the virus.

WHAT ARE THE SYMPTOMS OF AIDS?

Some of the symptoms of "full-blown" AIDS are caused directly by specific opportunistic infections. Symptoms include: extreme fatigue; recurrent fever; night sweats; swollen glands; obvious weight loss; thrush (a fungal infection of the mouth); and the dry, persistent cough and difficult breathing, characteristic of PCP; and/or the purplish blotches and bumps of KS. Most people with AIDS suffer some degree of neurological damage (e.g. disorientation, loss of coordination, memory loss, etc.), which is thought to be caused both directly by HIV and as a result of opportunistic infections.

HOW MANY HIV INFECTED PEOPLE WILL GO ON TO DEVELOP AIDS?

It is difficult to answer that question, as we are currently observing the "natural history" of this disease. As time continues to pass since AIDS was first identified in 1981, the estimated incubation period for this disease has progressively lengthened. This translates to mean we do not yet know exactly how long it takes for the symptoms of AIDS to occur once a person is infected with the virus, although it appears to vary from one individual to the next. This may be "dose-related."

Currently, it is estimated that about 40% of HIV infected people go on to develop AIDS. This figure may change as time passes. Some experts believe all people infected with HIV will eventually develop AIDS.

IS THERE A CURE FOR AIDS?

At this time, there is no cure for AIDS. A drug called azidothymidine (AZT) is now available in the U.S. This is not a cure, but it does offer people with AIDS the possibility of a slightly longer life. Other drugs and possible vaccines are being researched.

The AIDS virus mutates frequently, which makes the pursuit of a vaccine or a cure more difficult. **Prevention** is considered the greatest hope in controlling this epidemic.

AIDS

IS AIDS PREVENTABLE?

Yes. Thanks to the information gained since 1981, AIDS is now a preventable disease. The two main ingredients necessary to protect yourself against AIDS are knowledge about how the disease is transmitted and the motivation to adapt responsible behaviors based on that information. Let's take a look at each possible means of transmission and some positive preventative measures.

1. Sexual Contact

The first lines of defense here are *abstinence* or a *long-term monogamous* relationship. Those who do not find those alternatives feasible should *always* use *latex condoms** for vaginal, oral and anal sex, with a *water-soluble spermicidal (nonoxynol 9) lubricant and avoid multiple partners. Rubbers dams* may be helpful for oral sex with a woman. *Know your partner* (people infected with AIDS do not *look* different).

*Condoms must be used properly to be effective. Use only new condoms. Do not store in a wallet or a glove compartment. Check the expiration date. Unroll the condom carefully onto the penis as soon as it is erect (the virus can leak prior to intercourse), leaving a small recepticle at the tip. Withdraw the penis and remove the condom before the erection passes.

2. IV Drug Use

The safest way to avoid exposure in this area is by not shooting drugs. Those who are unable to stop using IV drugs should *clean their needles* (even if thought to be new) by boiling 15 minutes, soaking in rubbing alcohol 15 to 30 minutes or soaking in liquid chlorine bleach (1 part bleach to 9 parts water) 30 minutes. Needles should *never be shared.* (Additionally, alcohol and recreational drugs are known to weaken the immune system. Therefore abuse of any drug may increase your chance of getting AIDS. Your best bet is to avoid drugs altogether.)

3. Blood Transfusions

The American Red Cross began testing all donated blood for HIV antibodies in March of 1985. Transfusions are now considered *safe.**

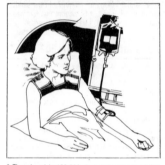

* There is a 1 in 100,000 chance of contracting AIDS by transfusion.

4. Mother to Child

About half of the babies born to HIV antibody positive mothers are themselves HIV antibody positive at birth or shortly after birth. Women who are known to be antibody positive should *avoid* becoming pregnant. Pregnant women who are antibody positive should seek *counseling.* Mothers who are HIV positive should *not breastfeed* their babies.

All high risk behaviors have been addressed and alternative behaviors identified. If you have concerns over your degree of risk, take the short test inserted in this booklet and determine your risk quotient.

AIDS RESPONSIBLE
ACTIVITIES CHECKLIST

Place a checkmark in the box representing each activity in which you currently participate, even if it is only occasionally. Sexual activities within long-term monogamous relationships need not be counted. Add up the numerical scores for each activity checked. This will give you a risk quotient.

Your risk quotient is a rough approximation of how risky your present behaviors are and should not be considered a totally accurate predictor of your risk of getting AIDS.

I participate in the following behaviors:

(0) Casual contact with strangers

(0) Hugging

(0) Massage

(0) Fantasy

(0) Romantic talk

(0) Lip kissing

(0) Caressing

(0) Body-to-body rubbing

(0) Bathing or showering together

(0) Mutual masturbation

(1) French kissing

(1) Protected sexual contact (using latex condom, spermicidal water-based lubricant, rubber dam or latex square)

(2) Sexual activities while under influence of recreational drugs/alcohol

(3) Sharing of razors or toothbrushes

(3) Fellatio (oral sex on male) without condom

(3) Cunnilingus (oral sex on female) without rubber dam or latex square

(4) Sharing of needles

(4) Using unsterilized needles

(4) Vaginal intercourse without protection

(4) Anal intercourse without protection

(4) Watersports

(4) Fisting

(4) Rimming

(4) Sharing of toys (e.g. dildoes, vibrators, etc.)

( ) *My Risk Quotient*

Key to Risk Behavior Score:
0 = You are now practicing safe, responsible behaviors.
1-2 = Your behaviors are fairly safe. (Your risk increases with number of partners and frequency of contact.)
3 = Your behaviors are risky.
4 or more = Your behaviors are irresponsible and unsafe. You need to reevaluate your lifestyle and make some positive changes.

If you have questions regarding your score, please call the Health Education Office of the Health Services, 486-4700.

THE UNIVERSITY OF CONNECTICUT

APPENDIX 4

DIRECTORY OF AGENCIES CONCERNED WITH AIDS*

━━━━━━━━━━ **AIDS HOTLINES** ━━━━━━━━━━

PUBLIC HEALTH SERVICE NATIONAL HOTLINE
800-342-AIDS
CENTER FOR DISEASE CONTROL (CDC)/AIDS
ACTIVITIES
404-329-3311
NATIONAL GAY TASK FORCE CRISIS LINE
800-221-7044
NATIONAL AIDS NETWORK
202-546-2424
NORTHERN CALIFORNIA AIDS HOTLINE
800-FOR-AIDS

SOUTHERN CALIFORNIA AIDS HOTLINE
800-922-AIDS
SAN FRANCISCO AIDS HOTLINE
415-863-AIDS
AIDS INFORMATION LINE
203-549-6789
AIDS INFO LINE — YALE NEW HAVEN
203-785-5305
TELEHEALTH (24 HRS)
203-549-6789

━━━━━━━━━━ **NATIONAL** ━━━━━━━━━━

AIDS Action Committee
Fenway Community Health Center
16 Haviland Street
Boston, MA 02115
(617) 267-7573

AIDS Institute, New York
State Department of Health
Corning Tower, #1931
Albany, NY 12237
(518) 473-0641

AIDS Program, Haitian Center Council, Inc.
50 Court Street, #1001
Brooklyn, NY 11201
(212) 855-7275

AIDS Project/Danbury
(203) 426-5626

AIDS Project/Hartford
(203) 247-AIDS

AIDS Project/New Haven
Box 7
North Haven, CT 06473
(203) 624-AIDS

Connecticut Alcohol & Drug Abuse
Commission (CADAC)
(203) 566-3403

Department of Health Services
AIDS Coordinator
150 Washington Street
Hartford, CT 06106
(203) 566-5058

Federation for AIDS-Related Organizations
506 West 42nd Street, E5
New York, NY 10036

Foundation for Health Education
P.O. Box 51537
New Orleans, LA 70151
(504) 928-2270

Gay Men's Health Crisis, Inc.
Box 274, 132 W. 24th Street
New York, NY 10011
(212) 807-6664

Hartford AIDS Advisory Committee
(203) 722-6791

Hartford Gay Health Collective
218 Collins Street
Hartford, CT 06105
(203) 567-4111

Health Crisis Network
P.O. Box 52-1546
Miami, FL 33152
(304) 634-4780

K.S./AIDS Foundation
3317 Montrose Box 1155
Houston, TX 77006
(713) 524-2437

Lambda Defense and Education Fund
132 West 43rd Street
New York, NY 10036
(212) 944-9488

National Coalition of Black Lesbians & Gays
930 F Street, N.W.
Washington, DC 20004
(202) 737-5276/5278

National Jewish AIDS Project
2025 Eye Street, N.W.
Washington, DC 20006
(202) 387-3079

New York AIDS Action
263A West 19th Street, #125
New York, NY 10011
(212) 807-0699

Northwest Connecticut AIDS Project
(203) 724-5194

Nurses Network on AIDS
155 West 85th Street, #5D
New York, NY 10024
(212) 496-7648

Philadelphia Community Health Alternatives/
Philadelphia AIDS Task Force
P.O. Box 7259
(215) 545-8686
Hotline: (215) 732-AIDS

The University of Connecticut
AIDS Education Network
(203) 486-4700 (x215, 268, 240) or
486-4738 or 486-4130

Washington Area Council on Alcohol and
Drug Abuse (WACADA)
1232 M Street, N.W.
Washington, DC 20005
(202) 783-1300

Women's AIDS Network
San Francisco AIDS Foundation
54 Tenth Street
San Francisco, CA 94103
(415) 863-AIDS

This is only a partial list of all available agencies.

©*The University of Connecticut Student Health Services, Health Education Office, 1987. Permission is given to duplicate this pamphlet in its entirety, if credit is given to originator. Bulk copies may be ordered at cost by calling 486-4700. (Pamphlets supplied free of charge to The University of Connecticut departments).*

APPENDIX 5

THE
UNIVERSITY OF
CONNECTICUT

Department of Molecular and Cell Biology
Box U-125, Room LSA 205
75 North Eagleville Road   September 22, 1987
Storrs, Connecticut 06268

TO: Faculty: Molecular and Cell Biology, Ecology and Evolutionary Biol-
          ogy, Physiology and Neurobiology

FROM: Tom Terry, Associate Professor of Molecular and Cell Biology, U-44

SUBJECT: Suggested Guidelines for laboratory exercises involving blood sampling
          and/or saliva to minimize possible transmission of AIDS

     Several laboratory exercises that have traditionally been used in under-
graduate biology courses involve the testing of student blood or saliva. These
exercises include blood typing for ABO antigens, the use of blood for microscopic analysis, the use of saliva as a source of amylase for enzyme assays, and
others.

     The epidemic status of AIDS raises important concerns about the safety of
such exercises. Guidelines issued by the State Dept. of Health indicate that
the AIDS virus can be transmitted via blood from an infected individual by need-
leprick or by inoculation through cuts and abrasions on hands. Even though the
number of AIDS virus carriers among our students is likely to be extremely
small, we must ensure that any laboratory involving blood sampling does not
expose any student to possible infection from another student's blood. Risks of
contamination from exposure to saliva are much less than for blood (a majority
of patients with acute AIDS do not secrete detectable virus in saliva, and the
likelihood of infection via saliva even through human bites or intimate kissing
is very low), but caution should still be observed.

Precautions.

     1. If alternative experiments of comparable didactic value are avail-
         able, those not involving student blood sampling are to be pre-
         ferred. For example, prepared blood slides, or the use of one
         volunteer blood sample rather than a sample from every member of a
         class would minimize risk.

     2. If blood sampling is practiced, the following precautions should
         be used:

         (a) Sharp items (needles, coverslips, lancets) should be
             considered as potentially infective, and should be han-
             dled with extraordinary care to prevent accidental inju-
             ries.

         (b) All sharp items should be placed in puncture-resistant
             containers located as close as possible to the area in
             which they are used. To prevent needlestick injuries,
             needles should not be recapped, purposely bent, broken,
             removed from disposable syringes, or otherwise manipu-
             lated by hand.

271

(c) Any objects which come in contact with blood should be disinfected immediately after use. This includes lancets, glass slides, disposable pipets, coverslips, cotton swabs, all of which should be discarded in disinfectant jars. Microscope lenses which touch blood slides should be disinfected by wiping with a swab soaked in disinfectant. Bench tops should be wiped thoroughly with disinfectant immediately after such exercises.

(d) No individual engaged in assaying his/her own blood should share any materials with another person. It is safe for others to look through a microscope, but a slide containing a blood sample should not be handled by anyone except the blood donor.

(e) If there is a foreseeable risk of exposure to another's blood, disposable gloves should be worn. Hands should be washed immediately and thoroughly if they accidentally become contaminated with blood.

(f) Acceptable disinfectants approved by the State Dept. of Health are:

1. Ethyl or isopropyl alcohol (70%)
2. Phenolic germicidal detergent in a 1% aqueous solution (e.g., Lysol).
3. Sodium hypochlorite with at least 100 ppm available chlorine (1/2 cup household bleach in 1 gallon water, needs to be freshly prepared each time it is used).
4. Quaternary ammonium germicidal detergent in 2% aqueous solution (e.g., Tri-quat, Mytar, or Sage).
5. Iodophor germicidal detergent with 500 ppm available iodine (e.g., Wescodyne).

3. The risk associated with exposure to saliva is far less than for blood. The shedding of virus in saliva occurs infrequently among AIDS patients. Nevertheless, it would seem a wise precaution to extend some basic precautions to the handling of samples of saliva (e.g., cheek or tooth scrapings used in microscopic exercises). At a minimum, saliva samples should not be handled other than by the donor, and all relevant materials should be disinfected after use.

4. If these precautions are made clear to students and laboratory supervisors, there should be no danger in using blood or saliva samples in laboratory exercises. The danger comes from lack of preparation and failure to observe safety precautions. Please be sure that laboratory T.A.'s are thoroughly informed of these precautions.

Ref. "AIDS Guidelines for State Personnel", available from CT State Dept. of Health.

APPENDIX 6

Books and Articles for Further Reading

1. *Living with AIDS and HIV*, David Miller, Macmillan Press, Houndmills, Basingstoke, Hampshire, Great Britain, 1987. Paperback, about $15.00. A practical manual for people with AIDS, for those who are antibody-positive, and for careers and counselors. Available from Macmillan Press in U.S.

2. *AIDS: The Ultimate Challenge*, Elisabeth Kubler-Ross, Macmillan, New York, 1988. Interaction of author with AIDS patients.

3. *Understanding Immunology*, Alastair J. Cumingham, Academic Press, San Diego, California, 1987. Paperback, $17.50. A thinking person's introduction to the science of immunology; written for the nonspecialist.

4. "The Bubonic Plague", Colin McEvedy, in *Scientific American*, vol. 258, no. 2, 1988, pp. 18-123. Magazine article.

5. *Current topics in AIDS*, Volume 1, edited by M.S. Gottlieb, D.J. Jeffries, D. Mildvan, A.J. Pinching, T.C. Quinn, R.A. Weiss, John Wiley and Sons, New York, 1988.

6. *"And The Band Played On" Politics, People and the AIDS Epidemic*, Randy Shilts, St. Martin's Press, New York, 1987.

7. *CRISIS: Heterosexual Behavior in the Age of AIDS*, William H. Masters, Virginia E. Johnson and Robert C. Kolodny, Grove Press, New York, 1988. Controversial book claiming, among other things, that the general heterosexual population is rapidly spreading AIDS.

8. Collection of 8 articles on AIDS, *Science* **239**, 573-617 (1988).

9. "AIDS and the Single Woman", *People*, March 14, 1988.

INDEX

surgeons, special problems with AIDS carriers, 219, 220

surgery, and blood transfusions, 81

surgical masks, as protection against AIDS transmission, 126

survival from AIDS
    statistics on, 145, 146
    women, blacks and hispanics fare poorly, 145

Sweden, campaign against gonorrhea, 124

symptoms of AIDS
    repression of, factors affecting, 142
    time of appearance in women and men, 140, 142
    See also Chapter 6.

syncytia, giant cells formed by HIV, 41

syphilis
    and AIDS, **155-157**
    causative organism, 155
    facilitation of AIDS by, 155
    increase in New York City cases, 155
    increased intensity in AIDS, 155
    Kaposi's sarcoma in, 156
    mandatory testing for, 103
    opportunistic infections in, 156
    stages of, 155
    standard treatment of, 156
    standard treatment failure in AIDS patients, 156
    symptoms resemble AIDS, 156

Szoka, Archbishop Edmund, stand on AIDS, 237

Taguchi, H., theory on spread of HTLV-I, 11

tat I
    and *tat* II protein of HTLV-I and -II, difference from *tat* III of HIV, 50

tat III gene
    of HIV, 50
    stimulation of protein synthesis by, 49

tears, AIDS virus in, 75, 76

teen-agers, proposed testing with vaccine, 190

testing for AIDS virus
    in blood, 80
    California Supreme Court ruling against, 85
    direct for AIDS virus, **97**
    how done, **97-101**
    importance of, 96
    indirect for antibodies to AIDS virus, 97
    in individual states, 108, 109
    other tests for virus, 98
    other tests for virus antibodies, 100
    in other countries, **114-119**
    positive test, what to do in event of, **209-210**
    prospective employees, test not allowed, 239
    in semen, 76
    by sports teams, 112, 113
    in the U.S., 88

testing for AIDS virus antibodies, **97-102**
    arguments against, **106, 107**
    arguments for, **104, 105**
    bills before Congress, 119
    government's view on, 102
    public's views on, **103, 104**
    Reagan administration's policy on, 103

Thompson, James, R., Governor of Illinois signs AIDS bill, 109

thrush, opportunistic infection of oral cavity, 27

thymidine
    binding by Carrisyn, anti-AIDS effect, 177
    relation to azidothymidine, 168

thymosin (alpha-1)
    hormone important to immune system, **196, 197**
    levels in AIDS patients, 196

thymus gland
    for maturation of T cells, 53
    production of thymosin, 196

Wong-Staal, Flossie
nucleotide sequence of HIV, **63, 65**
test for AIDS virus, 97
Wyro, Pete, Lt. Col. in Army,
Pentagon spokesman, 114
Yersinia pestis, bacterium causing the
Black Plague, 3
Young, Frank E., Commissioner of
Food and Drug Administration,
165

Zagury, D.
long term culture of HIV infected
cells, 39
testing of experimental vaccine on
himself, **191, 192**
Zaire, sex ratio of AIDS patients, 16

Zidovudine, trade name for
azidothymidine, AZT
See azidothymidine, 168-172